The Prairie Keepers

ALSO BY MARCY HOULE

Wings for My Flight
One City's Wilderness

Marcy Houle

The Prairie Keepers

Secrets
of the
Grasslands

ADDISON-WESLEY PUBLISHING COMPANY

Reading, Massachusetts · Menlo Park, California · New York
Don Mills, Ontario · Wokingham, England · Amsterdam · Bonn
Sydney · Singapore · Tokyo · Madrid · San Juan
Paris · Seoul · Milan · Mexico City · Taipei

PUBLISHER'S NOTE

The following story recounts the author's experiences while studying a remote native grassland prairie in northeastern Oregon. Some place names and many personal names have been changed to avoid any unintended embarrassment. All scientific facts are documented as written, but conversations in the book reflect the memory of the author.

Library of Congress Cataloging-in-Publication Data

Houle, Marcy
    The prairie keepers : secrets of the grasslands / Marcy Houle.
      p. cm.
    ISBN 0-201-60843-X
    ISBN 0-201-40821-X (pbk.)
     1. Buteo—Oregon—Zumwalt Prairie. 2. Birds of prey—Oregon—Zumwalt Prairie. 3. Prairie ecology—Oregon—Zumwalt Prairie.
    4. Zumwalt Prairie (Or.) 5. Houle, Marcy.
    I. Title.
    QL696.F32H68   1995
    598.9'16—dc20   94-42434
                                               CIP

Cover design by David High
Text design by Linda Koegel Design
Set in 11/14 point Garamond 3 by Don Dewsnap

1 2 3 4 5 6 7 8 9 -DOH-0099989796

First printing, March 1995
First paperback printing, February 1996

To my dear husband, John,
And to Mother and Dad
with all my love and all my thanks

Chapter One

A PIERCING WIND rattled the brittle grass, like a hand shaking a maraca. On the vast north slopes, last year's growth of Idaho fescue formed a grassland sea that swept across the rolling hills. On the drier, south-facing benchlands, bluebunch wheatgrass sent its roots deep into the untilled soil. The immense land was locked in the last vestige of winter—but not for long. Wisps of green and pointed new growth were sprinkled among the golden grasses. A pale April sun threatened to break through the veil of clouds that cast a pallor over the landscape.

Spring was about to burst on the Zumwalt Prairie.

The cold pricked my hands like tiny stars, and I rubbed my palms together to try to warm them up. The skittering movements of a few brown sparrows and ground squirrels seemed lost on the wild grassland that lay unbroken except for rocky outcrops sprinkled here and there and isolated stands of ponderosa pines and aspen trees tucked away in secluded valleys.

For an instant, the sun split the clouds, torching the prairie with flames of color. Hidden somewhere in the reddish glow, a long-billed curlew broke into song. But the moment of sun belied the ominous clouds still holding over the mountains and threatening snow.

I pulled my down coat closer around me, feeling its icy collar wedged against my neck, and tried to remind myself again why I was here, just what I was sent to do. The problem was, the answers were mostly ambiguous, especially to me.

I focused my eyes on a little grassland flower just emerging from the soil. The pale pink bud was tangible and concise, unlike everything else facing me, it seemed. Two months ago I had been hired jointly by the U.S. Fish and Wildlife Service and Oregon State University, where I was doing graduate work in wildlife biology, to investigate a highly remote and unstudied prairie in northeastern Oregon. Indications from various sources suggested that an abundance of native plants and animals might be inhabiting the vast grassland, known locally as the Zumwalt Prairie. A year before, a biologist of some repute had journeyed through the area and been intrigued by what seemed a high density of birds of prey living in the region. He couldn't explain why. No one could.

I was here to find out. But at the moment, just how I was going to do that eluded me. I knew from cursory investigation that the Zumwalt Prairie was a wild expanse of untilled ground that spanned nearly two hundred square miles. On a map, its size was equal to one-fifth of the state of Rhode Island. It lay like an isolated island locked in on three sides by mountains; its fourth border—the eastern flank—plunged into a cavernous river gorge. The prairie, almost entirely under private ownership, was managed by cattle ranchers. National forest land touched on its northern boundary, and the Wallowa Mountains and Eagle Cap Wilderness flanked it on the south. That the Zumwalt Prairie was also one of the last of the native grasslands that historically had covered a large part of North America interested me deeply.

Cultivation and the impoundment of large bodies of water had obliterated most native prairies in the country, and years of overgrazing by livestock had irrevocably changed many that remained. How these ecosystems functioned was poorly understood; little was known about the life histories of many of the species that lived here and about their interrelationships. Of growing concern was the damaging effect that the alteration and destruction of native prairies might have on the habitats of many native grassland species.

One of the last of the native grasslands—the thought rolled over and stuck in my mind like the thistles to my socks. This new venture seemed such an unreal change from my life at the university. My focus was moving dramatically, from people and papers and tests to an austere and distant land. Yet I was excited to be back in the wild. All my life I had wanted to explore and understand something of the subtle workings of nature. Our family home sat at the edge of a native forest of hundred-year-old Douglas fir trees. The inspiration of their towering beauty and the quiet animals that lived among them had been one of the driving forces in my choice to become a wildlife biologist.

For several years after college, I had worked for the Colorado Division of Wildlife, living in the mountains of Colorado and observing wild peregrine falcons, an endangered species. Studying these striking birds of prey only deepened my thirst to learn more about other native species. After four years, I had decided it was time to broaden my background and enroll in graduate school.

The job offer came while I was deeply involved in my studies, and I jumped at the chance. But now, seeing the prairie firsthand, I felt a sinking sensation in my stomach, for I was alone. The Fish and Wildlife Service had made it clear at the outset that there wasn't enough funding to hire anyone else.

Generally, the solitude wouldn't have bothered me; I had lived and worked alone before and in places just as wild. But after seeing the vastness of the Zumwalt, I began to doubt my ability to complete what I was realizing would be a massive undertaking.

With a sigh, I zipped the neck of my jacket to keep the cold wind from sneaking down my shoulders. The sun had disappeared again, and a bleakness shrouded the immense and lonely prairie. I glanced at my watch. It was half past three. I had driven for seven hours on rutted back roads and still not covered even the perimeter of this northeastern Oregon grassland.

A tearing motion cut the air above me like a scythe and caught my attention. Grabbing my binoculars, I tried to follow the fleeting image—a golden-hued prairie falcon—that was shooting like a hurled boomerang in pursuit of a large red-tailed hawk. The poor lumbering red-tail flipped upside down, then righted itself in an effort to beat quickly away. The prairie falcon wheeled over, empowered by victory, then directed its aggression at a golden eagle circling west above a grove of aspen trees.

With the falcon gone, the red-tail again enjoyed a few minutes of peaceful, oscillating flight. Unfortunately, his sortie led him straight into the territory of a ferruginous hawk—the largest of all North American hawks. The regal, eagle-sized ferruginous pursued the red-tail, not giving up the chase until both had disappeared across a dim canyon.

The blood began racing in my veins. Here were the birds I was after: ferruginous hawks and red-tailed hawks—the buteo hawks of the prairie. These were important inhabitants of the grassland, as was their cousin, the Swainson's hawk, who would arrive in a few weeks after a long migration. Buteo hawks, unlike the slim and sleek falcons I had studied, were distinctive for their broad, round-tipped wings; husky bodies; and wide-fanning tails. Both the ferruginous and the Swainson's hawks were believed to be declining across the nation, for reasons no one understood.

One of the few concrete tasks in my job description was to locate every buteo hawk nest on the Zumwalt Prairie. Within the confines of four walls of the university, that had not seemed a problem. But now? How was it possible? I took a deep breath and tried to fight off the panic I had been feeling on and off all day. I must give it my best shot. The information was essential because time was running out. Native grasslands were near the top of the list of threatened ecosystems in North America. If I could document that the Zumwalt Prairie had an abundance of native hawks sequestered within it and then discover why—what lay behind its strange prosperity—this knowledge could then be translated to other places. Management strategies could be designed for grassland regions where native plant and animal species were suffering declines.

A poker-faced badger popped its head from a burrow and nosed the air side to side. Its flat, striped face caught my scent; it promptly disappeared into its hole again. For several minutes I waited for it to reemerge, but only a kestrel swooped low over the field where the badger had been.

The wind picked up again, sweeping the flatland. With a sudden epiphany, I realized I had been standing in the same spot, watching the ground and sky, for nearly an hour. Two hundred square miles to go and I hadn't yet explored all lying at my feet.

Chapter Two

FOR THE THIRD TIME in twenty-four hours, I hit my head on the crystal chandelier dangling from the ceiling in the middle of the upstairs bedroom. I was, undoubtedly, too tall for this farmhouse, owned by a middle-aged schoolteacher, where I was renting a room. Outside, fog, rain, and hail heralded the dreary morning of April 23, my first official day of work. Inside, I heard Mrs. DeLacy shouting from downstairs to wake up her sixteen-year-old son, who was late for school and still sleeping.

I had quickly found out that no apartments were available in the tiny town of Joseph, which was a predicament, for the Fish and Wildlife Service didn't provide housing for employees in far outreaches. For several days last week I had roomed at the only motel in town while searching for a more permanent place to live. My inquiries were generally met negatively; no public housing existed, and the sparsely populated region was made up primarily of family-owned cattle ranches. On a fortuitous tip from the motel owner, I had contacted a local schoolteacher, a widow, who lived with her son in a large Victorian farmhouse south of town. The house had plenty of empty rooms, for the woman, having raised eight children here, had only one son left at home.

She had met me at the door with reservations. Of medium build, with graying dark brown hair, she studied me carefully without inviting me inside. She looked to be in her mid-fifties, perhaps slightly younger. Her face, which in her youth must have been extraordinarily pretty, softened slightly after she learned I was a graduate student at Oregon State University, which fortunately was her alma mater. She then invited me inside the front door, under the front hall light, to scrutinize me more thoroughly. I had learned a little bit about her from the motel owner. Dorothy DeLacy was a survivor. She had studied to be a schoolteacher, but stopped working when she married and then bore eight children. When her last-born son, Donald, was an infant, her husband, Drake DeLacy, died in a car accident. Unwilling to split up her children, Mrs. DeLacy supported her family by taking a teaching job at the local high school, and successfully raised all eight children herself. She never remarried.

I also knew that now that Donald had only one year of high school remaining, she wished to go back to school for her master's degree. With her hands set on her sturdy hips as she stood soldier-like in the hall, Mrs. DeLacy raised this subject, explaining that the university was five hours away and she planned to make numerous trips back and forth in her spare time this summer.

I suddenly realized, because of her continued queries, that she was inspecting me as to my capabilities as house sitter and potential high-school chaperon. With no other housing options available, I had no choice but to accept her qualified offer, which she clearly stipiulated would be on a month-to-month basis, depending on how well I "worked out."

Flat walls of rain blurred the upstairs windows, as if someone were pouring water from large buckets off the rooftop. Grabbing my coat and a pile of topographic maps, I walked downstairs and tried to skirt the rain to my truck, a rather pathetic example of a U.S. Fish and Wildlife Service government vehicle. The 1974 Dodge pickup, with ninety-five thousand miles under its hood, didn't look as if it could hold up for another season of back-road use. The rust coating the bottom gave a two-toned appearance to the truck's copper hue, while inside, the beige vinyl seats were worn and shiny from use, and only barely hid springs under tell-tale lumps. The cracked knob of the gearshift lifted off with the lightest touch, which made shifting dubious.

As I darted inside several more times to fetch my equipment—an assortment of paraphernalia that probably made little sense to anyone other than a field biologist—Mrs. DeLacy looked down, unsmiling, at the wet path I was trailing on her hallway oriental rug.

"Oops—sorry," I apologized. "Tomorrow I'll try to be more organized."

"Typical Joseph weather," she said, watching the rainwater drip down my cheeks. "No one in his right mind would be out in it."

Overwhelmed with the research task laid out before me, I didn't quite feel in my right mind. Conscientiously, I backed out onto the porch to keep the entryway from getting wetter. "Mrs. DeLacy, how long into the spring does this rain and snow usually last?"

"Oh, the rain and snow, they come and go. Come and go. Usually by the end of May the snow is gone."

"Whew! That's good news."

"Then it rains—hard—from June to the end of July."

Mrs. DeLacy watched from the window as I climbed into the truck and tried to start it. This was always an ordeal, but today the onerous thing apparently didn't wish to start at all. The engine churned repeatedly, refusing to catch. Resting against a seat that felt as if someone's elbows were thrusting into my back, I shoved over all my gear that had been spilling into my lap. I waited a minute. Then I tried to start the pickup again. It sputtered, wheezed, and died. The odor of gas wafted around the driveway. Mrs. DeLacy, I noticed, had moved from the window, opened the front door a crack to watch, and was holding her hand in front of her nose and mouth to protect herself from the fumes. Why the devil didn't she go eat her breakfast or something? Or yell again for her son to get out of bed?

I refused to make eye contact with her. The maps had tumbled to the floor on the passenger side, and I took a moment to rearrange them. Once they were back in order, I cranked the starter one last time, while pressing the accelerator flat to the floor. Instantly the truck exploded with a blast, taking me completely by surprise, and reviving Donald, whose head appeared at the upstairs window.

Well, at least he was awake now.

My first appointment of the day was with the officials at the Oregon Department of Fish and Game. I planned to introduce myself and to discuss with their nongame biologist some of the research I hoped to conduct over the next seven months. They knew I was coming, and Dr. Charles Henny of Oregon State University had informed them of what I intended to accomplish. I reviewed mentally some of the principal objectives, a central one being a complete inventory of every red-tailed, ferruginous, and Swainson's hawk nest on the Zumwalt Prairie. Each nest must be visited several times, first to discern how many eggs were laid, later to verify how many hatched and fledged. Then the goal was to find out *why* the species occurred in the numbers they did.

Of course, trying to unscramble such a complex natural system had as much probability of success as making complete sense of a black hole. And, at the end of my meeting with the Department of Fish and Game biologists, I was nearly positive that what I hoped to accomplish was impossible.

The senior biologist, Glenn Smith, was a tall, sinewy man with a heavy head of wavy brown hair lightly threaded with gray. His thin face was finely chiseled, although wrinkled from years of exposure to sun and wind. He first impressed me, as he stood in his office glancing over a thick stack of papers, as a keen and ruthless observer. His unsmiling brown eyes, I guessed, could quickly discern a horned lark from a lark sparrow or tell the age class of a deer from one hundred meters. They also easily took me in all at once.

Fumbling with wet clothes, I removed my coat so it wouldn't drip rainwater all over the desk or chair, and introduced myself.

"So you're the one they sent," he said cryptically, putting down his papers and fitting a stubby pencil behind his ear. "I was under the impression you were to have been here two weeks ago." For such a large man, his voice sounded surprisingly high-pitched.

"Yes, I was. I mean no, I couldn't," I answered, a bit flustered. "The GSA motor pool in Portland had some trouble finding a truck for me to use. It seems all of them were spoken for, so I had to wait for one to come back in."

Glenn shook his head disapprovingly. "Should have been here two weeks ago. The aspen trees and cottonwoods are about to leaf out. Then you won't be seeing a thing in those trees." He walked around to the other side of his desk and sat down, taking a sip of coffee. Six other used, brown-stained cups, with varying levels of old moldy coffee, lay scattered on his desk. "Who you working with?" he asked, while tipping his cup.

"No one." The question surprised me, for I thought he had been told about the lack of funding for an assistant. "It's just me."

"You?" he said, absently putting his coffee on the desk next to the other cups. I wondered how long this cup would stay there. "Just you? How in hell do you think you'll cover the Zumwalt?"

"I'm going to try."

"And I sure as hell can't spare anyone."

"I'm aware of that."

"Damn fiscal policy," he muttered under his breath. "The U.S. Fish and Wildlife Service just expects me to drop everything I'm doing and let you have one of my people on a regular basis. Well, I'm not going to do it. Maybe once or twice, but that's it."

"I don't mean to inconvenience you in any way."

"Those two clowns from the Forest Circus may be able to help you. They were here last week looking for you."

"If they haven't given up on you," interrupted a stocky man, about my height, frowning at me from the doorway. He wore the standard tight-fitting, olive green Fish and Game garb, and sported a tightly cropped crew cut. Right now he was busy twirling his cap round and round on his index finger. His hands and wrists looked very large compared with the rest of his body.

"Hey, Sparkey," said Glenn Smith, standing up again and leaning back against his desk. "You're a bird man. Grab a chair."

Sparkey wheeled a chair toward the table and settled down comfortably. Stretching out his arms, he put his squarish hands behind his head and rested his muddy boots on Glenn's desk.

"This here's the researcher who's studying the Zumwalt hawks. Think she'll find all those red-tails nesting in the cottonwoods?"

"No way. Too late in the season."

"That's what I told her."

I didn't need to be told that the deciduous trees were about to leaf out and obscure the stick nests of the hawks, generally red-tails, that preferred to nest in the crotches of old cottonwoods and willows. Early in the season, their nests showed up easily as black globs against the twisting lines of gray branches. When the trees were fully clothed with foliage, however, my task would become infinitely more difficult.

"How big an area you thinking of covering?" Sparkey asked, with his eyes still resting on Glenn.

"The entire Zumwalt."

He choked and quickly sat upright, his boots knocking some papers off the desk. But no one seemed to care. "The entire Zumwalt? You crazy or what? You'll be lucky just to get to some of the big ranches near town. It's a helluva big area. You seen it?"

"I drove part of it yesterday."

"I drove part of it yesterday," he mimicked in a tone that made me wince. "You know it's almost two hundred square miles? You're out of your mind."

Sparkey shook his head and picked up his feet again to rest them on Glenn's desk. "Now if I was doing this project," he said, with an air of authority, "I'd stick close by. I'd hit the farms. I'd drive all around the cultivated areas and set up my spotting scope and look for activity. When I found a nest, I'd take out my notebook and write down the productivity parameters. You know what productivity parameters are? That's pro-duc-tiv—"

"Yes, I know what they are."

He acted as if he hadn't heard me. "Productivity parameters

means how productive the nests are," he continued. "You check the nests to see how many little eggs are in them. Then you check how many of those little eggs have hatched into little birds. Then you check again and see how many of those guys actually flew 'bye bye' from the nest."

"Yes, I'm fully aware—"

"You've also got to see what mamma and dadda bird are feeding the little tykes. Ever collected pellets? Or do you know what a pellet is?"

"Of course I—"

"That's all the junk the birdies can't digest. You know, fur, feathers, bones, and teeth of rodents and birds, good stuff like that. But," he went on, with a big yawn, "I would have started a month ago. Early nesting red-tails are already coming back to the county. You're too late."

Glenn Smith suddenly changed the subject and asked the one question I was dreading: "How are you going to climb all those trees to find out if the nests are active?"

"That's right!" Sparkey agreed. "Some of those red-tail nests are up sixty feet high or more. Got your spurs?"

Not an experienced tree climber, I had discussed this problem with Dr. Henny before leaving the university in Corvallis. He had assured me that the biologists from the Forest Service could help me if some of the trees were too difficult for free climbing. But I knew this would not go over well with some of the men at Fish and Game.

"You *can* climb trees, can't you?" Sparkey asked slowly.

"Some trees, most trees, yes."

"Familiar with spurs? Spurs and ropes?"

"No, not really."

"Jimmeny Crickets—you mean they hired for this job someone who can't climb her own trees? That's a helluva note. Can you haul a forty-horsepower outboard motor for a half mile over a set of fences?"

This was pure nonsense; I wouldn't need a boat for the project.

"Any man here can," Sparkey added, removing his feet from the desk to pick the dirt from the cuffs of his pants. "And what's more, I know at least four guys who had their eyes set on the job you got."

"Climbing trees or hauling outboards is not the whole point of my job."

"Don't count on us to hold your hand and climb your trees for you," said Sparkey, turning toward Glenn. "What'd I tell you? That's damned equal opportunity for you."

"Well, I must be going," I said, trying not to sound as eager as I felt.

"Where you off to now?" asked Glenn, not unkindly, while searching the assortment of coffee cups for his freshest one.

"I must let the Forest Service biologists know I'm here, and then I have to stop by an automotive shop. Can you recommend one?"

"What's wrong with the rig?"

"When the Motor Pool gave it to me in Portland, they told me it needed a valve job."

"A valve job!" cried Sparkey. "Well, whoop-de-do. That means your truck will most likely conk out at any time. Probably when you're the farthest away from civilization. Right, Glenn?"

Glenn only said he would like a look at the truck. The two men accompanied me outside in the rain, Sparkey peppering comments every step of the way.

"Where's the spare?" Glenn asked, while walking around the rear of the pickup.

"Isn't it there? Is it underneath?"

Glenn bent down to look. "Nope. Not there."

"You mean she's got no spare?" said Sparkey, muffling a chuckle.

"I've completely run out of patience with those idiots at the Motor Pool," said Glenn. "They're all urban fools. Just where do they think she's driving? Ten blocks away to downtown Portland?"

I should have known, considering all the backcountry I would be driving, to check whether I had a spare tire.

"Call GSA today and tell them to send it here. Or, better yet, tell them to send you a new truck. This one's not going to last out the summer."

"We don't want to have to send out the search party because you're broken down out way the hell out in the Snake River District," warned Sparkey. "Remember, your AAA membership does no good in the Zumwalt."

As I drove away, in the rearview mirror I spied the men joking between themselves, probably, I conjectured dismally, about me. By the time I reached the Forest Service in the tiny town of Wallowa, twenty miles away, my head was splitting. I was actually relieved, even though it was an inconvenience, to find that the Forest Service biologists had checked out for the day. All I really wanted now was to go back to Mrs. DeLacy's and sit down, curl up with hot chocolate, and feel sorry for myself.

I turned around and headed back toward Joseph. The pelting rain had changed to clods of wet snow, which made driving not only fatiguing but risky, especially considering the truck's balding treads. The gloom was depressing. Even if I had begun my field research a week or two earlier, it wouldn't have helped much in weather like this.

Limping at last into Mrs. DeLacy's driveway late in the afternoon, I found that both she and Donald were gone. A note Mrs. DeLacy had taped on the refrigerator explained that they had left to visit relatives in Lewiston for the night.

After a dinner of leftover soup, I headed upstairs to relax in my bedroom. Images of weirdly shaped, monstrous cottonwood trees sprouting thousands upon thousands of leaves swirled through my mind. Completely hidden in branches towering eighty feet above me were all the hawk nests. Obscured. Inaccessible. Mocking.

Lost in thought, I hit my head, for the fourth time, on the chandelier. The impact didn't even faze me. Tonight, it seemed the least of my problems.

Chapter Three

THE SPOTTING SCOPE, tripod, and window mount were ready; binoculars, bird book, pencils, field journal, measuring tape, small plastic bags for collecting pellets, and lunch were stuffed in the backpack. I was careful to separate the lunch from the pellet collection. The camera was loaded with a new roll of film.

Between bites of Cheerios I leaned over to examine the topographic maps that lay sprawled out on the sunporch floor, and tried to decide where I should drive this morning. It was vital to take advantage of the break in the freaky weather. Today the bright sun, pouring in through the old glass windows, could trick one into thinking summer thoughts, although the air outside was still crisp and frigid, with brown lawns and leafless shrubs still fringed with snow.

On the kitchen floor next to the sunporch I had unrolled ten aerial photographs—their curling borders held in place with a medley of Mrs. DeLacy's coffee cups—that I had ordered previously from the Soil Conservation Service. The matching of the aerials with the topographic maps of the prairie required a map-reading finesse still beyond me. The topographic maps, with their tiny brown lines demarcating eighty-foot rises in elevation, seemed to have little in common with the aerials, which had been shot at such a high altitude that they looked more like a child's finger painting—gray smears on shiny paper, sprinkled with tiny black grains of sand. Only a device called a stereoscope and hours of eyestraining work would make the photographs jump into three-dimensional life and resemble hills and valleys and trees again.

These two sets of disparate maps then needed to be correlated with the Forest Service national forest and County Pittman maps I was using to find my way around. The Forest Service maps, of a completely different scale, of course, were divided into dozens of little quarter-inch squares like a checkerboard, each box representing a square mile. The only apparent resemblance between them and the topographic maps was that they were both white and green.

Right now, looking at the mess on the floor, I felt as if I were wandering in a foreign country without a guide. Somehow I needed to be able to read all the maps as easily as a book, and precisely associate them with the ground under my feet. Every hawk nest I found had to be pinpointed exactly, first on the topographic map, then on the aerials, with each buteo species demarcated by a different color—red for red-tails, yellow for ferruginous, brown for Swainson's.

As Glenn Smith had made clear yesterday, I first needed to search the areas heaviest in deciduous trees, notably aspen, cottonwood, and willow. From what I could tell from the maps and my cursory trips to the Zumwalt, approximately four-fifths of the prairie was native grassland and one-fifth was cultivated farmland. The cultivated land differed significantly from the prairie; people had altered, tilled, and intensively managed it. It also appeared set apart as a single unit within a thirty-square-mile radius surrounding the small towns of Joseph and Enterprise. Here all the ranchers resided—none lived out on the Zumwalt —and habitations were placed at nearly perfect intervals of one-half to one square mile, like a giant checkerboard. The rich bottomland habitat, ideal for growing alfalfa, winter wheat, and barley, was crisscrossed with irrigation ditches along which the giant old cottonwoods and willows grew intermittently.

A road survey needed to be conducted immediately. I would begin with the cultivated farmland, and then attempt to locate all the nests on the prairie. First I would record the nest distribution;

later I would return to climb to the nests to find out the productivity parameters.

This was something of a problem. My lack of climbing experience aside, the timing of my visit to a nest would be critical. A human visit too early in the nesting cycle, especially when buteos are incubating eggs, could cause irreparable harm. Swainson's hawks are known to abandon their nests after only one visit by a researcher early in the nesting season. Ferruginous hawks are equally problematic. The last thing I wished to do was drive away that which I wanted to observe. Unfortunately, I knew from experience that this sort of problem occurs far more often than any scientist wants to admit.

Observing the nests situated in low trees or on the ground would be less problematic, but I would still need to be cautious. Viewing them from above or from a distance with binoculars and spotting scope would be my alternative early in the nesting season, until the eggs hatched.

All species of birds tend to be specific about where they choose to build their nests, and hawks are no different. But scientists still had only a vague notion of what particular conditions rendered a habitat attractive to buteos. Therefore I needed to record precise information, beginning with what substrate—tree, ground, shrub—the hawks chose for their nests. Then I needed to note the height of the entire nest structure, as well as the height of the placement of the nest in the tree or shrub. Scientists speculated that different species of buteos chose to nest at different, yet specific, heights above the ground, like preferred spots in a condominium. Some were the penthouse nesters; others chose low to the ground for an easy escape. This kept the species separate, although it didn't appear to be discriminatory. The hawks just seemed to prefer a little privacy.

The roads I would travel, mostly gravel and rutted dirt, only zippered the extremities of this remote, geographic region. Locked inside were the real richness and mystery of the prairie and canyons, which required hiking long distances into areas without road signs or landmarks. To keep from getting inexorably lost, I would have to read the topographic maps perfectly.

Today I decided to explore Crow Creek first, by way of Dobbin Road. As I drove along, trying to get my bearings on the maps, I became aware of the rich shade of velvet green of the winter wheat as it reflected the sun's light. The blue sky, with a clarity found only in alpine regions, arched like a blanket thrown over the tops of the mountains and held taut at the horizon of the grassland. Cheeky ground squirrels darted to and fro across the road, only to vanish in silent holes as if a magician had suddenly zapped them to disappear.

By the time I had reached the junction of Prairie Creek and Dobbin Road, three red-tailed hawks were soaring over the plowed farm field that fit like a jigsaw puzzle next to a field of winter wheat. I recognized them easily by their chestnut tail and by the way they flew. They weren't built for speed, as were falcons. Their wings, broad and long, were engineered for soaring. When the winds picked up to speeds, like today, of ten to twenty miles per hour, red-tailed hawks could stay aloft, gliding effortlessly, for long periods.

Two tall cottonwoods, which stood out as straight and perpendicular monuments on the flat landscape, were of great interest to the hovering hawks. After I shut off the truck's engine, the only noise was the clattering of the trees' intertwining branches, sounding like a fencing match between two old men wielding wooden canes.

I reached for my field journal to make a notation. From the corner of my eye I saw two agile prairie falcons arcing a pattern in the east. Apparently they had irritated another, smaller raptor, possibly a kestrel, who was rapidly diving west.

Where exactly was I on the map? Holding the pencil in my teeth, I realized that this was all happening too fast. By the time I had flipped through four maps and figured my location, all six birds had vanished. Now, what looked like a rough-legged hawk wavered one hundred feet or so above a bare field to my left.

A problem with my note taking was developing. Trying to decode where I was while surveying all that was happening produced an inherent conflict. This had never been a problem before, but, I began to realize, perhaps never in my life had I seen so many raptors in the same general area at the same time of day.

After scouting approximately ten square miles, which took up the rest of the morning and part of the afternoon, I was thoroughly exhausted. Too many raptors were converging through the air at once, almost as if the hand of an invisible puppeteer were purposely directing a play of myriad players only to make my work more complicated. It wasn't just buteos that were flying. Looking over my hen-scratched notes, I stopped to check that I wasn't just imagining things:

Township 1 South; Range 45 East; Sec 25 ne, nw:
- One marsh hawk flying and hunting.
- One adult golden eagle flying and perching on rocky outcropping. Flies west out of sight.
- 2nd adult golden eagle flying from the east. Perches on rocky outcropping.
- Prairie falcon diving over a pair of marsh hawks.

Township 1 South; Range 45 East; Sec 32:
- Two red-tails hunting over field. No territorial displays.

Sec 33:
- One mature red-tail, flying near one immature red-tail and one prairie falcon. The immature red-tail chases a pair of pheasants.

Township 1 South; Range 45 East; Sec 12:
- Four unidentified raptors flying through area (red-tails? rough-legged hawks? or ferruginous?)

- Three red-tails, one dark phase, flying through area; not territorial.
- Two adult kestrels hunting, and perching on phone lines.

Township 1 South; Range 45 East; Sec 3:
- One red-tail alternately flying and perching on ground.
- Two red-tails, one very defensive. Appear to be rebuilding nest in cottonwood tree just south of farmhouse.

Township 1 North; Range 46 East; Sec 30 sw:
- Pair of ferruginous hawks, both sitting together and sharing a kill; small unidentified animal. One flies away about 100 yards, to preen. Other ferruginous still eating.
- Immature golden eagle sitting on ground. Takes off and flies over knoll.

Sec 42:
- One red-tail flying on hillside. Plane flies near him. Red-tail flips sideways when the plane turns. Red-tail returns to perch in a ponderosa pine tree.
- Same red-tail (I think) flies out; diving on a ferruginous hawk that flies within ¼-mile radius of pine tree. Stoops several times on the ferruginous, driving the ferruginous hawk away. Red-tail returns to the same pine, landing on top.
- Marsh hawk flies by, the same place the ferruginous hawk was five minutes earlier. Red-tail ignores the marsh hawk.
- Four marsh hawks (two pairs?) alternately dive, swoop, and strike with outstretched talons an intruding mature golden eagle. Eagle repeatedly

flips over to avoid attacks. Finally, eagle darts
swiftly to west.

Township 1 North; Range 46 East; Sec 19, center,
ne:

- Adult Swainson's hawk (an early arrival?) spotted
soaring above Crow Creek.
- One dark phase red-tail swooping and driving
away an immature golden eagle. Successfully
chases away the one bird, then another golden
eagle reappears flying from the west, diverting
the red-tail's attention.

I closed the notebook and rubbed my tired eyes. If this kept up,
one field notebook wouldn't do. But, I realized, many of these birds
were probably not breeders; undoubtedly, many had to be merely
"floaters" in the area—surplus birds that would disperse later, as
the breeding season got into full swing. Early spring was a betwixt
and between time, as the birds worked out among themselves their
nesting territories (areas they would defend from all intruders) and
home ranges (areas they would use to hunt and live out their daily
lives).

It was time to call it a day. Yet, how could I? Just now, two red-
tailed hawks, one with streaky brown plumage on its back and a
pale rufous breast, the other a dark phase bird, deep mahogany all
over except for the characteristic tail, caught my attention as
they worked together to repair a rather disheveled nest in a row
of cottonwood trees. In an adjacent tree, a perfectly good hawk nest
sat untouched. This would have seemed peculiar, had I not known
that buteo hawks regularly maintain more than one nest in a
season—an insurance, of sorts. If the wind blows Home Number
One from the tree and destroys it, you're okay if you have Home
Number Two. If it's early in the season, you can start laying eggs
again and get back to business. If it's too late, then work on your
home repairs for next year.

These little housekeeping matters were quite interesting, and I mounted the spotting scope on the car window. One of the pair perched out on a limb, its powerful, husky build clearly visible. I was so intent on the red-tails that I missed seeing the small woman striding down the gravel driveway in front of the two-story white farmhouse near which I was parked. She was almost at the side of the truck when I saw her, hands thrust deep in her jeans pockets, black hair swinging side to side, tied back in a pony tail with a red bandanna. From the clench of her jaw I realized immediately that I had crossed some important boundary.

I also had the uncomfortable feeling that I was just about to find out what it was in no uncertain terms.

Chapter Four

"YOU LOST?"

It was not a question but an accusation.

The husky voice belied the woman's small stature, and her large gray eyes shone like sunlit ice behind a dark fringe of lashes. Hurriedly I lifted the spotting scope from the car window.

"No, not lost. You must have seen me driving back and forth on this road."

"I certainly have. This, you know, is a private road." Her eyes moved down the side of the truck to scan the block letters: U.S. GOVERNMENT MOTOR POOL/FOR OFFICIAL USE ONLY.

"No, I didn't know. I'm sorry."

"Who in the hell do you think you're kidding?"

"Excuse me?"

"In the last six months at least a dozen people have come by our place for one reason or another—looking around and badgering us with questions. All you government people are running some kind of census or another or mapping this and that. Let me tell you, we're getting plenty sick of this!"

Surreptitiously, I nudged the maps to the floor with my leg. "Oh."

"You bring binoculars and trespass on our property without even the courtesy of a phone call. You leave our gates open and tramp on our newly plowed fields; I wouldn't put it past you to spy in our windows."

"I am sorry," I began again. "I won't cross your property if you prefer."

She paused to point out a fallow meadow lying directly west of us. "See that field there? Last spring one of you left the gates to that sheep pasture open and our ewes all got out. It took my husband and me hours to find the stock and get them back in the right pasture. That's the last thing we need at lambing time, especially with hungry eagles hanging over them like vultures over a dead body."

With the pointed toe of her cowboy boot, she kicked the ground. "And you damn well better not be studying eagles. For if you are, we'll kick your you-know-what out of this county faster than you ever saw."

"I'm not studying eagles," I said, somewhat unsteadily, wondering what the people in the county thought of hawks. As if reading my mind, the dark phase red-tail cavorted over the truck. It turned almost directly overhead and dove back to the grove of cottonwoods to perch on a branch above its mate.

"That pasture where all the sheep are grazing, the one with the hawks—is that part of your ranch?" I asked, praying it wasn't.

"Indeed it is. And this year those old trees are coming down."

"What—why?"

"Because those trees allow too many places for eagles to roost."

The two graceful red-tails were circling above the nest. "But eagles won't hurt your sheep," I said. "That's just an old wives' tale."

"An old wives' tale? Only an *idiot* would say that. Any fool who says eagles don't harm sheep has never lived on a ranch." Her warm breath against the cold air looked like smoke billowing from her mouth. "That's what's wrong with you, you government people. You don't have an inkling as to what really goes on out here."

If the hawks were to keep their home, I somehow had to calm things down. "Perhaps you're right," I averred. "So what does go on out here?"

The woman was taken by surprise; scrutinizing my face, she appeared to be trying to decide if I was being sincere or just patronizing. Winding her arms more tightly around herself, she leaned closer to the truck. Her oversized canvas jacket—probably her husband's—flopped about her like a sack.

"You really want to know? You want to know what life is like today living on a ranch? Well, I can tell you. It's a lot of things. It's *regulations*. The government regulates us so much that we can't do anything without its permission. It's *restrictions*. We're limited in what we can spray, where we can graze our livestock, how much water we can use to irrigate our fields. And finally, it's '*run you out*.'"

I didn't have a clue what she meant. "Run you out?"

"Inheritance tax. It breaks up the family farm, but that's what the government really wants all along." As a kind of challenge, she brushed back the bangs from her piquant face. Lines from wind and sun, and probably laughter, surrounded her bright eyes, but her face held no humor now.

"I don't understand," I said hesitantly. "There seem to be a lot of private ranches around here."

"Not for much longer. The days of the family ranch are just about over. It's corporate farms now—big-time operations. And they don't give a damn about the land." She shook her head in resignation. "You government people are the only ones that can afford to live here now, subsidized by your fat government paychecks."

I looked on, not knowing exactly how to respond.

"But why am I wasting my time explaining all this to you anyway?" she continued. "You people don't give a hoot about us."

"No, you have an interesting point."

"Oh, you think so?" she replied cynically, rubbing her red, chapped hands together to warm them.

"Well," I said, feeling as if I had just been clawed all over by a barn cat, "you look pretty cold. I apologize for driving on your road; I truly didn't know it was private property. I'll be going now." I turned to start the engine. "Please," I added, "please don't cut down your trees."

The woman's face softened slightly. She looked a little perplexed, as if she were trying to make up her mind about something. Then she laid her hand on the outside handle of the truck.

"Well, it's damned cold for April, isn't it?" she asked, pleasantly, as if we had merely been chatting about the weather.

"It—it sure is," I agreed, my hand still on the key.

"So why are we out here talking? You in there getting cold and me frozen stiff. You might as well come inside and have a cup of coffee."

The invitation caught me completely off guard. Inside for a cup of coffee? For a moment I was so incredulous that I could only stare.

"Well, are you coming or not?" she exclaimed, with a trace of a smile. Not waiting for her to change her mind, in one swoop I hoisted the whole jumble of equipment from my lap to the floor.

She shook her head quizzically. "I've always wondered under what rock the government finds you," she remarked, turning to step up the path leading to the black-shuttered, white farmhouse. "What a sorry lot."

The farmhouse kitchen was perfectly tidy, with a round oak table by the window, which overlooked the snowcapped Wallowa Mountains. Warmed by a large woodstove, now crackling with kindling, the room contained a cozy clutter of knickknacks jumping out from every corner. A milk pitcher on the counter was embellished with a gaggle of geese. A red clock the shape of a barn hung above the sink. Painted cows grazed peaceably on a ceramic cookie jar.

"Help yourself to a chair," she said, while running water to fill a shiny, stainless steel teakettle. "I'm Melanie. Melanie Deane. Sorry to lash out at you like I did. This kind of thing happens to us so often these days, we're just fed up to here." She motioned with a slash to her neck. "What'd you say your name was?"

"It's Marcy. What a lovely spot you have here."

"Why, thank you. I think so. Now what'd you say you're doing here?"

"I'm looking for hawks," I explained, girding up for the same reaction as that to eagles. "I'm working for Oregon State University."

"Why the government truck?" she asked suspiciously.

"Well, the Fish and Wildlife Service has given me a research grant."

"We like hawks," she said slowly, searching her cupboard for two mugs. "They eat the ground squirrels. Too bad, though, you've got that government truck; it'll be a strike against you. Folks will see that coming and think you're a locust—that's what we call the government workers. They come out every day at eight, go back in at four. Lazy louts."

The teakettle whistled and steamed from the heat of the woodstove. Mrs. Deane fetched a large jar of instant Folgers coffee and stirred up two hot cups.

"We love this ranch," she said, sitting down at the table. "Though it's anyone's guess how long we'll be able to keep it. Just about everything we have goes to payments and taxes."

"I can think of worse places to spend your time," I commented, gazing at the beautiful mountains surrounding her farm.

"Hawks, you say. Every year we have a pair of red-tailed hawks nesting in those trees you were pointing at outside. One dark, one light. We've enjoyed watching those birds raise their families. In fact, they've been here as long as I can remember."

I knew I had to dive in sometime. "Outside you said you might take those trees down. Then the hawks would have no place to nest."

"Like I said, those trees also give the damn eagles a place to perch."

"But what do the eagles do to you?"

Mrs. Deane banged her mug on the table, startling me. "What do they do? They kill our newborn lambs! It's all we can do not to shoot those damn birds when we see them lurking in the trees."

I sighed, thinking again about the beautiful golden eagles I had enjoyed watching soar over the farm fields. What kind of future did they have if all the ranchers felt as she did?

"I still don't quite understand," I continued, aware that I was treading on dangerous ground. "Over the years I've observed many eagles. Not to disagree with you, Mrs. Deane, but I think eagles have been given something of a bum rap. Have you ever seen them do it? Kill a lamb?"

She opened her mouth, poised to say yes. But suddenly she paused and took a sip of coffee. "One thing I've always prided myself on is in being honest. All right. I can't say I ever saw it myself. But Berl Stalp, a sheep rancher down the Imnaha River, says he sees it all the time." Her eyes brightened with vindication. "He's seen an eagle carrying away a squalling newborn lamb in its deadly talons."

She rose up and stepped to the cupboard to get some cookies and arrange them on a platter. "That's another one of your laws that's senseless. Protecting eagles. But it's also our right to shoot them if they're tormenting our livestock. That's the law, too."

I debated letting the matter drop. This woman could never be convinced to change her mind about eagles. Or could she? The biologist in me couldn't help trying.

"Mrs. Deane, everything I've read concludes that eagles never harm lambs. Eagles have been wrongly blamed and have suffered much persecution. Did you know that something like twenty thousand golden eagles were killed by ranchers in the 1940s and 1950s, before it became illegal?"

"That's good news."

This wasn't turning out the way I wanted. "One long-term study done in Montana, encompassing an area where there were more than thirty thousand sheep, found not one sheep ever killed by an eagle. I suppose they're big and fierce enough to do it, but they prey mostly on things the size of, you know, rabbits or marmots."

"If you plan on staying here very long," she cautioned, "I wouldn't broadcast your views too loudly."

"Oh, I don't mean to offend you," I added quickly. "But eagles have been blamed for so much, when it's probably foxes, coyotes, or dogs that are causing havoc."

"You really believe this, don't you?"

"Of course I do. I've studied birds of prey for many years. With your house being here so close, you shouldn't have any problem at all with eagles."

"And you want me to keep those cottonwoods for the hawks."

"To eat your ground squirrels," I added with a grin. "But speaking seriously, right now eagles are much too busy to be a problem. They're as hard workers as you. They're busy setting up their territories and building their nests and laying their eggs and trying to raise and protect their young. They won't bother your lambs."

Mrs. Deane didn't look convinced. She reached for a chocolate chip cookie for herself and handed one to me. "You're so sure about that?"

I garnered all the authority I could muster. "Without a doubt. On that, Mrs. Deane, you have my word."

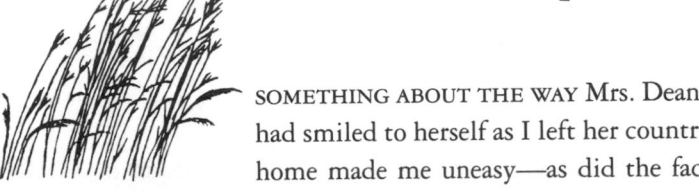

Chapter Five

SOMETHING ABOUT THE WAY Mrs. Deane had smiled to herself as I left her country home made me uneasy—as did the fact that three golden eagles were just now gliding effortlessly over the river a mile from the pasture where Mrs. Deane's young lambs were testing out their newborn legs. My expertise, I was well aware, did not really include golden eagles; what I had learned of their behavior and ecology was peripheral to the research I had done on hawks and falcons. But I knew some things about eagles, and I had observed many through the years.

The golden eagle is a majestic, dignified bird, a swift and agile flier with golden hackles adorning its proud head like a shimmering crown. Like the peregrine falcon, it was prized during the Middle Ages by kings in Europe for the sport of falconry. In a swift plunge to the earth, the golden eagle nearly rivals the peregrine in speed and spirit. With a wingspread of six and one-half to seven and one-half feet (held on its side with wings out, the bird could rival in height any NBA basketball player), the powerful eagle greatly benefits agriculture by feeding on injurious, prolific rodents, its favorite food.

Like many other raptors today, its status is somewhat questionable. Three main causes of its recognized decline have been identified, and these coincide with the decreasing populations of birds of prey in general: (1) restriction and degradation of their habitat; (2) contamination of their food sources by toxic chemicals; and (3) harassment by humans.

I was aware—but didn't mention to Mrs. Deane—that golden

eagles had on occasion been reported to kill mid-sized, adult black-tailed deer, and young or sickly fawns or antelope, but these were anomalies. As for lambs, the debate still raged hotly, with rumor and malice impugning the birds for acts they possibly never committed.

Still, I couldn't push aside the disquieting feeling that all was not quite right at the Deane ranch. I set my alarm for four o'clock the next morning, intending to drive back to the Deanes' place before dawn to begin work early, where I left off yesterday. I planned to check on the lambs and verify in my own mind that the eagles were long gone—quietly at roost in some old pine far out on the Zumwalt.

When I awoke, Mrs. DeLacy was banging around downstairs. This was somewhat astonishing; I had assumed no one else would be up at this hour, but come to think of it, Mrs. DeLacy didn't appear ever to sleep. Luckily, I was able to slip out of the house before she had emerged from her bedroom. I didn't care to have her question what I was doing, slinking off into the deep darkness with binoculars.

By the time I had reached my destination, the tree branches were just lightening up with the touch of dawn. Lambs and ewes resembled dark, moving ghosts skulking over the field. On the hill above, the house was still dark, and the calm of the early hour settled over the truck as I turned off the motor and got out to look around more closely.

It was then that I saw them. Five hulks roosting like repeat criminals in the cottonwoods that fringed the field of lambs. The ewes were beginning to baaaa; their innocent, unknowing offspring bleated in response. But the dark, sinister forms didn't move, only hunched forward to scrutinize more closely the situation from their lofty view. One especially large form stretched out a long wing to preen—and wait.

This was terrible. Tossing my binoculars on the car seat, I ran quickly to the field and hopped the fence, not caring that I was trespassing. The ewes and their babies began scampering and baaaing in all directions as I tore through the flock to reach the cottonwood grove. Thank God the house lights were still off. Unlike the frantic sheep, the eagles were unconcerned, as if I had been only the farm sheepdog.

"Get out of here!" I yelled, but not too loudly, for fear that someone might hear the commotion.

"Shooo! Scram!"

I could see the eagles craning their necks to get a better look at me, as they calmly shifted their position from foot to foot on the tree branches.

This wasn't working. "Dammit!" I shouted, jumping up and down and flapping my arms. "Get *moving!*"

At last, one of the giant birds flapped its lumbering wings and flew slowly, regally, toward the canyons dropping away to the east. Another followed it, and soon a third tagged along close behind. The last two eagles, however, only rocked back and forth on the branches, not at all eager to leave what I despaired were possibly their hunting grounds.

"Get going, you, and don't come back!" I howled, while flailing my arms and leaping about like a kangaroo. Finally, the recalcitrant eagles shifted about uncomfortably. With the entire pasture in a mayhem of running hooves of terrorized sheep, the birds reluctantly took off and disappeared somewhere out toward the Zumwalt. To my horror, the lights went on inside the Deane house. Dropping down low, I slunk back rapidly to the truck, praying they wouldn't come outside. Leaping the barbed-wire fence, I threw the key into the ignition and gunned the engine. Gravel flying, I sped away, with the sinking knowledge that the eagles *would* be back, if not today then tomorrow, unless something was done.

Unfortunately, Sparkey was hanging around at the Fish and Game office, pouring himself a cup of coffee, when I arrived an hour after my ordeal at the Deanes' field. He was the last person I wanted to talk to at the moment, and although I tried to walk past him after a civil nod, he followed me like a hound as I walked back to Glenn Smith's office.

"Glenn's not here yet," Sparkey offered, eyeing my frizzy hair wet with morning dew. "You here for the tire? It came in yesterday."

"Hmmm, that's good news," I replied, spying Glenn Smith arriving through the back entrance. Passing by Sparkey again, I walked over to Mr. Smith as he hung his olive down coat on the rack.

"Mr. Smith, I need your help; I've got a problem."

"Which *one?*" said Sparkey.

I ignored him and raised my chin. "I was at Melanie Deane's ranch yesterday, on Dobbin Road. She was going on about eagles pestering her lambs and wanting to kill them."

"Kill the lambs?" exclaimed Sparkey, grinning. "Ol' Ms. Deane wants to kill her lambs?"

"Oh, shut up, Sparkey," said Glenn. Sparkey merely smirked and took a sip of coffee.

"Kill the *eagles*," I replied, with a disdainful glance at Sparkey. "I explained to Mrs. Deane she had nothing to fear from the eagles—that they wouldn't harm her livestock—but then this morning when I went back, five eagles were roosting in the field."

"Just drooling over breakfast," added Sparkey.

"I tried as best I could to shoo them out of there, Mr. Smith, but I'm worried they'll come back."

"They will," said Glenn Smith coolly.

"But of course they wouldn't harm the lambs."

"You bet they could."

"But I thought—"

"We have a problem in this county," he said, picking up his list of messages, then putting them down again and sitting back in his black vinyl chair. "Every now and then eagles take a lamb, and it makes the farmers stark raving mad. Someone's got to take care of those eagles. Get her the shotgun, Sparkey. Let her be the one to do it."

I couldn't believe my ears. "Shoot the eagles?" I cried.

Sparkey fell over double with laughter.

"Blanks," said Mr. Smith. "We use shotgun blanks to dissuade the eagles from ever having a second thought about swiping a juicy lamb chop."

"But all the studies I've read have documented that eagles leave sheep alone."

"What'd I tell you, Glenn?" exclaimed Sparkey, munching on a doughnut from the coffee room. "The girl's had no field experience."

"It's a rare eagle who'll pick on livestock," Glenn explained to me. "A hungry bird, but it happens. The blanks should do the trick. Get the eagles when they're all roosting together, shoot a round. Deanes should have no problem after that."

Sparkey left the room, then returned wielding a gun in one hand and wheeling a fat truck tire in the other. Glenn stood up behind his desk to get a box of blanks from his shelf, which he handed to me.

"Better be careful what you say here," he warned. "Ranchers are funny people. They graze their cattle and sheep on lands that should never have been theirs to use in the first place. They let their animals defecate in streams already fouled by their fertilizers and pesticides. South of here, the Malheur River is just an agricultural sewer. When Indians were here, they lived in peace with the elk and deer; nobody worried about eagles or whatever. Now ranchers claim this land should be reserved only for their friggin' animals. In their opinion, elk and eagles have no right to share the range."

"Hey, you," said Sparkey with a nod to me, "you never said if you knew how to shoot a gun." Sparkey picked up the shotgun and tossed it a short distance in the air for me to catch.

"Yes," I said, amazed at how cavalier he was around firearms. "I can shoot."

He reached his hand in his shirt pocket to retrieve a canister of chewing tobacco and stuck his tongue in his cheek. "Well, don't get mistaken and go aiming at ol' Ms. Deane. She's one feisty lady. She'll have you down her gun barrel in a second."

With a well-practiced swipe, Sparkey shoved a wad of tobacco in his mouth. "And another thing. *She* won't be using no blanks."

Chapter Six

IT WOULDN'T DO for me to go back to the Deanes' place at midday with my shotgun. Too much chance I could be seen. Never again would I be dumb enough to give my word on anything about wildlife. Wild animals are too full of surprises, which makes studying them fascinating but unpredictable. We humans feel, seated on our lofty perch, that we know much about animals, but after observing wild creatures I know just how little we really understand. Everything one species does is interconnected with everything else; this has been problematic for all our management plans for wildlife. Even with our sophisticated statistics and computer programs, we have only scratched the surface of real knowledge of ecology. When people are added to the equation, defining the problems and coming up with solutions become even more muddled, for human actions impinge either directly or indirectly on all creatures and their habitat.

I found it difficult to concentrate on work the rest of the day. I was discouraged, too, that thousands of new shoots seemed to have appeared almost overnight on the aspen, willows, and cottonwoods along Liberty and Dawson Roads, making my search for hawk nests more arduous. Even if I had trouble finding nests, any four-year-old could point out the numerous hawks, however. In one square-mile section alone, I had observed one female red-tail making a nest in a large cottonwood just south of a farmhouse, two other adult red-tails hunting over a freshly tilled field, an immature red-tail chasing a pair of pheasants from a fence row, and still another red-tail perching on the ground.

Making sense of this seeming surplus of hawks was trying. Some of them appeared to be nesting, others just flying around. Some stick nests were being used, while other perfectly good ones were left vacant. What was determining the birds' distribution? Having run out of clean clothes to wear, I rolled back to Mrs. DeLacy's late in the afternoon, allowing time to get to the laundromat before dinner. I planned to spend a few hours afterwards charting on my maps all the nests I had located. In another two weeks I should be ready to start exploring the uncultivated, native prairie. The area was so vast that it seemed one could easily get lost in it and never be seen again—which probably was Sparkey's secret wish for me.

Mrs. DeLacy greeted me at the door when I arrived home. With a mother's trained power of observation, she commented on my red and strained-looking eyes, and kindly extended an invitation to dine with her and Donald, which I gladly accepted. Her pot of stew was mouthwatering, and I relaxed with a glass of red wine and some gossipy dinner conversation. Donald, however, was for the most part sullen during dinner, his inert enthusiasm only resurrecting when the phone rang.

"Family rule: no interruptions at dinner, Donald," repeated Mrs. DeLacy each time Donald jumped up to answer the telephone like a released prisoner. "It's almost scandalous what high-school girls are like these days," she added to me. "They call for Donald every night, with silly excuses like they misplaced the homework assignment. It's driving me absolutely batty."

Between the phone interruptions, Mrs. DeLacy queried me continually about my work, and actually seemed genuinely interested, although Donald was not. His pale, long face held an agonized look of boredom while we talked over research objectives and graduate school and the pros and cons of pursuing a Ph.D. Mrs. DeLacy liked to talk, and she had no qualms at all about saying exactly what was on her mind.

Between mouthfuls of light, crumbly cornbread, she brought

the subject back to home. "I've quite a few people asking about you, you know," Mrs. DeLacy disclosed. "They're asking why I took you in, you being a stranger and all." She paused for a moment to take a sip of wine. "I'm glad you filled me in tonight what you're up to, for people have been questioning why you're driving all over town peering at their ranches."

She smiled and took a second helping of cornbread. Mrs. DeLacy admittedly was no longer the svelte, five-foot-two brunette shown in the numerous pictures of herself as a young girl she had displayed around the house. Probably her excellent cooking had been her downfall.

"The problem," she continued, "is that big government truck of yours. I'll be honest with you; I'm embarrassed having it parked in front of my house. But after what you've told me tonight, I'm beginning to think a bit differently. I think others might too. Why don't you come with Donald and me to the Elks Club dinner social next week?"

"My God, Mom, I won't go to that thing! Those boring old people and their stupid stories—"

"That'll be enough, Donald. You will *go*. As I was saying, people could meet you there and you could explain to them about your work. And impress upon them that what you are doing is perfectly legitimate."

My stomach dropped at the thought. "Of course, Mrs. DeLacy, I'd be glad to go."

When my little wristwatch alarm went off at half past three in the morning, everything was dark and still. I had not slept well. Dressing quietly, tiptoeing around the room and carrying my boots under my arms, I crept down the stairs, not making a sound. In the upper part of my coat were the shotgun blanks; I was careful to keep one hand on them so they wouldn't rattle.

I had purposely left my pack and spotting scope in the kitchen, near the back door, which I slowly nudged open and then closed very gently behind me. No need to lock it. No one locked doors in this county. Mrs. DeLacy had once said she didn't even know if the house came with a key.

In forty-five minutes I was at the Deanes' farm. The silvery half moon shone a bit brighter this morning and illuminated quite clearly the farm field with its reposeful lambs—as well as an arrangement of five ghostly forms poised on twisted tree limbs hanging just above the woolly victims.

In the darkness, I felt for the shotgun, which lay hidden behind the seat. As I opened the truck door, a blast of cold air bit at my hands and face. Carefully I lifted the gun out and, placing it under my arm, walked over to the fence post and rested it while I jumped over the wire. The sheep were afoot now, becoming agitated.

The sweet, cold wind that often comes up just before dawn trembled the fallow field grasses. If I hadn't been anxiously skulking about like an armed miscreant on someone else's property, I would have relished the beauty of the crisp mountain morning. The shadowy black forms of the Wallowa Mountains rose up in two-dimensional shapes, outlined in a rosy fringe from a lightening southeastern sky. The moon tipped the silver coats of the spectral figures of lambs, and a pleasing scent of alfalfa and new earth touched my nostrils.

Before long, however, the Deanes would be awake; the shotgun blanks were burning a hole in my pocket. I headed straight for the eagles.

The flock of ewes began shepherding their offspring away from me as I moved in on the cottonwoods. Why they seemed more disturbed by my presence than by the band of eagles "drooling over them" was bewildering, but that wasn't my problem. To my dismay the five big birds seemed to have no fear of me whatsoever, and absolutely no intention of dispersing, even when I stood directly beneath them.

In the darkness I fumbled with the shells, dropping a couple from my pocket. I was anxious to get this over with, and I hurriedly loaded the gun, all too aware that my truck was well behind me, which meant there could be no quick escape. But not a single light burned in the Deanes' farmhouse windows.

The ewes had quit trotting and calmed down. A plaintive killdeer cried from the moist meadow across the way. Taking aim at the cluster of cottonwood branches and five dark hulks, I held my breath and pulled the trigger.

An explosion of giant wings beat from the trees, rippling out in every direction. Petrified sheep bolted every which way like mercury droplets dancing from a broken thermometer.

It worked, I thought guiltily. As rapidly as I could, I loaded up and fired again. Now everything was terrorized.

Tucking the gun back under my arm, I darted in the darkness across the field, crunching down the newly sprouting wheatgrass. The truck, wrapped in shadow, was only a hundred yards away. My lungs heaved. *I must get out of here before the Deanes discover me.* A light flicked on in the house—but there was the fence—I was upon it.

Dancing gravel spewed from the skidding tires of a truck screeching to a halt, and halogen headlights snapped on, blinding me. A large silhouetted form jumped out and pointed a flashlight in my face. A voice, stern and cold, bellowed from behind the light, and nearly brought me to my knees in surprise and fear.

"Don't move, and drop the gun," commanded the voice without a face. "You're under arrest—for trespassing on private property with a firearm."

Chapter Seven

"SHOULD WE HANDCUFF and hog-tie her, Eric, or give her a chance to explain first?"

"I can *explain*."

"Naw, let's just take her in, Austin. Sparkey'll know what to do with her. There's a hefty fine, jail sentence too, I think, for shooting at protected birds like eagles. Sparkey'll know."

Something wasn't right. How did these men know I had been after eagles? Sparkey's hand was in this.

"Could you please take that flashlight away from my face? I can't see," I said. "Who are you guys?"

Moving the light from my face and pointing it underneath his chin, the person bowed. The chiseled shadows created by the flashlight made his face look like a macabre, carved jack-o-lantern.

"Austin Scott, at your service, madam." He and his sidekick burst out laughing. "God," he added, "that's the best joke I've played in a long time!"

So that was it. Austin Scott and Eric Peterson, of the U.S. Forest Service—the fellows I was to meet but had never tracked down. The two jokers were the wildlife biologists who were to lend me a hand climbing trees and banding birds this summer; at this point I didn't think I wanted anything to do with them.

"How did you know I would be here at five o'clock in the morning?" I asked, chagrined.

"Sparkey passed on the news when we came looking for you yesterday afternoon. For nearly two weeks we've been trying to catch you."

"You nearly scared me to death. I thought you were Mr. Deane."

Austin laughed. "Speaking of the old fart, I think we better get out of here before he begins to wonder what's going on out here with his precious sheep. Why don't we all go in and get breakfast at the Circle T; we can talk there. But, Annie Oakley, put away that shotgun."

The day hadn't even begun and already I felt weak and spent. Enterprise's only twenty-four-hour restaurant was a busy place at six in the morning, evidenced by the slew of pickups parked out front. Seated at a table dusted with crumbs, in the flat, fluorescent lights inside, I got my first look at the two men, who looked to be in their twenties.

Austin was tall and husky, about six foot four, with straight, shaggy black hair that appeared self-trimmed, almost as if he had placed a bowl on his head for an outline. His brown eyes were bright, and beady like a robin's, and like a robin's they seemed to track everything quickly. One thing about his olive-complected face I liked: his thin lips had a positive upward twist to one side.

His partner, Eric, was fair and light skinned. Eric was also robust and tall, although not quite as tall as Austin. His long face was deeply sculpted, almost tight around the cheekbones. I found it difficult to read his eyes, which were ice blue and cold, although perhaps it was due to his silent manner—taking everything in but not giving back a response.

Austin had difficulty rearranging his long legs under the low table. "You've bitten off more than you can chew, you know," he said, finally getting settled, then adding, "These damn chairs are for midgets."

"We've talked about it, Eric and I, and given it a lot of thought. Your project's bound to fail," Austin continued. "Now, I'm not saying you shouldn't give it your best shot. Something is going on out there, and we're all curious why there seem to be so many buteos."

"Especially when we all know it's private rangeland grazed by a multitude of cows," added Eric.

Austin paused to take a slug of coffee, which dribbled a bit on his chin. He wiped his brawny wrist across his face. "It's those damn ranchers. They think they control the whole resource out there." He looked up to smile at a tiny, gray-haired waitress who placed a hefty four-egg Mexican omelette on the table in front of him. Apparently, Austin had little concern about cholesterol. My small dish of oatmeal looked anemic in comparison as I sprinkled on brown sugar and raisins.

"You macrobiotic?" Eric asked sarcastically.

Austin continued, talking with a mouthful of yellow eggs. "You're probably aware your boss, Chuck Henny, has asked us to help you. We've been instructed to gallantly devote ourselves to you when you need assistance banding the little buggers. But you better get yourself outfitted first. Shouldn't she, Eric?"

"Yup."

I took a sip of lukewarm, bitter coffee. "What do you mean," I asked, "*outfitted*?"

"Oh, the insects around here!" exclaimed Austin, for an instant putting down his fork to motion with his hands. "If you camp out, the sand fleas will crawl in your sleeping bag and have you for supper. The mosquitoes here are as nasty as their tundra cousins. After you've worked for a while out on the Zumwalt, you're goin' to look like you have measles, your ankles will be all swollen up, and your sleeping bag and clothes will have to be exterminated."

"Yeah, sure."

"And that truck of yours. I heard all about it. It'll fail, most likely when you're deep in the prairie. No one will know where you are, except for the badgers, who carry disease-infested ticks, and the plague-ridden ground squirrels. Lucky for you, you have us habitat guys to give you some tips."

I needed their tips as much as I needed Sparkey to help me refine my research goals. But I *was* curious about their terminology.

"Just what are habitat guys?" I asked, with a smile.

"Wildlife guys like Eric and me. You'll find there are two

types in this business. The habitat specialists and the wildlife biologist types. We're the first kind, more open minded, broader thinking. Guys like us generally work for the Forest Service, and sometimes for the BLM, but that's a two-faced outfit. Habitat types, like us, think it's just great that a girl like you would get involved in this kind of work. But the biologist types, now—you know what I'm talking about—they're tunnel visioned, Fish and Game guys, the good ol' boys. There's a lot of them out here. And they don't like the fact you're messing around in a man's job."

Austin, finishing his giant omelette and third cup of coffee, got up to use the rest room. Eric stayed at the table, but was quiet. I decided to disregard most of what they were saying as pure hyperbole, but a few things did seem to stand out starkly. The talk of grazing. What kind of condition was the Zumwalt in? And how detrimental had livestock grazing been to the area's wildlife? And then the different agencies around here—Fish and Wildlife, U.S. Forest Service, Bureau of Land Management, Soil Conservation Service—all having a stake in the same resource. From what I could tell, no one seemed able to get along with anyone else.

It was a relief to finally extricate myself from these habitat types and get on with my work. Ever since talking with Mrs. Deane, I couldn't rid myself of the belief that I had a moral obligation to try to contact the ranchers on whose property I would be traveling for the next six months. Her protest that government workers rarely asked for permission to conduct studies on private property— they just did it anyway—held too much truth, unfortunately, to disregard. I knew I wouldn't feel completely comfortable until I had spent some time at the courthouse finding out land ownerships, and had asked the property owners' permission, although I knew Chuck Henny would consider it a waste of valuable time.

Prominently situated in the center of Enterprise, the county courthouse cast an air of grace and dignity on the small sleepy town. Aside from the sprawling, two-story Forest Service compound that seemed to take over the entire west side of town, it was Enterprise's only significant building. The quiet demeanor of the federal-style brick structure was a marked contrast to the bustle and fumes of the Forest Service vehicles going in and out of the job corps across the street.

Once inside, I became unbearably aware of the courthouse's antiquated heating system as I reviewed all the county tax assessor's information. The air was suffocating, the thermostat conservatively set for at least eighty degrees. How could anyone breathe in this place, much less move around? The wool clothes against my skin, which this morning had felt cozy, were now simply miserable.

After six hours I had the names of seventy ranchers to call. Mrs. DeLacy would be home in a few hours, and I didn't relish the idea of her overseeing me in her kitchen, so I decided to quit and get home early to make my calls.

Fresh mountain air helped revive my skin, which felt like boiled crab, and I kept all the windows of the truck fully down for the entire thirty-minute journey. While driving down the highway, I tried to come up with a good sales pitch for the ranchers. But I quickly realized that the job might be trickier than I had thought.

"Hi there!" sounded too forward, too pushy, I decided at once. "Howdy" was worse, though. The cliché sounded like I wanted something from them—which, of course, I did.

"Hello" was much better. It was more professional, as long as I remembered not to sound too excitable.

Getting past the first word, I needed to come up with a suitable introduction.

"Hello. I'm Marcy Cottrell."

(Should I pause here? Absolutely not! Gives them time to hang up. Just dive right into something about Oregon State University; their kids probably go to school there, and that should make them sympathetic.)

"Hello! I'm Marcy Cottrell, a student from Oregon State University. I'm conducting a census—"

Oh, no. Not *that* inflammatory word. I must be sure not to slip up and use it. *Project* was the better word. Summer *project.*

That was it. "Hello. I'm Marcy Cottrell, a student from Oregon State University, and I'm doing a summer project on the hawks of Wallowa County. I was wondering if it would be all right if I could quickly check your property for hawk nests."

It sounded more like a spiel to procure items for an auction, but it was the best I could do.

Settling down comfortably in Mrs. DeLacy's kitchen nook, I arranged the note cards with the ranchers' names in alphabetical order and took a deep breath. Thank goodness her Donald wasn't home. I had forgotten about him.

Mr. Leonard Allen was my first prey. After my speech, he grunted "Yeh, okay," which, while not enthusiastic, at least was good feedback.

The next two ranchers who answered the phone gave the lame excuse that they needed to check with their husbands first. A child answered my fourth call. When I asked to talk to his mother, I overheard her in the background exclaiming "Who is it?" The child answered, "Someone selling something." His mother's response was plain: "Tell whoever it is we don't want any!"

This was not going well. I paused to fix myself a cup of tea and review my strategy. Perhaps, I thought, I had better go back to "Hi there."

My next call, fortunately, met with resounding success. Bob Boswell responded exuberantly to my plea, which was beginning to sound more timorous each time I used it.

"You just go out and look at all the hawks you want!" he cried vigorously. "Just be sure to keep the gates as you find them. We have problems, you know, with people leaving the gates open, but if you close them behind you, you're welcome to go on my property anytime you want!"

Clyde Cardwell also received me as kindly as if he had been the Welcome Wagon committee chairman. Betty Fazio (obviously liberated, since she said she didn't have to ask her husband and could speak for herself) gave a resounding yes, and went on to explain that a red-tailed hawk nested just outside her kitchen window and had been coming back to that same spot for over ten years.

"We love our birds," she exclaimed. "They're our friends."

With only a few exceptions, call after call was met with warmth, goodwill, and a willingness to lend a hand from the men and women who ran ranches in the county. Taking the time to call them first was probably the best public relations effort I could have made. Several said to stop by their houses first and they would give me a key to their locked gates out on the Zumwalt. A few even offered their horses to ride. Hawks, it appeared, were known in this area for their rodent control—certainly a different reputation from that of eagles.

My confidence swelled in proportion to the diminishing number of people left to contact. This really wasn't bad after all, I realized. But then I hit upon Cyrus Hockley, whose unusual reception made all the others pale in comparison.

"Who you callin' for?" he bellowed.

"I'd like to speak to Mr. Hockley," I said, then too quickly ran over my rehearsed dialogue.

"Hawg, you say? You're calling for Mr. Hawg? My name sure as hell ain't Hawg!" he laughed.

"Yes, Mr. Hockley, I know that," I replied, trying to sound cheerful. "I said I'm studying hawks—"

"I just told you," he cut in, beginning to sound slightly irritated. "My name ain't Hawg."

"Yes, I realize that, Mr. Hawgley—I mean Hockley." Damn, I was getting all messed up. "Please let me explain again. I'm looking at hawks."

"Hogs? I ain't got no hogs."

"Not hogs, Mr. Hockley. *Hawks.*"

"CAN'T YOU HEAR? I AIN'T GOT NO HOGS!"

"Yes, but—"

"I AIN'T GOT NO HOGS AND MY NAME AIN'T HAWGLEY. AND DON'T EVER CALL HERE AGAIN!"

The slamming down of the phone on the other end coincided precisely with the arrival of Mrs. DeLacy, who stood speechless at the kitchen door with Donald. Slowly I put down the receiver and gathered my note cards into a pile.

"I'm trying to touch base with some of the ranchers," I explained.

"Janet Worth, who owns the Laundromat, just stopped me all in a huff. Seems you left your clothes in her washing machines all night long," Mrs. DeLacy said, obviously ruffled herself. "Folks there complained so she had to take them out and throw them in a heap on the only table in the place—the one they use for folding their clothes. Tying up everything like that ruins her business, don't you know. She's quite irate, demanding you get your clothes out *now* or she'll toss them in the trash barrel."

"Let me tell you a secret," she continued, putting down a stack of homework papers to grade later and shaking her head. "You've got a lot to learn about how to 'touch base' with people here."

Chapter Eight

IN LESS THAN A WEEK of scouring the back roads of the prairie for hawks, it became increasingly apparent that something unusual was going on. I had studied hawks before; I knew something of their distribution and general abundance. But here, on the Zumwalt, I was seeing more hawks, of different species, all mixed up and interacting together, in numbers that were contradictory to the usual "one buteo nest to several square miles." It seemed, from cursory observation, to be more like "several buteo nests per square mile."

Although trying to differentiate the medley of hawks and find their nests was exciting, I found myself, my first days on the Zumwalt, not looking up at the birds but down—down at the prairie, one of the last native prairies in the United States.

Most of the nation's native grasslands have been transformed into continuous fields of wheat, corn, or barley. The Palouse Country of southeastern Washington and northeastern Oregon—of which the Zumwalt Prairie is one large piece—was no exception. The rich, productive soil of the Palouse had made it a farmer's dream in the nineteenth century—a dream that still exists today. In the last century and early in this century, record crop yields sprang from the plowed fields that once had been native grassland. In time, the area became one of the most productive grain-growing regions in the world.

But the dream had an unfortunate snag, irreversible and permanent. All of the productivity of the Palouse, all of the huge harvests, had created a potentially fatal monster: soil erosion.

Soil erosion has always been associated with farming, but when tractors replaced horses and more and more land was taken up for farming, its effect on the Palouse accelerated dramatically. From 1939 to 1977, the Palouse region lost 360 tons of soil from every acre of cropland. Outpouring of chemical fertilizers and chemical weed sprays had, in the short term, counterbalanced the loss of soil's effect on productivity, but as one scientist commented, unless a breakthrough occurs in conservation, the effect of continuing erosion will undeniably create a decline in productivity in the Palouse that no amount of technology will be able to offset. Other scientists studying the region gave farming in the Palouse only another 120 years.

The Zumwalt Prairie is one of the last native grasslands in the Palouse. It has been by and large free from the plow. It is clothed with bunchgrasses—perennial native grasses that come back year after year. These are the heart and soul of the prairie. In the ecological scope of view, I knew there was an infinite difference between an ancient prairie and wheatfield. A prairie is a complex system, a mixture of perennial plants that built up and protected the soil. In contrast, the shallow-rooted wheatfield or cornfield is a monoculture—one species only—that needs to be tilled and reseeded each year, a practice known to easily erode and wear out the soil.

The long-lived native grassland is held together by thousands of roots of the ancient grasses. In many cases, roots of indigenous bunchgrasses extend twenty-five feet or more into the earth. In the untilled prairie, often only the top 15 percent of the grass can be seen; the majority of plant is invisible beneath the surface—collecting nutrients, recharging the soil, allowing the plant to live through cycles aboveground, growing in the spring, dying back in the late summer or fall. Some of the deep rootstalks live to be more than a hundred years old.

The "old ones" of the Zumwalt, the things that give it texture and substance, are an assortment of native species of grass: Idaho fescue, bluebunch wheatgrass, Sandberg's bunchgrass, Kentucky bluegrass, tufted hairgrass. Bunchgrasses, so named because they grow in individual clumps having a bunched-up appearance, are perennial grasses with deep, extensive root systems, thus making them excellent soil binders. Reproducing solely by seed and not by rootstalk or runners like sod grasses, bunchgrasses are in danger of dying out if their seed is not allowed to mature and spread.

"Bouquets" of bunchgrasses growing from one to four feet high fill in the Zumwalt Prairie carpet. Two species in particular are plentiful and are displayed in the landscape at predictable places, like a paint-by-number portrait. Bluebunch wheatgrass, the most important range plant in eastern Oregon and Washington, has swept the drier, southern flanks of most hills, benchlands, and rocky canyons with shallower soil. Idaho fescue, another choice forage plant relished by livestock as well as by deer and elk, has taken over the slanted hillsides facing north, as well as the softly undulating rolling hills with deeper soils. I had learned to tell the two apart mostly from their location on the prairie, as well as from the simple fact that bluebunch wheatgrass is bluish and sports a red collar where the leaf joins the stem, and Idaho fescue has skinnier, almost fine leaves and, if I became desperate to identify it, is the only grass with black roots.

Mixed throughout the green bunchgrasses of the Zumwalt are hundreds of early spring wildflowers, growing in profusion, almost as if an invisible, giant hand had sown them freely from a bottomless can. The names of the flowers are both lyrical and descriptive: arrowleaf balsamroot, blue camas lily, shooting star, pink plumes, purple-eyed grass, pussytoes, among countless others that were just emerging when I was there.

The Zumwalt, with its plentiful grasses, flowers, shrubs, mammals, and birds, teems with intricate interrelationships. Seeing all the parts, and trying to make some sense of them, reminded me of an old Navajo saying that my favorite professor, Dr. Charles Warren, had once told me: "The greatest sacred thing is in knowing the order and structure of things." Dr. Warren had stressed to his students that to be a scientist of any measure, one must not see a biological system simply as an isolated parcel. A biological community must be thought of as a system of simple parts—parts that relate and whose relationships form a whole. This whole is, in essence, ordered, unified, and harmonious.

Somewhere in this whole, I suspected, lay the answer to the mystifying abundance of hawks. But to find any answers would require knowledge of all of the variables that make up the hawks' habitat. And my background in rangeland resources was limited. I was aware that a chief problem with today's method of biological education is that it prepares biologists in the special knowledge of their disciplines—in my case, raptor biology—somewhat at the expense of adequate education in integrative perspectives and procedures. As a consequence, many of today's management plans for fish and wildlife easily break down under implementation. All too often, foresters manage only for Douglas fir populations and cut down the trees on rotation, without understanding its effect on the entire forest community. Too often game biologists manage deer and elk populations without knowledge of livestock grazing regimes, which predetermine the quantity and quality of important food sources. It is a rare mammalogist who crosses over with a raptor biologist, yet as all raptor specialists know, hawks depend on ground squirrels for their sustenance.

Overseers of resources generally manage solely for populations of specific things—for populations of geese or pheasants or salmon, for example. Yet, if plans for the species are ever to have long-range viability, those who write and implement management plans must understand how the species in question fits into the bigger picture—into the entire community species pool—within which it lives.

From my superficial view of the Zumwalt Prairie, without yet having discerned the true quality of its rangeland, it seemed a polycultural sea of greens—springtime mint greens, forest greens, shamrock greens near the large stock ponds, bluegrass-of-Kentucky green by the creeks. They were every hue and shine—pale, bright, dull, and verdant—and always changing from the height of the sun in the sky, or the volume and cover of roving clouds. The wind changed the color, as did morning and evening dew; morning color was heightened, noontime was flat, and late afternoon shone gold-green and shadowy. Woven between the green, like blue yarn on the loom of the prairie, was water. Seasonal creeks and stock-ponds—round, placid, sparkling lakes built by cattle ranchers for their thirsty livestock—were plaited throughout the Zumwalt. Surrounding these riparian areas were lush grasses, primarily tall, willowy timothy and "white man's foot grass," as Native Americans called Kentucky bluegrass, for wherever the "white man" walked, this grass later grew to mark his footprints. Grebes and ducks frequented these waters, making graceful, moving punctuation points on the flat surfaces.

The bewildering thing about this serene picture was that something was missing, something I had expected to see moving about everywhere on this rangeland—cattle. I knew very well that all the people I had spoken to used this land to graze their livestock, but in early May, few, if any, could be seen. In their place were hawks, sleepy owls, deer and elk, skittering ground squirrels and industrious badgers creating hole after hole in the prairie. Coyotes ranged freely the hills; porcupines scuffled slowly along the willow groves. But mile after mile displayed no cattle.

My perplexity only heightened during the first weeks of May. By May 19 I had located sixty-four active raptor nests: thirty-eight nests belonged to red-tails, eleven were ferruginous, six were Swainson's hawks, eight were great horned owls, and one was a golden eagle. This amazing number did not include nests I had found of marsh hawks, short-eared owls, barn owls, and kestrels, all of which frequented the grassland knolls, fields, and abandoned barns.

Like a recurring theme that plays in your mind and creates

irritation because you can't shake it, some of the things I was seeing refused to integrate.

I had learned, from books and newspapers and talking to a variety of knowledgeable people, that grazing was destroying the native prairie, but here I saw no cows. I was duly warned that ranchers would complain about me traipsing across their private lands for a government study, but in most cases, I had been genuinely welcomed. I was well aware that ground squirrels, the hawks' mainstay, were a hallmark of overgrazed lands, but on the Zumwalt I saw hundreds of Belding's ground squirrels emerging after their long winter estivation, seemingly thriving in the succulent Zumwalt grasses.

To the ancient Greeks, beauty was a relation of parts in a unified whole. The Zumwalt parts did not add up. The outline of this beautiful prairie portrait was not filling in as the picture I had been trained to see.

Chapter Nine

"DONALD. . . DONALD!. . . DONALD DELACY!!"

Mrs. DeLacy's theme song for her son rang through every room in the house, as it did every day before school, but now it was to hurry him up to dress for the Elks Club dinner social. The refrain began sweetly, then rose in multiple decibels, at last erupting as a scream. Like a springer spaniel trained to respond only when the commands threaten action, Donald knew he didn't have to move until the last, harrowing screech.

I was already dressed and waiting downstairs in the velvet green parlor chair, while a fire blazed cheerfully in the unscreened fireplace. I didn't recognize my legs, for I hadn't seen them in over a month, clothed as they always were in blue jeans and long gray wool socks. Resting my nylon stockings and pointed, heeled dress shoes on the velvet foot stool, I enjoyed looking at the shiny black party shoes—ladies' shoes—and feeling the satin of my beige blouse against my skin, a delightful contrast from everyday cotton flannel. My long hair was clean and brushed, and hung down freely across my shoulders, instead of being restrained in braids. I had even donned lipstick and mascara, to make me even further unrecognizable to myself.

"You look—different" was all Mrs. DeLacy said. However she meant it, I took it as a compliment and hopped up to get my coat, after first smoothing the pleats of my gray brushed-wool skirt. I couldn't seem to get away from wool, but the dark gray satin lining made the well-cut skirt feel elegant as it caressed my legs.

"Donald, your bow tie's crooked and we're going to be late if you don't get your shoes on," said Mrs. DeLacy, with a twist to secure the belt of her purple raincoat. "We'll ride in my car and Donald, you can sit in the back, just move the books to one side. Your hair looks becoming that way, down but off your face," she said to me as we went out the door.

"Oh, thank you, Mrs. DeLacy. What about the fire?" I asked a bit hesitantly. "Shouldn't there be a screen in front of it?"

"Never's been a problem. The old screen broke a few years ago. I'll replace it sometime. Donald, for the Lord's sake, take off that grimy leather jacket and put on something decent!"

I had never been in an Elks Club before, but somehow I knew just how it would look. And it lived up to my expectations. Following Mrs. DeLacy and Donald through two solid wood doors, I saw at once that the room was something of a cross between a dark and smoke-filled cocktail lounge and a lively diner. It had the architectural feel of a remodeled 1950s ranch-style house, long of length, short of ceiling, but open and spacious, too, and jazzed up with newly refinished hardwood floors. Off to one side were rectangular tables festooned with white tablecloths and stainless steel utensils, with little burning candles floating in wax as undersized centerpieces.

Most of the action was coming from the center of the large meeting room, the "lodge" part, where men and women and some teenage children laughed and shot the breeze with probably the same people they saw at all these functions. The clink of glasses rose from the bar as people were provided with wine, beer, and cocktails. Many of the men wore bow ties, like Donald, or fancy bolo ties, and the great variety of Stetson hats riding on their heads rivaled that of a western clothing store.

Mrs. DeLacy bought me a glass of white wine and, for Donald, a 7-Up after frowning at his request for a "Bud."

"Now, you're going to be meeting many ranchers tonight, and I hope you won't get them going on Fish and Game policy," warned Mrs. DeLacy. "Remember, you're representing Oregon State."

While Mrs. DeLacy chatted with someone she knew from school, I stole a glance at the people in the room. Perhaps it was an illusion produced by the low plaster ceiling, but the people here looked tall; I could swear a majority of the men topped six feet. The weathered, ruddy faces of the ranchers were in direct contrast to the pallid skin of urban Portlanders; these people exuded health, whether or not the vision matched reality. But it was a fact that people here, by matter of choice and occupation, were outside more, living beside and with the land. Perhaps it was just the soft lighting, but their cheeks looked rosier, their hands rougher, their faces more lined but with brighter eyes than many folks in Portland.

"Good evening, Dorothy!" cried a tall, slender man dressed in a fancy white suit with a ruffly shirt while accosting her with a hug around the waist. "Glad you could make it. Hello, Donald. And this must be the bird girl."

Mrs. DeLacy flinched. "Marcy," she corrected.

"Brad Lucas, Marcy, and this is my wife, Janice."

"Pleased to meet you," I replied. My fingers crumpled in his staunch handshake.

"You're looking well, Dorothy. We missed seeing you at the last grange meeting."

"I know," she said with a sigh. "I've been just too busy. Lately all my time has been taken up grading papers."

"I think you would have been amazed at the reaction your girl's calls set off," Mr. Lucas said, with a kindly smile. "She was the talk of the meeting."

"What calls?" Mrs. DeLacy asked slowly.

"You know Bill Deane's wife, Melanie, was taken with her. She even told ol' wild Bill he'd better keep his hands off the shotgun and let the eagles be."

"Melanie said what?" exclaimed Mrs. DeLacy.

"You know something, Dorothy? Your bird girl was right. That band of marauders that have been pestering the Deanes all spring just flew off somewhere a couple of weeks ago, never to be seen again. Just like she said was going to happen." He looked over at me, and smiled again. "Maybe you know something we don't know."

Mrs. DeLacy's brows were knitting together. "You were talking about the grange meeting, Brad."

"Oh yes, I was. Well, Bill talked to Clyde and Bruce and got them to agree they wouldn't plow under those nests of the ground-nesting hawks anymore. Apparently your girl, Dorothy, convinced them that the hawks did a darn good job picking up after their gophers."

"There's Clyde and Bev now," Mrs. Lucas interrupted, with an almost imperceivable jerk of her shoulders.

Mr. Lucas, at nearly six and a half feet, towered above almost everyone else in the lodge. He waved his arm above all heads and pointed down at me.

"Clyde, come meet the bird girl!" he yelled above the din; I could feel my face visibly reddening. "Dorothy's new girl!"

Mrs. DeLacy's face blanched. The woman named Bev rushed over to kiss Dorothy on the cheek. "Dorothy, dear," she gushed, "that makes nine, doesn't it?"

"Eight children is all I can handle."

"But you've only got one left at home," said Clyde. "Isn't that right, Dorothy?"

"Having Donald at home is as much work as the other seven children combined." Donald was standing by the table with peanuts and pretzels talking with friends and completely ignoring his mother.

"How nice that Dorothy took you in," Bev said to me. "You being a stranger and all."

"It's only for a short time, until she finds a more permanent place," Mrs. DeLacy reported hastily. My sip of wine suddenly stuck in my throat as I remembered that I was only on trial. I had forgotten Mrs. DeLacy's original warning that if life became too hectic with company and visiting children in June, when school let out, I must find a new place to live. Relocating then, my busiest time, would be a dreadful strain.

"Next thing, Brad," said Clyde, handing his wife a martini, "this bird girl will be trying to convince everyone that we shouldn't shoot coyotes."

"Clyde, you know damned well if you only would calve later in the spring, not in January, you'd cut your coyote problem in half," replied Mr. Lucas.

"Don't believe a word of it."

"Clyde, you old coot, like Doc Hatfield said at the last Coordinated Resource Management meeting, bringing in helicopters to kill coyotes is asinine, when we all know that coyotes help keep down the rodents. If you just time your calving when the rodents are out, you reduce the danger to your calves."

"You're beginning to sound radical, Brad," warned Dorothy.

The bell rang for dinner, and, carefully shuffling Donald and me along to our table as if we might otherwise turn into wayward goslings, Mrs. DeLacy seated me between herself and her son. Once situated, she queried me in a whisper as to what "calls" I was making, but before I could reply, two couples had joined us at the dinner table. Ted and Betty Martin and Sam and Anita Russ were ranchers with large holdings at the edge of the Zumwalt near the Imnaha River border.

On being introduced, Mr. Martin, who I recalled had seemed interested in the hawk study, began asking questions that surprised me with their sophistication.

"Do you pronounce the kinds of hawks you're studying boo-*tay*-o or boo-*tee*-o?" he asked as a green salad overflowing with creamy blue-cheese dressing was being placed around the table by waitresses dressed in scalloped pink blouses and pleated pink skirts.

"The emphasis is on the first syllable. *Byu*-tee-o. But it's not *boo*, it's *byu*, like in *beautiful*."

"What in the world is byu-tee-oo?" asked Mrs. Russ, somewhat astonished. "What in heaven's name are you talking about, Ted?"

"Byu-tee-o is a cream my wife puts on her face at night to make her beau-ti-ful," he said with a squeeze to his wife's shoulders. "No, really, Anita, it's a bird. Hasn't Sam told you about the bird girl?"

"What's a bird girl?"

"Let her tell you," said Mr. Martin, with a wink at me. Mrs. DeLacy wore the same pained look she had had on all evening.

I put down my water glass and smiled. "I'm here, Mrs. Russ, from Oregon State studying the hawks of Wallowa County. Buteo hawks, like red-tails, are the big, open-country ones that have broad wings and tails."

Mrs. DeLacy put her fingers to her lips. "Quiet everyone," she whispered, with a frown at me. "His Highness is about to speak."

People began to bow their heads in prayer as His Highness, whoever that was, uttered a slow grace, and then afterward announced we should all dig in and enjoy the wonderful food.

"Like that steak," whispered Mr. Martin, with another wink at me. Mrs. DeLacy prattled on about school, her students, her plans to take some graduate courses this summer. I wondered if she suffered from a touch of loneliness. Always among teenagers, she must have welcomed the chance to be with her peers.

While the dinner plates were being removed and dessert served, "His Highness" got up to give a synopsis of the Elks Club annual report and to introduce new officers to rounds of applause. Dessert was left mostly untouched, for the "floating islands," or whatever they were called—floating somethings in a sea of green liquid—were concocted from unrecognizable ingredients and too closely resembled the floating candle centerpieces.

After "His Highness" had stepped down from the podium, people began rising from the dinner tables to congregate again and socialize in the main lodge hall. This time, I noticed, everyone's speech seemed to be louder, and livelier, resulting from good food and friends and several rounds of drinks.

Our table partners also dispersed. Mrs. DeLacy excused herself to go to the rest room, Donald vanished, and I found myself suddenly alone by the pretzel table.

Feeling out of place and something of a hypocrite, I stuffed my mouth with a handful of pretzels. Hidden under my party clothes was a closet environmentalist amid a swarm of conservative Republican ranchers. When would I be forced to "come out"?

Eyeing me from several tables away, a young man about my age with sunny blond hair proffered a smile. Not knowing what else to do, I reached over for another big handful of pretzels.

To my dismay, the young man, obviously misreading my signals, strutted over confidently. He wore a gray sports jacket with a black leather bolo tie clasped together with a fetish of silver and turquoise. His new cowboy boots knocked out a two-step rhythm on the hardwood floor.

I scanned the room quickly for Mrs. DeLacy or Donald. They were nowhere in sight. The man came up beside me and helped himself to some pretzels.

"You're with Dorothy, aren't you?" he said, by way of an introduction.

I nodded, my mouth too full to speak.

"Ben McPherson," he said, reaching out his hand to shake mine, which was gritty with salt crystals. "I think you spoke to Dad the other day. Lloyd McPherson."

Lloyd McPherson, if I remembered correctly, had several thousand acres of rangeland on the Zumwalt flanking Swamp Creek. "Oh yes, yes I did," I replied, trying to swallow all the pretzels, which was difficult without the aid of a glass of water.

"Dad told me about your project. It intrigued him. You see, we're all kind of fanatical about birds in our family. I'd be happy to lend you a hand if you ever need it."

"Thank you. I'll remember that."

He smiled warmly, and I felt myself relaxing. "Dad and I got to talking about where we've noticed the most hawks. We both came to the conclusion that it was out around Findley Buttes. Have you seen the buttes?"

"No, not yet. There's still a lot of land I need to cover," I said, clearing my throat.

He looked at my empty hands. "Can I get you a glass of wine or something?"

"Oh, no thank you. I'm not sure how long Mrs. DeLacy intends to stay."

"Well," he continued, "Findley Buttes is northeast of Joseph, about fifteen miles as the crow flies. The two buttes together span about six or seven square miles. Prettiest country you'll ever see, though this time of year it can be wet and soggy on the back roads because of snow melt. You have four-wheel drive?"

"Don't believe a word he's saying!" a florid, older gentleman interrupted. Sidling up to Ben, he gave him a hearty slap on the back. "Hello, young Mr. McPherson." The man was obviously intoxicated. "Better be careful, young lady. This lad will say anything to a pretty girl."

Ben shook his head and smiled sheepishly at me. "Cyrus Hockley, you're full o' beans. No one can believe a word you say. You can talk the tail off a hog."

Hogs? Hockley? Good grief! This was one individual I'd hoped never to run into. And now he had his arm around Ben and was heaving nuts in his mouth.

"Well, who is this little lady?" he mumbled to Ben, and I cringed, looking for Mrs. DeLacy, who must have been swallowed up in the rest room.

"Don't know her name yet," replied Ben, grinning, "but they call her the bird girl."

"Birdy, you say?"

Surreptitiously trying to back away before my true identity

was revealed, I bumped into Mr. Martin, who, unfortunately, had brought over still another rancher to meet me.

"Whoa! Not so fast; don't run off yet," said Mr. Martin. "Stan Ferris wants to meet you. Stan owns the ranch next to the Russes; you might be seeing him next week when he starts moving his cattle."

With relief I saw that Mr. Hockley was being pushed farther and farther back, as Mr. Martin and Ferris intruded.

"Stan is interested in hawks, and wants to know more about your study," said Mr. Martin, while Ben crowded in to hear. All of this curiosity about hawks was really quite marvelous. I could feel myself relaxing, enjoying this surprising attention.

"I'm going to take her out someday and show her the buttes," Ben was saying, as several others came around.

Outside of this circle of concerned landholders I could just barely see Mrs. DeLacy's short form, at last resurrected from the rest room. Just now she was trying to get my attention by agitatedly motioning something to me with her hands. I tried to respond, but she became lost to my sight when Ben McPherson shifted his long legs to stand like a pillar between us.

"Take her to the buttes to show her the hawks?" asked Mr. Martin.

"The Swainson's hawks; they're all over the place in June," replied Ben. I realized this cowboy did indeed have some knowledge of birds.

"What in God's graces is a Swainson's hawk?" asked another man, with a handlebar mustache, sidling over to join the group.

"It's a bird, Nathan," answered Ben, while I still tried to look past all the people for Mrs. DeLacy. "A hawk."

"Someone call me?" hollered Mr. Hockley from the rear.

"Tell me more about your project," said the mustached cowboy, who stood a little too close, but I was backed up by the table of pretzels again and had nowhere else to go.

Suddenly pushing her way through the circle like a resolute

bulldog, Mrs. DeLacy came forward and reached up to drape my coat over my shoulders.

"Why it's the Fairy Godmother coming for Cinderella!" cried Mr. Hockley, growing more drunk by the minute.

Mrs. DeLacy was not smiling as she escorted me across the floor to the exit door, while bidding brusque goodnights to her associates.

"Remember my offer to drive you around Findley Buttes," yelled Ben, as the door closed between us.

It had been a rather Cinderella evening, I thought, especially the last part, with the rancher's attentiveness and eagerness to discuss the hawk project, which came as a delightful surprise. Mrs. DeLacy pounded down the outer stairs in silence. Her reaction seemed curious, but I shrugged it off as merely the result of a long tiring day.

At the bottom I turned to face her, putting my hand on her sleeve. "Thank you for including me," I said genuinely. "I really enjoyed meeting your friends. Their interest in the hawks is wonderful."

"Your *blouse*," she replied cryptically, fumbling through her purse for her key. She opened the door on her side of the car, and then slammed it behind her. Donald crawled silently onto the back seat.

My blouse? Opening my coat, I looked down and gasped. The top four buttons were unfastened, having somehow worked their way loose during the evening. Tonight I had unknowingly exposed to the world a pale bare chest and the flimsy top half of my old lacy bra.

Chapter Ten

BECAUSE MRS. DELACY never mowed her lawn, by mid-May it was dandelion heaven in her one-acre backyard. The golden fairy bonnets shook their sassy heads and splashed her vibrant lawn with sunny yellow. Mrs. DeLacy wasn't the only one whose property sported dandelions; throughout the cultivated fields where horses grazed and frisking lambs, foals, and calves tested their new legs, the ubiquitous plant grew thick and unruly, reflecting the sun's rays back to the broad cerulean bowl of sky.

Fruit trees of all varieties were bursting into bloom in the county; shadowy, quiet roads were draped by the burgeoning leaves from stately old trees. The blue Wallowas, ten thousand feet high and capped with spring snow, closely encircled the cultivated valley five to six thousand feet below. The native prairie extended north and west from the valley for mile upon mile, escaping from the cultivated lands like a child running from her mother, with waves of grass for hair and colorful wildflowers for a cloak.

Mrs. DeLacy was right; freaky hail or snowstorms infrequently spoiled spring's pretty picture. Wallowa County's twenty inches of annual precipitation occurred mainly from October to June, and much of it in the form of snow. Some days I would awaken to three to four inches of snow on the ground, or find myself caught far out on the Zumwalt when a cloud from nowhere would catch me by surprise, and thoroughly drench the landscape as if a thousand-gallon plastic water bladder had just been popped by a sky god playing a joke.

After starting to hike long miles in the expansive interior

country, I quickly learned that a prairie is far from flat. Its hills and valleys are significant, although at first they all look the same. Each infinitesimal brown line on the topographic map represented eighty feet in elevation—and there were many lines. Each one meant another chance to get turned around and lost. Every ravine, hill, and creek had to be checked for hawk nests—a task that I soon discovered was akin to hunting for the pot of gold at the end of a box canyon.

For the first several days, I scaled every hilltop to keep sight of my truck so I wouldn't get lost. After a week I relaxed, gaining confidence in reading the maps, and let myself go, usually ten miles, sometimes twelve to fourteen, to the heartland interior. There were no rattlesnakes to worry about on the Zumwalt. No people to surprise you around the next bend. Walking alone, mile after mile in this wild country, was a pleasure and invoked a feeling of security more penetrating than any stroll down a city street.

The prairie "dangers" were actually mere inconveniences: mosquitoes, twisting an ankle in the battlefield of camouflaged badger holes, or catching one's skin trying to get over or through barbed-wire fences. After two days, I had more than twenty large mosquito bites on my back, a bandaged arm from a bad cut from a fence, and a four-inch rip in the seat of my new jeans from trying to crawl under barbed wire.

Today, May 18, I parked twelve miles up the Zumwalt Road and across from Hadley's Corral, an old vacant farmhouse still demarcated by a weatherworn, wooden signpost nailed to a fence alongside a long-overgrown driveway. I planned to explore Pine Creek, a winding waterway lining, like the graceful mark of a blue calligraphy pen, a clutch of hills laden with wildflowers. Green frogs created 360-degree sound, rivaling Bose stereo speakers, while everything seemed to be calling to everything else. The peep of the ground squirrel echoed back to the yodel of a meadowlark; the whisper of grass spoke to the fretful cry of a kestrel.

Pine Creek's enfolding hills at turns expanded and closed as the miles took me deeper into the interior. Deer and elk footprints tiling the game trails were easily visible and so abundant that it seemed the animals must have been rushing off to a game convention. Buteo nests appeared down the canyon at regular intervals spaced about a mile apart, although the snaking route of Pine Creek kept the hawks' visibility to each other at a minimum.

I tried to catch sight of the hawk nests before the landlords saw me, but I generally failed. This time of year the birds were on guard. I felt victorious whenever I caught a pair unawares, as I did the incubating female red-tail sitting tightly on her nest in a ragged aspen tree. Her mate, flying up-canyon, dangled a Belding's ground squirrel in his talons and, once alighted beside her, picked up the food in his beak and handed it over. The hungry female took it and soared to a nearby tree to eat, while her dutiful mate carefully positioned himself on the eggs. This transfer of attention to the eggs or young was a buteo trait.

These birds paired for life, and would take another mate only if their original partner died. They shared equally the labor of nest building, and together participated in incubating the eggs and feeding and raising their young. Buteo hawks could be used as a paradigm for modern couples.

The sound of my boots slicing through the bunchgrass was like fingers running through a soft bristled brush. Both sod and bunchgrasses are generally perennial species that are excellent soil binders, but whereas the sod grass is more lawnlike, its dense network of rootstalks making the soil and grass one entity, bunchgrasses show the scalp of soil in between, allowing for a bright palette of wildflowers to take root, like a sweater made with multicolored, nubby yarn.

The wealth of Zumwalt plants made it nearly impossible for my eyes to integrate them. In a native prairie, 220 species or more can exist together in a single square mile—a feat made possible by several delicate interworkings. Plants share soil at different depths. They obtain light at varying heights. They make their demands for water and nutrients at different seasons of the year. And they work for each other's benefit. Tall growing plants protect lower ones from overheating and drying out. The sod formers and low-growing species reduce water loss by covering the surface of the soil. Leguminous plants supply nitrogen to the soil, which benefits all their neighbors.

At some seasons of the year, a few species seem to eclipse all others. In spring on the Zumwalt, two-foot-high arrowleaf balsamroot flowers cast a gay yellow blanket that could put any field of dandelions to shame. Each balsamroot grew from a long stalk, topped by one large yellow flower nearly five inches wide. At its base was a cluster of silver-gray leaves, each blade approaching one foot long with the shape of an arrow. Arrowleaf balsamroot liberally flanked south-facing hills with thousands of sunflowerlike blossoms. Indians prepared medicine from its roots, and its oily, ripe seeds were a source of important nutrients for nearly all western Native American tribes. Captain Lewis of the famed Lewis and Clark Expedition wrote in 1806 of a bread the Indians made from the seeds of the plants mixed with dried service berries.

Pine Creek's hills were a colorful mixture of yellow, purple, white, pink, and blue-violet, the latter, in mid-May, coming from fields ripe with beautiful camas lilies. In historic times such meadows were considered tribal property and jealously guarded. The plant's onionlike bulb was plump and nutritious, and was probably the most important food of many Native Americans. Cooking of camas bulbs, an involved procedure of steaming in fire pits, was so delicate that, according to some historians, only the oldest and most experienced women of the tribe were trusted with its care. Wars had been waged over disputes among rivaling tribes about who possessed particular camas fields. With such import placed on this lovely, hyacinth-looking flower, it is not surprising that Native Americans were unable to fathom the white man, who felt it his prerogative to take over these possessions and destroy the bountiful meadows with his plow.

Other flowers, abundant but easily overlooked because of their delicacy, pressed in between the grasses. Fritillaries, or yellow bells, shook their elfin heads with the slightest wind. The dainty flowers were only four to twelve inches high, and their tiny yellow blossoms only about a half-inch long hanging down like little fairy bells from the top of the stalk. Prairie smoke was another small, bell-shaped flower whose pink, urn-shaped cup dangled from stalks sixteen inches high. Later in the spring, the cup would amazingly turn upward, and white, feathery plumes would grow from the pistils, like little wisps of smoke.

Nearing the headwaters of the west fork of Pine Creek, the terrain climbed up to the mesa of the prairie. The land seemed to stretch out, flatten out, dry out, without the benefit of the small watershed. It was still green, filled with flowers and tall bunchgrass, but there was more space between the vegetation. Few trees grew. A few outcroppings of rock stood as pillars dropped incongruously on the flat sheet of prairie. With little to obscure vision, it was easy to see an oversized, ferruginous hawk nest spilling out of an available crevice in the outcrops.

It was easy for the bird to spot me also. A handsome male flew from the rock and appeared to be heading my way, but turned. Something else had come between us—a noisy, taunting raven. The hawk jibed his wings, soaring to discourage the sooty, intelligent pest. The raven wasn't disturbed. He boldly continued his afternoon jaunt to the hawk's outcrop, where he calmly perched. The ferruginous hawk proffered a fly-by to vent his frustration, but the raven still sat, unmoving. Finally the hawk gave up and returned to join his mate at the nest.

I left the estranged neighbors to their private vexations and turned diagonally to cross a series of softly undulating hills toward where I had come from this morning. Still another ferruginous hawk, perched on a badger mound, rose powerfully into the air, the sun tipping a crown on the bird's white head. It was becoming easier for me to identify them from a distance, if only I could catch sight of their undersides. Ferruginous hawks' typically white bellies contrasted with their reddish brown legs, which, when held back in flight, showed up as a dark V shape.

The bird swooped down swiftly to swipe an unlucky ground squirrel. In what seemed one motion, the bird attacked, grasped, and lifted off again with its prey to return to its nest. I wandered closer to peer into the old stick nest placed prominently on a rock bluff. Three young hawks—about two weeks old, judging from their primary feathers already unsheathed about one half inch— sat well protected in a bed of downy feathers. Six uneaten ground squirrels lined the periphery, as though the birds had just stocked up at the grocery store.

Catching the east fork of Salmon Creek on the return trip, I discovered three more active buteo nests, which meant, after nearly ten miles of searching, that I had located a satisfying total of seven nests. With eager anticipation, I tried to imagine how this one piece of the Zumwalt puzzle would look filled in on the base maps. What patterns, if any, might be revealed? Why did the birds choose to nest where they did, and how did they decide to separate themselves? Some nested closer together, some farther apart. Yet they all seemed to be going after the same food. Were there enough Belding's ground squirrels to go around for everybody? And just why were there so many of the funny little rodents, anyway?

My feet were tender and my legs sore; I needed to work up to this. I had never suspected, before this spring, that a native prairie could be so diverse, full of color and surprises. Plants and animals, soil and water, landforms and climate—all were mixed together like some magical concoction in a giant cauldron. I could only wish that these disparate ingredients, if left to settle for a while in my mind, might separate out, like oil, vinegar, and spices in a dressing, to help me come up with answers before they were shaken up again.

I crossed two fields, jumped over four more barbed-wire fences, and then paused to read the topos, which told me I was only a half mile from my truck. Crossing up and over the last ridge, a fresh gust of wind hit my face. There was the truck; I had come out at almost exactly the same spot I had started. Now all that lay between me and relaxation was a wire fence stretched out for miles to the north and south, and across the fence, a bucolic field of hay about a quarter mile in width, and then a second wire fence separating the meadow from the road.

There was only one problem. Positioned in the center of the hay field, eyeing me contemptuously, was the largest Black Angus bull I had ever seen.

Chapter Eleven

I IMMEDIATELY REMOVED my red bandanna. Whether or not bulls are colorblind was an issue I didn't care to test at the moment. Something like smoke was coming from the animal's cavernous nostrils, which were pierced by a large steel ring. His puffing breath sounded more like a groan, and I felt my stomach turn, wondering how I would ever reach my truck without passing through this horrid beast's pasture.

My eyes scoped up and down the barbed-wire fence separating us, hoping to see some sign of cross fencing somewhere, but the unbroken line extended straight for miles in each direction. Pivoting myself perpendicular to the bull, I feigned unconcern and strolled leisurely northward several hundred feet. To my dismay, out of the corner of my eye I could see that the grotesque animal, so large and oddly shaped that it seemed to be dragging its bulky underside along the ground, was trailing me almost step for step.

This was ridiculous. A lone bull couldn't stop me from getting to my truck. If I waited for a few minutes, it would lose interest in me and return to grazing the succulent green sod grass being trampled under its splayed, cloven hooves.

Throwing my backpack aside, I sat down. Clouds were rolling in, throwing multiformed shadows across the prairie. Gliding by unperturbed on the glass of an unfenced stock pond were two horned grebes, colorfully adorned in breeding plumage. The orange feathered wisp of "horns," starting at its red eyes and growing back to the middle part of its head, were adorable on the little robin-sized waterbird.

They were not adorable on the giant bull. In fact, they looked utterly torturous, each measuring about two feet in length and ending in a sharp, sabrelike tip.

The rising, plaintive "coorloo" of the long-billed curlew came from the shining waters. The bird flew up from the grass, led, it seemed, by its long, slender beak, which looked more like a pencil. The sweet song lent a placid quality to the scene, which was ruined when the bull lumbered over to drink from the same spot where the curlew had been.

Seeing his attention diverted, I slowly picked up my pack and walked noiselessly in the other direction. The bull did the same. How fast could these brutes go? I wondered. Was it safe to try to outrun him? As a test, I began to jog slowly. The bull also picked up its pace.

I began to worry that this silly game might go on until nightfall, but at last something unseen by me caused the bull to pause and sniff the air. Were bulls like dogs, ferreting out scents? The nose ring trembled, and the animal turned its head, which looked about as intelligent as a tomato. Shuffling his short front legs, which looked incapable of hauling around such a massive neck and chest, the bull lumbered back toward the pond.

I wished the ugly animal good riddance. Springing up and paralleling the fence downwind, I watched for just the right spot to hop over and make my getaway. The bull was still pursuing some invisible feedlot when I grabbed hold of the metal fence rod and lightly placed my boot on a line of wire. Leaping over fences was similar to vaulting up on a bareback horse, and I was getting better at it with practice. So as not to ruin the wrought tension of the wire, I tried to exert as little weight as possible, and quickly jumped.

Three thousand pounds of biomass slowly veered around. I began striding with long but quiet steps straight across the quarter-mile field, feigning confidence while feeling mortally exposed. A shocking-yellow meadowlark, perched safely on a post, belted out its melodious whistle, while the squashed, coonlike face of a badger poked up out of a burrow. The badger was making a mess of the meadow, digging large holes in pursuit of ground squirrels, its preferred food.

I must be careful not to trip in these miniature moonlike craters, I thought to myself; this was the last place I wished to twist an ankle. Keeping my sights on my goal, I was making acceptable headway, when I noticed something dark and sinister following me.

The clumping steps began to pick up speed. In similar fashion, my feet moved. The pace increased. The brute with the monster horns adroitly lifted his powerful legs to trot; for all its bulk, the animal deftly missed every badger hole in the pockmarked field.

Fighting panic as the adrenaline pumped through my veins, I considered running, but wondered if that would only further entice this *thing*. Although not familiar with the temperament or territorial behavior of bovines, I could still read this one's body language. It meant business.

I ran for my life.

The huge animal charged through the delicate tufted hair grass, as enraged as if I were a matador. Where are the picadors when you need them? The ground was actually shaking from the animal's pounding hooves.

My only hope was the fence. As I closed in on it, the bull had shortened the distance separating us to only a few terrifying yards. Sprinting for dear life, I reached the fence and in one motion vaulted it single-handedly.

The black behemoth, only feet behind me, halted abruptly, his vacuous gaze dumbfounded by the wire between us.

"Why did God ever make horrible creatures like *you?*" I cried out loud, as the bull's rheumy eyes, too little for its head, still stalked me.

The voice that came from behind me was nearly as frightening as the bull: "God made bulls to scare the daylights out of folks who trespass on private property!"

Spinning around, I saw a bronzed man with a Stetson tipped over one eye, laughing from behind the broken gate of Hadley's Corral. He pushed up the hat and revealed eyes the color of a prairie stock pond.

"No, that bull won't hurt you none," he said. "Henry's as gentle as a kitten."

"What was he doing chasing me, then?" I asked, out of breath. "And I wasn't trespassing. I have permission."

"Henry's just gettin' his exercise. He likes a good joke." He removed his Stetson to scratch his bald head. "You're the bird girl, aren't you? The one who spoke to my wife last month."

I nodded and tried to calm my pounding heart. The man smiled and reached out his crusty ranch hand.

"I'm Larry. Larry Hadley. Noticed your truck here when I got here this morning. You've been out exploring all this time?"

"Yes," I replied, panting but softening a bit under the spell of his easygoing demeanor. "Looking for hawks."

"You know, hawks are important to us. They really help us out." Mr. Hadley scratched his head one more time and then repositioned his cowboy hat. "We've got a terrible red-digger problem out here; the damn squirrels take so much of our grass, they're competing with our cattle."

"They eat your *grass?*"

"What else do you think they eat? In a few weeks' time, there's going to be thousands of 'em. You can't shoot or poison them all. That's why those hawks are sacred to us. They're the best red-digger control we got."

Judging from the looks of his field full of holes, I didn't think the hawks were doing a good job at all.

"The diggers and the badgers. Their holes are so damn large, a horse or cow can fall in it and break a leg. You know, one family of red diggers can eat as much grass as a full-grown steer."

I found this difficult to believe but kept my thoughts to myself.

"You must be mighty thirsty after your day's trek and run," he said, looking back down at the gate to examine the busted hinge.

"Oh no, not really. I have water in my pack. I just need to catch my breath."

"It's been a hot day and you're as red as a beet. Mabel!" He shouted up at the house. "Anymore iced tea in the thermos?"

No answer came, and Mr. Hadley turned to explain. "My wife, Mabel, is inside, tidying up the place. After a whole winter away, the dust is something awful. We're only out here, you know, in summer and fall, when we move the cattle."

"Mabel!" he cried again, cupping his hands to his mouth. "What you say, Mabel?"

"For the Lord's sake," a high voice replied at last. "Yes!"

Mr. Hadley opened the squeaky gate, which tilted at a sixty-degree angle, and touched his hand to his hat, motioning to the house. "Why don't you come on in for a spell. You look like you could use a rest." He laughed to himself. "And so does poor ol' Henry."

Resting my pack against the fence, I followed Mr. Hadley up to the house, where Mabel stood in the doorway with a broom. I felt no sympathy for poor ol' Henry. In fact, I quite enjoyed the thought of Henry, several years hence, hanging in the local butcher's meat locker.

Chapter Twelve

BEFORE THE COMING of white man, Native Americans inhabited the canyons and prairies of this remote section of northeast Oregon for more than ten thousand years. They became known, in modern times, as the Nez Perce tribe, whose lands spread into southeastern Washington, northeastern Oregon, and central Idaho. The Wallowa band of the Nez Perce lived in the beautiful Wallowa Valley and on the Zumwalt Prairie; their history is one of the saddest chapters in the opening up of the Northwest.

It was the all too common story of treaties made between the Indians and the U.S. government—treaties that were later broken by the white man. The Wallowa band of the Nez Perce, of all the tribes in the Northwest, was possibly the least desiring of war, the most willing to work with the white man, and, at the last, the most betrayed.

In 1855 the Nez Perce and the U.S. government crafted a treaty to set off Wallowa County as an Indian reservation. But in 1860, when gold was discovered on Nez Perce land, miners poured into Indian territory with little concern for the promises made to the Indians. By 1863 the Indian leaders were again talked into giving up more land to the white man. Four years later, the Wallowa Valley, too, was declared open for settlement.

The next ten years, with the Indian attempting to meld with the white man, were strained, but quarrels were amazingly minimal. The Nez Perce chiefs of the Wallowa band had always promised peace, and they did their best to live up to their word. But in 1877, Chief Joseph's band was given thirty days notice to leave their beloved Wallowa Valley to move forever to the Nez Perce Indian reservation at Lapwai, Idaho. Other Nez Perce bands, driven from their homelands in the Snake and Salmon River country, and from the beautiful Camas Prairie, would join them.

In the summer of 1877, the Wallowa Nez Perce band, led by Chief Joseph, began the long trek to Lapwai. Chief Joseph and other chiefs of the Wallowa band had never actually signed a treaty giving up their valley, and they were on their way to Lapwai to convince the government to let them return to their homeland. A skirmish erupted between some settlers and a few renegade Nez Perce during the journey, however, and it developed into a major war with the U.S. Army. The war ultimately affected all the different bands of the Nez Perce, including the Wallowa tribe.

Trying to escape bloodshed, the Wallowa Indians fled east, and then north to Canada. Their flight was a terrible ordeal, for they were constantly pursued by the dogged General Oliver O. Howard, who refused to give up until the Nez Perce were captured and sent to the reservation.

For four months Chief Joseph's tribe successfully evaded the army, traveling more than twelve hundred miles, mostly in poor, wintry conditions. On several occasions soldiers caught up with the Indians, but they could never completely overcome the Nez Perce, who continued to escape them due to superior strategizing. Only thirty-nine miles from the Canadian border, however, with freedom achingly close, the Nez Perce were at last trapped by General Howard and, exceedingly weary, finally surrendered.

"Our chiefs are killed," said Chief Joseph, speaking for his people. "It is cold and we have no blankets. The little children are freezing to death. From where the sun now stands, I will fight no more forever."

The brokenhearted Nez Perce were forcibly taken to Indian territory in Oklahoma, then later transferred back to reservations in Lapwai and Colville, Washington, where Chief Joseph died, never again setting eyes on his beloved Wallowa Valley.

I thought often of the Nez Perce Indians as I explored the prairie. The haunting quality of the wind, the vast expanses, the ring of mountains protecting the valley, all seemed to speak of a different prairie that had existed only little more than a hundred years ago. The Nez Perce had inhabited all this land, but their presence here had never seemed as vivid and real to me as it did when exploring remote Lightning Creek Canyon, which turned and twisted to reach the flanks of the deep Imnaha River gorge. This arid fringe of the Zumwalt had shallower, stonier soils and myriad hidden rocky ledges, and seemed more lonely and forsaken than the rest of the prairie.

Yet here the voices of the past echoed more clearly and strongly in the empty miles of undulating bluebunch wheatgrass. Lightning Creek and the surrounding canyons had been a transition spot for the Nez Perce—a resting place in their annual migrations between the winter grounds, which encompassed the warmer canyons of the Snake and Imnaha Rivers, and the summer lands, in the lush Wallowa Valley and prairie. On these rocky trails, the Nez Perce made their twice yearly journey of twenty or thirty miles, bringing with them their many horses and cattle, several thousand head, which they acquired and built up in later years.

The Nez Perce had shared this country with wildlife—deer, elk, and hawks. Before the arrival of the white man, the plow had never touched the prairie; miners had never split open the ground for gold. Many of the northwest Indian tribes could not understand and had a distinct aversion to the way the white man manipulated the earth, as elucidated by a Northwest Indian named Smohalla:

"You ask me to plow the ground? Shall I take a knife and tear my mother's bosom? Then when I die she will not take me to her bosom to rest. You ask me to dig for stone? Shall I dig under her skin for her bones? Then when I die I cannot enter her body to be born again. You ask me to cut and make hay and sell it, and be rich like white man! But how dare I cut off my mother's hair?"

What had the land looked like during the reign of the Nez

Perce? What, in the presettlement landscape, had been the native species' composition and abundance? As scientists were beginning to realize, a biological community of interacting species was not something that could be observed at a single moment in time. It incorporated, rather, a sequence of stages that extended back into the past and into the future. Single measurements of a system, such as inventories, were important, for they provided information about how things were at one point in time. But scientists also need to understand how things were apt to function under various conditions. Only by trying to understand a landscape's capacity could scientists hope to make appropriate management decisions that would positively affect the entire biological community in the long run.

It all came back to the "whole picture" approach. All parts needed to be retained in working order for the machine to keep running. The goal of ecology was to somehow maintain the cogs and wheels, screws and levers, so the capacity of the system could overcome any short-term imbalance or poor performance.

It was my guess that in historic times the Zumwalt Prairie closely resembled what I was seeing today. There must have been native grasses growing here, ancient ancestors of today's bluebunch wheatgrass and Idaho fescue, and possibly the same species of wild-flowers. Undoubtedly, there were hawks and eagles, although their abundances may have been different.

The diaries of the early pioneers revealed a highly diverse pre-settlement landscape. And it was still debatable whether large herds of roving bison had historically occurred in Oregon, as they had in other parts of the West. But range fires—some naturally caused by lightning, others deliberately set by Indians who burned the land in successional cycles—were known to have occurred often in historic times, and played an important role in the height of the grassland vegetation of the West.

The early settlers' attempts to put a stop to all prairie fires pos-sibly effected more change in the landscape than any other early management activity. Concurrently, settlers also began grazing large herds of cattle, which, in some respects, kept the grasses down in a similar fashion to the fires of the past. There was a difference, however. With the demise of the range fires, vegetative succession started and, where there was adequate water, trees and shrubs began to grow in places that before had been only grass. In addition, settlers planted trees around their homesteads—trees that remained long after the homes were gone, and provided nesting sites for many species of birds, including hawks.

A golden eagle lazily banked overhead and caught my eye. The huge bird drifted easily in the wind over the hazy reaches of Lightning Creek Canyon. Slowly I began my careful descent down the steep basalt slopes, watching my footing. Volcanic rocks of all shapes and sizes lay exposed and randomly strewn about the canyon, like some ancient being had blithely tossed the boulders about like marbles. This was perfect ferruginous hawk country—grassy, open, unpeopled, with an abundance of rocks on which to place a nest. Now the question was, which rocky outcrops were currently being used?

This took certain detective skills honed from long months spent in the field. With so much country to cover on the Zumwalt, some tricks could save an inordinate amount of time. Hunting for whitewash was one tried-and-true method that could slice time from looking over each outcropping for a nest; although birds could easily sequester themselves from view, splashes of their whitewash on the rocks were not easily missed.

Whitewash, another term for bird waste, varies from species to species. Golden eagles leave a large, white mess, almost as if a painter had used a wide roller to cover the walls. Peregrine falcons, in contrast, leave long, pencil-thin streaks of white dripping down cliff faces. Smaller birds, such as sparrows, leave spatterings of small drops, like spillovers from a paint can.

Hawk whitewash, however, is neither thin and separated, like the falcon, nor wide and extensive, like the eagle. It looks merely like a common brush stroke of coconut-white living-room paint stuck to sticks and rocks. The more years a nest has been in use, the more the buildup of whitewash.

Using this technique, I was able to track down a ferruginous hawk nest fairly quickly. Greeting my intrusion, four little downy heads of baby hawks, only about a week old, peered over the immense stick nest as I looked down from above. With both parents circling agitatedly above, I quickly retreated from the big-eyed, hooked-beaked balls of fluff, with gaping mouths that seemed larger than their heads.

A mile farther up the canyon, another prominent nest hugged the top of a rock outcrop. A slender, gray coyote ran along the rimrock just to the north. As I neared the nest, hearing no familiar cries of a defensive ferruginous hawk, I realized what had happened. The nest was unattended. Inside were only egg fragments, still fresh with yolk and white and blood on the interior of the shells. Below the nest was another eggshell, scored with the marks of canine teeth.

Lightning Creek continued winding precipitously to enter Little Sheep Creek, which dove into the Imnaha River Canyon and, in turn, plunged down to the Snake River chasm. The sight of the red rimrock canyons folding into one another as they dropped away from the prairie was arresting. How could anyone climb up and out of this rugged country? How could the Nez Perce have made yearly pilgrimages from the bottom of the deepest gorge—Hell's Canyon of the Snake River—up to the Wallowa Valley?

This same route had been used for thousands of years by Indians; the white man didn't lay eyes on the Zumwalt Prairie until 1839, when Nez Perce leaders led the Reverend Henry Spalding up the worn trail. Old Chief Joseph had guided Spalding through the Zumwalt's grassland meadows to the flourishing Wallowa Valley, the Nez Perce's cherished homeland. Reverend Spalding, not known for his responsiveness to natural beauty, was overwhelmed by what he beheld—the quality of the soil, the rich growth of grass and clover. After viewing it, he wrote in his diary that "it is the best land I have seen in this country." White settlers now grazed their livestock on the same rich prairie lands where the Indians had set up their camps. But the Indian presence was still here, and something of the tragic events that had occurred a century earlier still hung in the quiet spots. The press of their footprints, the whiz of their hunting arrows, could be felt along the sparkling creeks and among the remnants of ancient grasses.

I knew that some of the nesting locations of ferruginous hawks had probably been used by successive generations of birds for hundreds of years. These birds used the same nest again and again, especially if it was in a sturdy tree or rocky outcropping. Some nests were known to exceed even those of golden eagles and reach twelve to fifteen feet in height. Therefore, the snapshot of the nests I was seeing today failed to reveal all that must have taken place here years ago, when the ancestors of these present-day hawks lived on a prairie inhabited by the Nez Perce.

I wondered at the relationship between these two "native Americans." I suspected the ferruginous had been valued by the Nez Perce for its skill at hunting and its regal decorum, its grace in flight and eaglelike fearlessness.

The final nest in Lightning Creek Canyon more keenly impressed me than the other two. As I scooped around for fresh hawk castings beneath the stick nest that towered over four feet tall, I happened to feel something poking me under the soil. Digging down a few more inches, I discovered the tip of a piece of glossy obsidian. I carefully removed the dirt around it and lifted up a perfect, small arrowhead.

Blowing away the loose soil, I turned it around in my hand; the polished surface reflected the lowering sun like an exquisitely chiseled black diamond. Although obsidian was a hard igneous rock, the diminutiveness of the arrowhead, the size Indians used for hunting birds, made it appear delicate, almost fragile. This small piece of glass, formed from rapidly cooling lava and later by the skilled hands of some unknown Nez Perce, spoke to me more eloquently of a rich past, now inexorably gone, than any other time during my wide travels of the Zumwalt.

Past, present, and future: I saw more clearly now that any one aspect of time taken alone cannot fully characterize a biological community. Biological systems, including humans, are on a trajectory. Softly I placed the arrowhead back in the ground and covered it up again with soil. Although I wanted to keep it, I knew it would not be right. It belonged here. It belonged with this historic old nest. It was our past, speaking to our future.

Chapter Thirteen

THE ROAD TO CHICO CUTOFF was deeply rutted and slow going. Intermittent spring rainstorms had created potholes of gooey mud, waiting, like quicksand, to drink truck tires, especially worn tires on an underpowered two-wheel-drive government wreck. Actually, the truck and I were starting to understand each other, and if we were both patient, I felt reasonably assured that it would take me where I needed to go. Avoiding hidden sinkholes was my responsibility, but it was difficult to watch two places at once—the air and the ground ahead.

Chico Cutoff marked the northern boundary of the Zumwalt Prairie, where the pure stand of grassland ended and dense groves of ponderosa pines and aspen began. It also marked the end of private land, which merged with huge holdings of public property, overseen by the Forest Service. It was highly remote, visited only now and again by ranchers and Forest Service workers. In these forests lived rare goshawks and great gray owls, who, on this edge of two habitats, interacted with great horned owls and buteo hawks.

Scouting for hawks along the fringes of Chico Cutoff was tedious, for the area was deeply etched with pockets of aspen groves, each growing in a protected reach of enclosing hills. Buteo nests were often tucked away in the groves, which meant that every stand of trees needed checking by foot.

Already this morning I had checked three groves. Each had been separated from the other by a couple of miles, and each had housed a different buteo hawk nest. All three species had reacted differently to my intrusion.

The red-tailed hawks had chosen to place their nest in a partially dead tree. This adaptable species was capable of using a wide variety of habitat types, as I was finding. From cottonwood trees near town, to outcrops of rock, to lone trees, to open forests, the red-tail made its home. It had the widest ecological tolerance of any hawk in North America, which would be its saving grace in times of shrinking habitat.

The matriarch of this particular family swooped over me in alarm and cried out to her babies, who sat in the nest puffed out and immobile, looking like little stuffed prizes at a carnival. Her mate picked up the defense, as she swung low, preparing to land on top of the ducking nestlings. The graceful approach seemed one liquid movement, as she stopped her forward motion instantly by closing her wings forward in front of her, almost as if she were clapping her hands.

In contrast to the artful display of the red-tails, the ferruginous hawks that nested about one mile away chose to sit tightly to the nest. The mother bird refused to leave her small downy nestlings and stood above them with her wings outspread, shading her young from the direct sun. She called out, however, her displeasure at my intrusion.

The Swainson's hawks were so quiet as I hunted the grove that I would have overlooked them if not for a mischievous magpie who flew over to tease the serious hawk. While the female Swainson's sat perfectly still on a rather fragile-looking mess of sticks crammed inside the arms of a small aspen tree, the shiny black and white marauder zipped over to torment her—and perhaps to snitch an egg or two.

The gentle hawk put up with this nonsense for several minutes, but finally lunged from the tree, sending aspen leaves fluttering down in her wake, to mortify the magpie and teach it a lesson.

Continuing my exploration into the rolling prairie hills, I began to realize that something about the land was different. Something new seemed to have sprouted up overnight: cattle. In all directions, cattle, just delivered to summer pasture, were sampling the succulent spring grasses. From a distance they looked uncannily like little sprinkles of black pepper shaken all over a giant green plate.

I sighed and hoped I wouldn't encounter any more frisky bulls like "ol' Henry."

Standing at the edge of the prairie, with the retreating river gorges dropping off to the east, the Wallowa Mountains and Eagle Cap Wilderness encircling the south and west, and the Chico pine forests at my back, I was suddenly struck by what a self-contained unit the Zumwalt Prairie really was. For all the Zumwalt's expanse, it was still an island. The grassland habitat was effectively ringed in on all sides by completely different ecosystems—mountains, river canyons, and dense pine and fir forests. The Zumwalt was set apart, making it "doable" in terms of a research site, but incorporated in that was an inherent biological threat. All island habitats face the same problem: if anything happens to the populations of animals inhabiting an island, whether that island is surrounded by sea or disparate ecosystems, replacement of the animals is difficult because they are cut off from any renewing source.

There didn't seem to be any cause for worry on the Zumwalt at this time. The great numbers of breeding hawks, as well as a high incidence of extra birds with no nests, seemed to indicate a plethora of individuals. Yet, as a scientist, I was aware that natural catastrophes could and did happen. Virulent disease, devastating storms, or massive mismanagement by people could greatly affect a population, to the point of reducing its numbers to a dangerously low level.

Long-term survival of any species requires the presence of thousands of contiguous acres of suitable habitat, or habitat parcels that are connected via naturally occurring wildlife corridors linking healthy ecosystems. The fragmentation and isolation of natural habitat is the most serious threat to biological diversity today. Worldwide, virtually all habitats are becoming surrounded by human activity. Humans are creating thousands of "islands"—fragments of once large, homogenous ecosystems that are now surrounded by urban, suburban, or agricultural lands.

One major result of humans' carving up habitat into fragments smaller than the home range sizes required by an animal is that those species tend to disappear. First to be wiped out usually were more specialized species—those that moved widely and existed at low densities, such as black bear and elk. This has been documented repeatedly in the northeastern and southeastern regions of the United States. When large areas of contiguous forest were broken into small islands, native species began to vanish, including wolf, elk, black bear, bobcat, and cougar, all of which never returned. Songbirds, too have been declining at an alarming rate throughout the United States, caused, in part, by the fragmentation of forest habitat. Because of the loss of the top predators—the hawks, bobcat, bear, and cougar, for example—middle-sized omnivores such as opossums, raccoons, and skunks are burgeoning in the United States. These opportunists, all of which coexist well with humans, prey on native warblers, thrushes, vireos, tanagers, bluebirds, and meadowlarks.

Worldwide, one half million to two million species will become extinct by the year 2000, according to the *Global 2000 Report to the President*. The rate of extinction is expected to increase from one per day in 1980 to one per *hour* by the end of the century. As I looked on the bustling Zumwalt, however, these predictions seemed utterly impossible.

I felt incapable of gloomy musings on a day filled with sunshine and fields of wildflowers and cattle. Stupid cows. Just now they were congregating in a hollow exactly where I needed to go—milling around a stock pond and trampling everything to death. I counted seventy-five Black Angus steers, many of whom had turned to watch me as I was watching them through my binoculars.

There didn't appear to be a bull in the bunch, thank goodness.

Taking a deep breath, I boldly sauntered in their direction, intent on examining the six aspen trees that stood in the hollow behind them. What silly-looking, immovable creatures cows were, standing as if rooted to the water's edge, digging their big hooves deeper into the prairie soil.

A flat stretch of grassland, devoid of trees but rich in fescue and hundreds, possibly thousands, of dainty pink flowers, lay between the cows and me. The rosy blossoms, commonly known by the beautiful term *prairie smoke*, made the prairie blush. I stooped to observe the delicate pink flower the shape of a bell, which hung gracefully from thin reddish stalks about a foot high. Some of the plants were in the height of bloom, but others were already going to seed; as the flowers were fertilized, the pink urns turned upward, and plumes began to grow from the pistils. The filmy haze from their feathery seed pods created the effect of a layer of smoke on the grassland, which gave the landscape an ethereal aura.

The cows were on the move, I noticed, but this time I knew I had nothing to worry about. These guys were all steers, and steers, were, well, not bulls, not cows, but altered to be little more than steaks on hooves. Yet I had to admit that they looked surprisingly massive when they were in bulk, as now.

Something was stirring them up, I could tell. Their awkward forms made me think of the cattle stampedes I had seen on reruns of old westerns, and I laughed out loud. Where were my lariat, boots and spurs, and quarter horse?

The beasts were actually trotting now. I looked behind me to see what they were after; there was nothing but more grass. To the south another stock pond glistened, but they weren't heading in that direction. The ground beneath my feet jiggled slightly with the weight of the galloping cows. Do cows really gallop? I watched the moving wall of bodies coming closer. Yes, they were galloping now, and they seemed to be heading straight toward me.

I quickly turned around to scan the landscape. All the fence lines, I noticed with a sinking heart, were miles away. This was cowboy country, open range, and the wild cows knew it. The vibration of the earth was increasing with the closing-in of hundreds of hooves. Suddenly I saw visions of being trampled to death by a herd of stampeding steers. Without knowing exactly where I was going, I broke into a run, trying to stay ahead of the roaring torrent, hoofbeats pounding in my ears.

In something of a panic, I spied a lone, decrepit aspen tree growing, just over the ridge, like an artesian well in the middle of the grassland desert. With the foul breath of the bovine "predators" almost upon me, I reached the tree just in time to climb it to the top and split the befuddled herd in two, as they continued running blindly on either side of the tottering tree.

For a few moments longer, the animals continued on in their helter-skelter fashion, then slowly calmed down, realizing that what they were after had seemed to disappear. Then one saw me hanging onto the tree and stopped. Gazing up at me with mournful eyes, the beast snorted and mooed, and unfortunately attracted the attention of his buddies. The whole lot slowed to a shuffle and turned to look blankly up at me in the tree.

I stayed clasped to my precarious perch for nearly an hour, worrying equally whether I would be trampled to death if I dared descend or whether a rancher on horseback would happen by, find me hanging in the tree, and think me stark raving mad. My arms grew tired, and I shouted at the animals, hoping to frighten them, but they huddled beneath the tree, taking turns munching grass and resting.

Cows have no business here, I thought savagely.

With the beginning of my second hour in the tree, the problem took on new proportions. I couldn't stay here all night, and the cows seemed to have no intention of moving. At one point I moved down a few feet, but the animals responded by closing in. Just what in heaven's name did they think I was?

It was well past lunchtime, and watching all the cows enjoying their cuds, I actually felt hungry, and, resting back carefully on the uncomfortable limbs of the tree, I finagled my sack lunch from my backpack. It was an exacting maneuver to hold on to the tree and still get my food out without dropping it or losing my grip. My water bottle, however, accidentally fell out, and generated a stir among the cattle, who squashed the canteen without a trace of compunction.

Whether from growing thirst or disinterest, the herd of cows at last, to my great relief, decided to move on. I watched them follow a lead steer, hardly letting myself breathe for fear they would perk up again, and swagger away in neutered-male camaraderie. Their little minds seemed to have forgotten what had intrigued them for half a day.

I scampered down from the tree and jogged without stopping for a half mile in the other direction, pausing to glance now and again over my shoulder to make sure they weren't after me. At last reaching a fence, I hurdled over and flung myself into the grass on the other side.

My body ached; my head spun around with dizziness. I closed my eyes, and the warm touch of the lowering sun on my face and the sweet smell of wild grass filling my nostrils helped me to relax from the ordeal. A lone meadowlark melodically bubbled from a nearby fence post, while the mournful cry of a killdeer rose up from the wetlands.

Cows were the bane of my existence, I decided flatly. No one had told me that humble livestock could move as fast as a raging panther and be just as fierce, just as predatory.

I sighed. No one would believe me either.

Chapter Fourteen

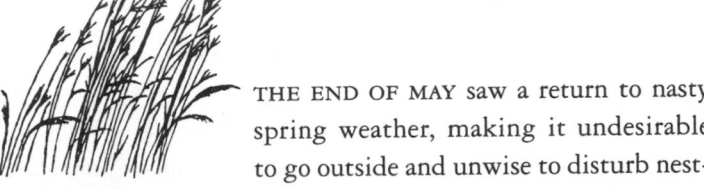

THE END OF MAY saw a return to nasty spring weather, making it undesirable to go outside and unwise to disturb nesting hawks, who, in their agitation, might leave their young unprotected and subject to chilling. It was a good time, though, to catch up on scientific reading and to review notes and maps for emerging patterns. I was amazed at how much land I had already covered, revealed by the colorful flecks of little red, yellow, and blue dots growing across the smooth, wide interior of the Zumwalt. A big chunk of unexplored territory remained in the far northeastern section, however—two rounded mounds, each one several square miles in diameter—the Findley Buttes.

By sheer coincidence, Ben McPherson, one of the ranchers I had talked to at the Elks Club, called and offered to drive me around the buttes the last weekend of May. His family grazed cattle on one portion of the hilly rangeland and would soon be driving their herd to summer pasture; he could check some fences while I looked for hawks.

"You wouldn't want to trust your old truck out on those roads," said Ben. "After these last few days of rain, they'll be slick with mud. You'll need big, high-ridin' tires and four-wheel drive. My new Chevy pickup has them both."

On a sunny spring morning heralded by song sparrows and a raspy flock of pine siskins descending in waves on the swelling Douglas fir cones in Mrs. DeLacy's yard, Ben swung up in his metallic-gold, three-quarter-ton Chevy. It was hard to say which was brighter: the sun's reflection off the pickup's cab and wheel rims or Mrs. DeLacy's pool of dandelions.

Ben helped me load my equipment into the backseat of the cab. "You can forget about your sack lunch," he said. "I've packed a lunch both of us can enjoy out on the buttes."

I spied a large wicker picnic basket on the floor behind the seat. The floor of the cab was so clean that I was almost afraid to climb inside with my dirty boots.

"You're going to like the buttes," Ben continued. "This time of year, after a rain, everything livens up. I don't know the names of all the flowers, but there are more there than anyplace else I've ever seen."

Together we drove nearly twenty-five miles of backcountry along the poorly maintained Zumwalt Road to reach the flanks of the southernmost butte, passing in a blur fields of bunchgrass and wildflowers. Gone now were the early spring varieties: the wispy purple-eyed grass and the camas lily. The sunny paint stroke of arrowleaf balsamroot was also fading. In their places were blue penstemons, pink carpets of sticky geranium, and purple larkspur. A few cows were visible, but not many, and those seemed swallowed up by the high rolling hills.

"A dozen cow elk, over there," exclaimed Ben, pointing. "Look there, three more cows and two yearlings. This is good country for elk."

"I've always wondered something," I said, hearing my voice go up and down with each pothole he struck. His fast driving on the rough road obfuscated all the wildlife for me. But I had always been curious about the coexistence between elk and cows on the range. I knew Ben could give me the rancher's view.

"Elk and cattle," I began. "Just how well do they mix? I mean, are they competitors?"

"If the land's being mismanaged, yes," Ben answered thoughtfully. "But I know for a fact if livestock grazing is done properly, the two are actually quite compatible."

"What do you mean, properly?"

"Because of the way the grass grows out here, most ranchers don't put out their cattle until the first two weeks of June. That gives the grasses a chance to precondition, toughen up. They're not so likely then to get trampled or overgrazed as they are if you let out your cows early spring, when the bunchgrasses are just coming up. The bunchgrasses are too fragile then, and easily hurt by too much grazing—cow or elk."

"So the cows and elk kind of share the range at different times?" I asked.

"Generally speaking. The elk will make for the high country in summer."

We drove a while in silence, until two huge mounds began to rise out of the prairie like small volcanoes emerging from the ocean.

"There they are. The Findley Buttes," said Ben. "Just where do you want to park and start walking?"

It was easy to see that both buttes couldn't be covered in one day. Even one was too immense. On my map I had partitioned out a section that I thought might make a fun five-mile hike through the aspen and pine groves that sliced up the sides of the thousand-foot hills. As we got out of Ben's truck, I was struck by the chill in the air. Ben's truck, with mud and dust splattered all over the wheel rims, certainly didn't look as clean as it had, but Ben didn't seem to care. He busily pored over my maps as I collected gear and binoculars.

"Here, let me bring this," he said, lifting the spotting scope from my hands and hoisting it over his shoulder. What a peculiar picture he made, carrying the equipment together with the over-sized wicker picnic basket that looked straight out of *Better Homes and Gardens*.

We had walked less than a quarter mile when I saw, perched on the ground between two big bull thistles only one hundred yards away from us, a ferruginous hawk, deeply intent on some chattering Belding's ground squirrels standing up in the wet grass. What foolish little animals to dart around almost at the talons of an imposing predator! Or perhaps the ferruginous had just nailed one of their siblings.

I gently placed my arm on Ben's to stop him. Seeing us, the big bird took off clumsily; with a screech, it began to circle above us.

"Think he has a nest nearby?" asked Ben, watching.

"Probably. Let's go up over that ridge first. Then we can cut around the back and hit all these trees. Ben, are you sure you want to lug that picnic basket all the way? We could eat later, back at the truck."

"It's no problem. When we get to the top of the butte, we can stop for lunch, and hiking makes me real hungry."

Whether or not our foreign presence was the reason, the ferruginous hawk remained agitated. When a brown, placid Swainson's hawk happened to wing up and over the summit, the ferruginous swept over to strike and, with a loud wail, tore at the smaller buteo with talons outstretched. The Swainson's quickly responded. Rolling over on its back to avoid the fighter, the hawk swooped in a giant S curve to rise through the air and fly above the ferruginous. Then, without pausing, the Swainson's hawk stooped five successive times on the ferruginous hawk, at last darting like a mouse for its hole to a black pine tree several hundred yards north.

The war-weary ferruginous hawk backpedaled south, disappearing over the next canyon's ridge.

"There's got to be a Swainson's nest in that pine," I said enthusiastically. "Let's see if there are any young, then follow the direction of the ferruginous."

"Sounds fine with me. What made them go at each other like that?"

I explained to Ben that generally birds like ferruginous and Swainson's hawks were separated from each other by virtue of their different selections of habitat. Ferruginous hawks preferred the stark, uncultivated native prairie, whereas the Swainson's hawk tended to nest in shrublike trees in the open. As I talked, it suddenly dawned on me that the Zumwalt Prairie, although appearing to be one entity, was subtly eclectic—a rich potpourri of trees and soil, rocks, climate, and topography that allowed species that were competitors for the same resource to live together. It was something akin to elk and cattle being able to live together, yet I found it difficult to equate the two ungulates, one bovine, one exquisitely wild, together in my mind.

The last few days of rain, I noticed, had visibly softened the land. Blades of vibrant green grass, sparkling with water droplets, quivered in the slightest wind; many of the wildflowers, on close inspection, hung nearly prostrate on limp stalks. The heavy clay soil adhered to our boots, making every step a weightier one than the last. Continuing our climb up the buttes, the soles of our boots became stacked three or four inches thick with mud. Ben's fancy cowboy boots, which looked totally uncomfortable anyway, had become sorry caricatures of shoes, with the boot heel gaining height in mud and thus shifting his weight forward, something like ladies high heels. He paused to kick off some mud on a sharp stone.

"What's that big bird just sitting in the field over there? An eagle?" he asked, setting up the spotting scope.

Ben was right. A huge immature golden eagle, its youth identifiable by its broad white tail band and white wing patches on the undersides of both wings, was quietly resting on the ground, eyeing four marsh hawks—two pairs, I guessed—flying across the soggy, sloping meadow to the west. He seemed to have trouble making up his mind if he really wanted to fly or just linger for a while longer in the warm sunlight. He sleepily watched the hardworking birds wheeling low to the ground in four slim arcs of motion. Two of the birds were gray males; the other two, coppery females. Of all the hawks, they were probably the simplest to identify for they had a telltale, white rump that always showed up when they flew.

The eagle extended its long wings and, with broad pumping motions, lifted off. The wake of air he left behind actually ruffled the grass and flowers on which he had perched, like a miniature helicopter gushing wind on a tiny heliport and faerie bystanders. His carefree jaunt didn't last long, however, Spotting the golden bird almost twice its size, a single male marsh hawk turned to dive fearlessly, with sharp, arched talons, almost landing on the back of the hapless eagle. The eagle rolled over on its back to miss the air strikes, and seemed to have everything under control, when the three other marsh hawks raced over to join their friend and, in rapid fire, attacked the big bird mercilessly. It was a perfect example of power in numbers, and the eagle knew he had gotten himself in over his head. Swiftly careening a one-eighty, he sped east and vanished as a small dot over the canyon country.

"Did you see that?" cried Ben. "Those four pipsqueaks just humiliated that poor bird. Now he's off to take out his frustrations on some tender white lamb. Look, the summit's just above us. Let's stop and eat. I've had too much excitement."

Ben opened the wicker basket to reveal a handy tarp to sit on, in addition to a lunch the likes of which I hadn't seen for a long time. "I didn't make all this," Ben said sheepishly. "Mom packed it for us."

It seemed funny for this man of twenty-five or so to have his mother still packing his lunch, but I didn't care and felt grateful. The meal included cheese, ham, pepperoni, tuna and peanut butter and jelly sandwiches, potato chips, peanuts, dill pickles, radishes, three kinds of yogurt, four granola candy bars, and two slices of chocolate cake.

"Hope you're hungry," said Ben with a twinkle in his eye.

"I've never seen such a picnic lunch! Do you always eat this way?"

"No," said Ben, "but from the way you were stuffing your mouth with pretzels the other night, I figured I better bring a lot of food. Now," he said, arranging the tarp on the ground and holding out his hand, offering me a place to sit down first, "what do you think of this spot?"

The plunging Imnaha River Canyon took the eyes down, then up again, across the canyons, to the jagged edges of the Seven Devils Mountains of Idaho. To the south were the majestic Wallowas; to the north and west, the prairie sent out scores of rippling hills like a silverscreen etching. The place was so beautiful that I almost didn't want to eat.

Ben laughed, thinking I was having trouble deciding what to eat first. "You know, Marcy, you can eat as much as you want." He helped himself to a peanut butter and jelly sandwich and a thermos of juice. "Do you enjoy this," he asked, sitting back and stretching out his long legs, "watching hawks?"

I nodded. "There's something about this prairie—I can't define exactly what it is—but it mystifies and excites me. I was told, before I came here, there were hawks, but nowhere near in the numbers I've found them. And there's something more—something that just seems to work here. I guess I was expecting a grassland to be a bit, well, a bit dull, after living in the mountains for four years. But the richness of this whole system is fascinating to me. What's more, its beauty is just as exquisite as any mountaintop. But I still don't really understand why it works as it does."

"And it's private land," added Ben.

"What does that have to do with anything?"

"A lot. A whole lot. Better eat up before the sun goes behind those clouds. I can feel the air cooling down as we speak."

The earthy, fragrant scent of pine needles grew stronger as a frosty breeze picked up. I decided not to remove my jacket after all. As Ben reached into his backpack for water, I unwrapped a tuna sandwich and looked at him. His clear blue eyes were rimmed with some of the blackest lashes I had seen. His blond hair looked shiny and healthy, revealing some red highlights in the sun. Like most of the ranchers I had met, his skin was ruddy and tanned, his hands brown, chiseled, and rough. The cowboy look was there, all right—with the big silver belt buckle, tightly fitting western shirt, and those pointed boots, which had something grotesque, like faux alligator, stitched on the top. Yet, for all the stereotype there was about Ben, he had a distinctive urbanity, a warmth and innate gentleness, that didn't seem to fit with the media's version of the cattlemen of the wild and woolly West.

The sun was strongly illuminating certain areas, like a giant, trained spotlight, but shadows were beginning to dance across the flatland as we finished our lunch. The warbling song of meadowlarks had diminished, which didn't portend well for the weather, but a few diehard songsters were attempting to take over for the rest. I suddenly began to feel an urgency to see more of the buttes. Ben seemed to read my mind.

"You know, there's an old road that winds around the back side of the southern butte. We use it sometimes for moving cattle. We might be able to cover more ground if we head back and circle the butte by truck. You might miss a few spots, but you'd get a great overview."

Ben's idea was a good one. Most of the hawks we had been seeing had disappeared around the east end of the butte. "Sounds fine to me," I replied, then added, as an afterthought, "How's the road condition though, after all the rain these last days?"

"No problem for my truck," Ben answered confidently as he folded the tarp.

We hiked down the butte, reaching the truck in record time, spurred on by a growing sense of an imminent weather change. Quickly we loaded up and headed out, backtracking a few miles to a road I had overlooked. It looked more like a dirt path that hadn't been used for quite some time; much of it had revegetated, although deep muddy ruts, which for my truck would have been utterly impassable, were visible in spots. Ben, however, disregarded them.

"Let me just hop out and get this fence," Ben began.

"No, I'll get it," I said, with an eye still on the condition of the road. I jumped out of the truck, hoping my new skill at opening persnickety barbed-wire gates would pay off. This gate, however, was a monster, and I found myself struggling with the wooden lever—acquiring a deep splinter in the process—trying to pull the two posts together closely enough so I could lift off the tethering loop of nasty barbed wire. Just when I heard Ben getting out to help me, the thing blessedly released, and I pulled back the fence for his truck to drive through.

"You can leave it open," Ben said through the window. "We'll be coming back this way, and the cattle aren't out yet."

Ben put the truck in four-wheel drive, and we started up what remained of the old road. The east side of the butte was stonier, with more veins of pine trees and aspen groves fingering down from the top as a result of hidden springs and snow pockets that had accumulated from winter storms.

We stopped to explore the first sizable grove of ponderosa pine and Douglas fir trees, which grew just off the road. After a half-hour search, we finally discovered a red-tail nest with four young, half grown. In the same grove of trees was a great horned owl nest with two yellow and brown balls of fluff snapping their wicked, small beaks at us while their silent winged parents watched close by.

Red-tailed hawks and great horned owls are at best dubious neighbors. The large owls are notorious for usurping red-tails' nests in spring and, at times, making a meal of their young. Red-tailed hawks have to put up with the dangers because the two species of birds prefer similar habitat.

"You say you're planning to come back later and band all these guys?" Ben asked with disbelief. "How are you going to do it?"

"Yes, I'm going to band them, starting soon, as they're almost big enough," I answered, wondering how in the world I would cover this prairie a second time, in the period of a week or two, before the young birds fledged. Until now, the aluminum bands used by the Fish and Wildlife Service to identify birds would have been too large to fit on the birds' skinny legs and would have slipped off. But the nestlings were growing daily and soon would be of a suitable size for banding.

"How many hawks do you figure you have to band?"

"Oh, a couple hundred, maybe."

"Couple hundred!"

I feigned confidence I didn't have. "As my major professor has said, one must shoot for the high, the unknown—be willing to fail. A scientist must not do only those things she knows she can do, or already knows the answer to. One must do what one thinks is right."

"So how you going to do it?" he asked again, coming back to the point.

"I don't have the faintest idea."

We walked in silence back to the truck. The weather indeed was changing, with feathery clouds shining ominously, encircled by rainbow-hued ice crystals.

"Let's get that ferruginous hawk nest. Then I think we better head back," Ben said. "I'm betting snow."

"Snow? Now? The end of May?"

"When you've lived here long enough, you'll understand those mountains can make any weather they want, at any time of year."

The road ahead was worse—deeply rutted, soggy, and overgrown with weeds, mainly marsh marigolds, indicative of moist places, on either side.

"You think you can make it?" I asked Ben.

"Remember, I'm in four-wheel drive," he replied, lunging ahead. The repeated sound of mud spraying the sides and hubcaps was like artillery.

"Ben, maybe we should turn around."

"This road's no problem for my truck. It's a cinch to get through this sinkhole."

"Through? Shouldn't you go around it?"

"Sure; around it. On the left."

In my inexperienced opinion, it looked more prudent to veer to the right, but I kept quiet. Ben obviously knew what he was doing.

"Hold on!" he said with a smile, then gunned the engine down. All eight of the truck's cylinders roared to life like a charging lion as the oversized wheels dug through the slime, mining a hole, deeper and deeper. I could feel us going down, sinking with the marsh marigolds, while the tires spun around, going nowhere.

"A little more to the left and we've got it," cried Ben, but we remained stationary, making no progress.

"To the right!" he said jovially, yanking the steering wheel but putting us only deeper into the pit.

The truck, already in four-wheel-drive low, could muster no more force. Frustrated, Ben put it in reverse, which was a mistake, for now all four tires mired completely.

"Damn it," said Ben under his breath. "Don't worry. I'll just dig a bit and we'll be on our way."

He got out to produce a shovel from the flatbed. I jumped out to help. "You're going to get yourself mighty dirty," Ben said.

"I don't mind. I'm the reason you're here in the first place."

We dug around the tires, together making trenches for the wheels to proceed forward, to escape from the well of mud. Unfortunately, as we shoveled—Ben with his hands, I with the shovel—the channels we were making quickly filled up with water—slimy water mixed with mud, like chocolate pudding. Inadvertently, we both realized at once, we had been driving on a spring.

Neither of us said anything. Ben went to gather rocks, while I tried to bail out the upwelling water. When he returned, carrying an armload of rocks, we arranged them in front of the tires to produce a makeshift bridge. Our hands, arms, and faces were a mess of mud after nearly an hour of work.

"That should do the trick!" said Ben, trying to sound encouraging. But his eyes were tired. "Now, stand back."

I moved, but not far enough. As the truck groaned, the tires spun like a whirling top out of control. In a few seconds, I was covered with streaks of mud from head to foot.

"I'm so sorry!" Ben shouted, leaping out while the engine still ran.

"Oh, it's my fault," I said, at this point not really caring what I looked like.

He stood back to look at me and couldn't withhold his laughter. "Marcy, you're a walking bucket of brown paint. Do you want the water bottle to wash some of that off?"

I shook my head, resigned. "It'd just make it worse."

"Well," he said, putting his hand on my soiled shoulder, "let me try again. But this time stand far off to one side."

Ben got back in the truck and stormed the engine a second time, but the obstinate Chevy refused to budge. For another hour we dug, bailed, and piled stones around the tires, but, like a stubborn mule, the pickup only shoved its heels in deeper. Ben finally admitted that we were hopelessly, irretrievably stuck after two and a half hours.

I could have told him that after ten minutes.

"What about your CB?" I asked, while he stood, mute, gazing at the pathetic-looking vehicle, which bore no resemblance to the powerful machine it had been that morning.

He walked dejectedly to the truck. "Good idea," he said dully, hating to admit defeat and having to call for help. I could hear him in the cab switching channels, trying to get anyone's attention. But we were too far out. None of the twenty-three channels could drum up even a faint response.

Ben got out with a stupefied look on his face. I understood. We were on the back side of Findley Buttes, twenty miles from the nearest habitation. The time was half past four.

And the first snowflakes were just beginning to fall.

Chapter Fifteen

"THIS IS ALL MY FAULT," Ben said grimly. "I should never have tried driving through a spring."

"You didn't know it was a spring. And anyway, I always enjoy a good walk."

"It's too long for you. You better stay here while I go for help."

"Too long? I've been hiking all spring, remember?"

"But the snow—"

"I could just as easily freeze to death right here in this truck," I said facetiously. "Ben, if we hike three miles an hour, we'll reach a farm before midnight. The snow doesn't seem like it's going to stick. It looks like a fast-moving storm." I zipped up my jacket and put my water bottle in my backpack, while Ben packed up what remained of the lunch.

"I still feel like a lout."

"Don't be silly, Ben. A fellow named Sparkey, at the Fish and Game, predicted this would happen, so if he ever hears about this, which I hope he doesn't, he'll be tickled." (I imagined all that Sparkey would say.) Ben stared pensively at the truck, which, sunken down with mud lapping at the rims of its wheels, more closely resembled a flat-bottomed boat than a pickup truck.

"You're going to need a winch to get that out, aren't you?" I asked gently.

"I'm afraid so," he said. "It's nearly cemented. Unfortunately, Dad doesn't have a truck with a winch."

My dilapidated government truck certainly wasn't equipped for this, but I knew one that was. "I know two guys," I began slowly, "from the Forest Service. Their truck has a winch, and I'm sure they'd be happy to help us."

Ben continued to look downcast.

"Oh come on, Ben. This is nobody's fault!" I cried, with a quick look at my brown stained hands and clothes heavily streaked with dirt. "At least you still look presentable. I look like a brown hippopotamus who's just finished wallowing."

He smiled at last, although weakly. "Yes, I'm afraid you do."

I hadn't been joking when I said I enjoy long walks. And the first few miles, before my feet began to ache, were pleasant. A hush had fallen over the prairie with the light dusting of snow. The rolling hills, mounded and smoothed, bowed into one another like a hundred gentle ski slopes. Hyperactive Belding's ground squirrels had all but vanished and retreated to the warmth and safety of their burrows. And the air was distinctly empty of birds, because most of them sat tightly on their nests, keeping their eggs and hatchlings warm.

For the most part, it was a long quiet walk, hour stretching upon hour, with neither of us saying much, for the spell of the prairie was strangely powerful. The miles, devoid of other people, were spotted with a rich diversity of wildlife that somehow, in the lowering light, seemed to embrace us. Beginning to hunker down were the diurnal species—the porcupines, pocket gophers, and the deer and elk, whose blurred forms nestled in the nooks of hills or under trees. A plain snipe broke the stillness with its wild, forlorn call, while Brewer's sparrows skirted the tops of the grasses when we approached too close. Brewer's were easy to identify with their flashing white outer tail feathers that looked like little white slips showing under a brown dress.

Meanwhile, nocturnal species were just gearing up. The ghostly figures of little brown bats haunted the air that spoke, from time to time, with the cries of range coyotes. Afternoon had already blended into twilight, and twilight edged into darkness, and still we walked, not stopping to rest, until our hunger overtook us. With what light there was from the elusive moon, Ben paused to look at his watch.

"Five after nine; we've been walking now for four hours," he said, yawning, and stretching out his arms. "Somebody's bound to get worried and come looking for us." Tossing off his pack, he unzipped it and threw out the tarp over the soaked ground. "Come on. Let's eat. I'm starving."

We collapsed on the mat and, like vultures, dove to eat what remained of lunch, which did little to assuage our raging appetites, but neither of us talked anymore about our hunger. The snow had stopped, and the air was beginning to warm slightly, but our bodies rapidly chilled down. I wished I had brought my hat. I always brought my hat. How could I have forgotten it today? Trying to give me the most room possible on the tarp, Ben stretched out his long legs on the ground, with the tip of his boots pointing up at the sky. It was painful to even contemplate how Ben could walk mile after mile in those torturous boots that were never designed for hiking, and although he never complained, I could see his steps becoming noticeably more mincing as we proceeded on our journey.

At any minute we expected to see searching headlights as the night wore on, but no one came. We continued walking, with increasing stiffness, and moved on, eight, ten, twelve miles, knowing there were many more ahead of us. The large black shadow of a short-eared owl startled us when it winged, low and silent, across the road. Shapes and forms moving in the darkness assaulted our dimming sensibilities; it seemed inconceivable that any animal could see when we certainly couldn't.

The gentle, rhythmic sound of our boots sluicing along was hypnotic and soothing. Falling into a natural stride, side by side, made walking easier, like energized molecules between us drafting forward without much effort on our parts. Wind pricked our cheeks, but its spike helped to keep us awake and alert. I was unwilling to let my body gain control over my mind. More than a walk, the ordeal was actually a thought process; as long as I took interest in the things around me, I kept at bay my awareness of the growing fatigue in my limbs.

"Do you want to rest again a bit?" Ben asked gently, his face lost to me in darkness.

"No, not now; I don't need to rest," I said with more energy than I felt. "I'm listening to the different sounds our feet make as we step on snow, then on grass, rocks, and dirt. Noise just seems to jump out at you at night."

"I wish we'd hear noise of someone coming for us. I can't believe no one's concerned, especially with the snow."

"Maybe it didn't snow much in town, since it's at a lower elevation. Well, one thing's for sure; Mrs. DeLacy won't be coming to look for us. She says she can't figure out my schedule at all, and is suspicious at what I'm doing all day traipsing around this forsaken country."

"Dorothy's a nice lady," offered Ben. "I had her for a high-school business class years ago. Everyone here respects her—how she fought to keep her kids with her after her husband died, refused to accept any welfare; she'd never let anyone pity her. She's always been one for standards, keeping her house up, though it's cluttered as hell, made her kids dress better than the rest of us. She'd never allow her girls to wear jeans to school."

I sighed, thinking of the sorry state my clothes were always in. "She must think I'm the perfect slob, then. But what about her yard?" I said, laughing. "That's not perfect."

"Oh, she'll hire some kid later this summer to take care of it after the grass and dandelions are three feet high."

As the moon rose higher in the clearing sky, we hiked on, in a growing haze, until at last I could just see the outline of a familiar sight ahead—the decrepit old house and outbuildings of Hadley's Corral. At this time of night, they eerily resembled phantomlike structures of an abandoned ghost town. The Hadleys, of course, had long gone back to town, and the only sounds were the creaking of the rusty gate as it blew back and forth in the wind, and the unexpected, low bellow of a cow. "Oh, God," I whispered under my breath. "It's Henry."

"Who?"

"That dreadful bull. I hate that bull."

"You mean Hadley's big Angus?"

"He nearly killed me. Chased me clear across the field."

Ben's hearty laughter rang out in the dark. "Why, he's a prize-winning stud! Old man Hadley's pride and joy."

"I don't care *what* he is; he's perfectly horrid and should be put to sleep."

"Just wait a little while and you'll be seeing a whole lot more cows and bulls on your daily prairie walks. Henry's actually more gentle than a lot of them."

I moaned, thinking about all my run-ins already with cows. "I'm so happy to hear that, Ben." In the dreamlike darkness, all the Henrys of the Zumwalt took on nightmarish proportions. To think that this gorgeous prairie would be stomped over and chomped down by the mouths of Henrys seemed nothing but a travesty.

"Aw, the cattle shouldn't bother you," said Ben. "The bulls are spread far apart and the cows just scatter, searching out grass, water, and salt."

"And destroying ponds and stream banks," I said, feeling slightly cynical as my energy continued to ebb.

"You really are an environmentalist, aren't you? Well, you are right in a way. Cows will concentrate near water, and eat up everything around it. The trick is to get the animals well distributed—spread far out. This goes for deer and elk, too."

"How do you do that? Fencing?"

"That's one way—fencing off the streams. But the abundance of stock ponds on the Zumwalt really helps too. Keeps the livestock on the move."

"But not all ranchers fence their streams."

"That's true, too, unfortunately," he said. "I'll agree, you'll find instances on public and private lands where resources are damaged under current forms of livestock grazing. But don't forget, there are lots of ranchers sensitive to protecting riparian areas. Don't lump us all into one."

"I don't mean to. I'm just getting tired, I guess. But I don't understand why those ranchers who do overgraze keep on doing it, when they know full well it's bad for the land."

"Too often management decisions are made on the basis of short-term profits," replied Ben. "Long-term values aren't given enough consideration."

"That's what I'm saying."

"But that's only part of the picture. Look around you. Look at the Zumwalt. What do you see?"

"I can't see anything." I knew what he was driving at, but it wasn't, really, what I saw that mattered—it was what I didn't see. I didn't see hordes of cows, or beat-up streambeds or dusty, dry plains. I saw healthy stands of native bunchgrasses, and herds of deer and elk. And dozens of raptors.

But it was too late and I was too tired to continue talking about range management and the private life of cows. Trudging ahead blindly, I missed seeing a rock in my path and stumbled. Ben caught my arm and held it.

"You're tired out, aren't you?" he said, helping me to my feet.

"No. Well, yes, a bit. Aren't you?"

"Yes, and it's nearly midnight. You want to wait here while I go get help?"

"No. It's not much farther. I can make it fine."

He continued holding my arm as we walked. "You know, for an environmentalist, you're quite game."

"For a rancher, you're quite nice, but this is silly—I love to walk, and I think this has been a great adventure. Will you please tell me something, Ben? Why does everyone in this county seem to hold such a grudge against environmentalists?"

He dropped my arm. "Because we have a lot more at stake in this than you do. You see this as some sort of debate, a theoretical exercise in public policy. But for us, it's our livelihood. The ranch is our family. We're on the verge of losing a way of life that for us has gone back generations. We know the land and love it."

We walked on in silence, a damper having somehow fallen on the end of the day. The tenor hoot of a great horned owl came from some old cottonwoods near a ditch, and the call of a screech owl, which sounded something like bouncing rubber balls, replied from a small stand of evergreens. Another hour passed, and still another, until at last a tiny flicker of a light wavered in the distance, like a mirage. It grew, it brightened, as we approached closer—pouring new energy and relief into our aching bodies, and also, on my part at least, a funny, swift twinge of sorrow.

"Pritchard's farm!" said Ben, grabbing my hand and pulling me along. "The old coot's probably still up watching reruns of the Johnny Carson show. Come on!"

Our feet, which had trudged so steadily for over twenty miles, suddenly seemed to sprout wings to fly across the last several hundred yards separating us from civilization. I wanted to reach it, and was running with Ben toward it. Yet something in my soul held back, still yearning to stay out with the night, the wild prairie, and not let it go.

Like all the doors of Wallowa County, the Pritchards' was unlocked, and Ben helped himself inside after giving the knocker a sound rapping. Mrs. Pritchard stood up in her brown terry bathrobe and orange slippers, in front of the blaring television.

"Why Benjamin B. McPherson," she exclaimed, with a bony hand to the mess of pin curls in her gray hair. "What on earth are you doing here at this hour?" She glimpsed me standing behind him and moved the hand to her heart. "And what in the name of heaven have you dragged in with you?"

Chapter Sixteen

SOMEHOW I WAS HOME, and too soon it was morning and Mrs. DeLacy was banging on my door telling me I was wanted on the phone. For a moment I wondered if yesterday had only been a dream, but as I tried to rise up out of bed, my entire body rebelled and I fell back to the pillow in exhaustion. Mrs. DeLacy yelled again. I felt I would have to crawl to the hall on my hands and knees, for my legs were like stone pillars, incapable of flexibility or movement. At the foot of the bed was a pile of dirty clothes that I noticed had muddied the hand-sewn quilted bedspread prized by Mrs. DeLacy. She called again, and I threw on a bathrobe and hobbled stiffly to the telephone alcove in the hallway.

Austin Scott's bombastic voice blasted from the other end of the receiver, telling me he would come by in a half hour with the aluminum bird bands that had come in yesterday from the Fish and Wildlife Service. "We'll start banding today," he said, assuming I had nothing else planned. "I'll show you how to do it and then you're on your own."

But there was one problem, of course. Carefully framing my words so as not to blame anyone, I mentioned that I needed to get a friend's truck unstuck out on Findley Buttes before I could do any banding.

"Whose truck?" queried Austin, suspiciously.

"Ben McPherson's, a local rancher."

"Those damn yahoos don't know a thing about driving around the backcountry!" Austin exclaimed. He continued to rant about dimwitted cowboys and their pickups, but I was too tired to defend Ben and merely held the phone away from my ear. Finally I took a breath and interrupted.

"Austin," I yelled back. "Can you help us?"

There was a moment of silence.

I started again, this time more moderately. "Please, Austin, Ben's going to need a winch to get him out of this mess, and I was the one that got him in it in the first place. Will you help me?"

There was a grunt, then a dead receiver. He had hung up. I quickly called Ben, who had left me his phone number last night after his father had dropped me off, to tell him to meet us here in short order, for my "friends" from the Forest Service had offered their assistance. I then shuffled back to my room to shower and dress.

Austin, Eric, and Ben all converged in Mrs. DeLacy's driveway within ten minutes of each other, and after brief introductions all around and rather toned-down explanations about what had transpired yesterday, the four of us packed tightly into Austin's rig for the journey back to Findley Buttes. Squashed in the middle between Ben and Austin, I waved to Mrs. DeLacy, who stood legs apart, in her routine position as gatekeeper to the front door. Austin revved the engine while backing out—which was totally unnecessary and served only to kick up a spray of gravel in the wake of his tires.

Looking over to pass a smile, Ben made no comment about my changed appearance, but I could see that he was clean shaven with fresh clothes, and, I noticed instantly, had forsaken the agonizing cowboy boots for Red Wing trail boots.

"Why the hell were you out on the back side of Findley Buttes yesterday, with the water table so high?" Austin asked with his customary tact. "Only an idiot would take a car there."

"Austin," I interjected heatedly, "that's not fair! We had four-wheel drive, and Ben was being, well, generous to offer to take me where I needed to go."

Ben surprised me, though, by agreeing with him. "You're

right. I didn't use the best judgment," he said, not defensively. "I was aware there could be hidden springs, but I guess I thought I could get around them."

Austin's shoulders relaxed somewhat, and for the first time all morning, he looked Ben in the eyes. "Well, maybe it's not as bad as I think."

As we proceeded down the back roads, it struck me how the Zumwalt of last night was a stranger to its complexion in the light of morning. The snow that yesterday had seemed our biggest hurdle now had nearly completely melted in the warm chinook wind that overnight had transformed the landscape. The shock of azure sky arching overhead like an immense parachute bore no resemblance to the flat, somber sheet of stratus clouds that had clung close to the earth less than twenty-four hours ago.

The birds, too, seemed to sense the difference. Ferruginous and red-tailed hawks were out practicing aerobatics in the wind gusts; they seemed to be grabbing a moment from the seriousness of their present duties to frolic as they did in early spring—being carried up in the hand of the wind, and released to tumble down, in arcs and swirls, spurning the proximity of the ground and challenging the wind to catch them again.

Orange-cloaked kestrels hovered in the air on small falcon wings, on the lookout for mice and snakes. Horned larks were back as sentinels—their round, fat bodies capping the wooden fence post.

More and more Belding's ground squirrels were emerging, and seemed to be racing about everywhere—the young ones with no regard for the dangers lurking about them, from predators to truck wheels. In fact, the ridiculous squirrels seemed to enjoy testing if they could make it just in front of our tires without being squashed—waiting until the last moment, when we were almost upon them, to dart quickly across the road on kamikaze missions.

My legs, stiff and sore, had trouble fitting between the big guys and the stick shift, and I repeatedly had to alter my position when they started to fall asleep. Austin commented that I was as squirmy as a red worm in a compost box, and was making it exceedingly difficult for him to change gears.

"Get your mind off how pinched you are," he said, "and see inside that bag on the floor by Eric's feet."

Leaning over everyone, I grabbed the brown paper sack and peered in. Inside, hundreds of small aluminum rings lay in the bottom of the bag; running my hands through them, they jangled like a booty of tiny silver coins.

"Also in my pack there's a bunch of forms for you to fill out. Each one of these bands has a number etched on it. The number corresponds to a computer listing back in Washington, D.C.," Austin explained. "Whatever you do, don't lose any. They're entrusted to your care, and you were lucky to get a banding permit in such a short time. Ever banded raptors before?"

"I've seen it done, but have never actually applied a band myself."

Austin winced. "You're really new to this stuff, aren't you?"

"Not really." Briefly I told of my four years in Colorado studying peregrines. But it made little impression.

"They shouldn't allow anyone to be a raptor biologist who isn't a falconer. I've been banding and flying birds since I was fourteen. You can never really understand a bird until you've actually flown one of your own—handled it, fed it, gained its trust, watched it fly, trained it to return to you on command. Novices can't begin to understand the amount of time and effort it takes to train the birds to "wait on.""

"*Wait on?*" asked Ben. "What's that?"

"*Wait on* means the bird circles in the air until quarry is flushed into the open," said Austin, with a condescending tone. "Falconry is time-consuming, unexciting, hard work, and lots of it."

"Why do you do it, then?"

"Why? 'Cause it's fun. Those that stick with it know that. But it's all for a relatively short period of flight in the field. Hawks and falcons aren't pets to be caged or to show off; they need to be worked. A lot of beginning hobbyists quit and the birds suffer in their care. But the knowledge that genuine falconers have gained from keeping their birds is the one thing that will save the birds in the long run from being creamed."

A few more miles down the bumpy road, Austin pulled off suddenly and without explanation parked. "What are you doing?" I asked, to which he replied, "Just get the bag of bands and come on."

I knew immediately the spot he was heading to—the rippled barked cottonwoods in the close-in draw held the nest of a great horned owl. "Austin, this is a horned owl nest," I said.

"Bejeezus, you think I don't know that? You've got to learn to band sometime!" Hoisting on his pack, he took off, his tall, black forester boots with the thick vibram soles scrunching the young lupine and yellow owl clover.

I put the sack of bands in my pack and watched all three men walk off together. Something about Austin's condescending manner was provoking; I was determined to show him I knew as much about birds as he did. Austin was already at the base of the sixty-foot-high cottonwood tree, where an agitated owl parent stood swaying and tired on a low branch of an adjacent tree. Awaking rapidly, it regarded Austin with malice and snapped its powerful beak, "woofing" at him, and then at us.

In great horned owl language, to "woof" at something is to herald great alarm; to our human ears, however, the sound was more akin to the muted bark of a muzzled dog. I was aware, though, of the terrible, swift force that a great horned owl, in its silent flight, could unleash on an enemy. The aggression level of each individual great horned owl is different, like that of goshawks; therefore, the degree of their defensive behavior is unpredictable, and explains why many raptor biologists have battle scars on their heads and arms from past encounters with these species' talons.

This pair of owls, thankfully, was more acquiescent and let us approach their nest without resorting to tactile hostility. Spurless,

Austin climbed up the tree with the powerful agility of a leopard. Watching from below, we could see two small heads suddenly pop up over a large stick nest. One bold nestling, in fear of the hulk getting closer and closer, stood up to jump, and half flew, half fell all the way to the ground in a fluff of wings. It hopped about unhurt on the bare soil beneath the nest, and Eric ran to grab it while Austin pursued its sibling, who had also jumped out of the protective arms of the nest and was sliding its feet farther and farther along the branch, keeping just out of Austin's reach.

"Here," Eric said, handing the owlet to me. "Hold it while I get the stuff."

The pint-sized edition of his distinguished parents rested on my arm as surprisingly lightly as a cottonball. Its huge yellow eyes stared me in the face, attempting to frighten me. He snapped his small beak, hissed as I tried to soothe him, and even experimented with a few "woofs." I thought again how this soft fluffball of feathers, still too young to have its "horns," was a winsome mixture of both wild defiance and ridiculous bluff, as he puffed himself like a balloon to appear bigger and more fierce than he really was. Ben looked at me gazing at the adorable little creature and laughed; Eric walked over to lift him off my arms and place him on my shoulder. The bird snapped his beak at Eric, then rocked back and forth on my shoulder, as if I were a new kind of tree. Standing tall, his white, feathered legs resembling pantaloons, the bird spread out his wings as far as they would go while keeping an eye on Ben and Eric. Seeing the young bird from the corner of my eye, I found it difficult to keep from laughing.

Beginning to tire slightly, it started to sag, and leaned over to rest his soft body against my cheek. I stood perfectly still, exhilarated by the very closeness of this beautiful animal, and not just a little nervous that he suddenly might become aware I was not a tree trunk at all and turn around to bite me.

Eric and Ben walked over to Austin, leaving me standing like a caricature of a snag. Austin was down, having caught the second nestling. He rolled his eyes when he saw me and, without a word, reached into his pack for pliers and the record book, and opened my pack to get the bands. Grabbing two, he walked over to preach.

"Listen up," he said, knowing I stood a captive audience. "First, Marcy, you write down the number of the band on this page. *Don't forget to do this* or you're out of luck once the bird's released. Write down all the data here—include the date, time, location, species, and everything else you need. Will somebody please take the damn bird off her shoulder? She needs to do this."

Something wicked in me felt secretly gleeful when the bird, who had been so trusting of me, bit Eric's fingers as he reached out to grab it.

"Come over here, Marcy," Austin ordered, "and take the pliers while I hold this guy. Now, all you do is pick up the band like this, making sure it's the same number you wrote down, and put it around the bird's leg. Don't worry; he won't bite you; I've got hold of him. Now, put it around, and with the other hand gently clamp down the two ends with the pliers. That's not enough; press them harder. There, that's good."

Handing the bird over for me to hold, Austin took the pliers. "Well, that's all there is to it. I'll watch you do the other owlet, then we'll put them on the tree limb."

"Why not back in the nest?" I questioned.

"You think I want to go back up there a second time?" exclaimed Austin. "Hell no. They'll be fine. They can get back up there themselves. They're on the verge of fledging anyway. Mom and Dad will make sure they get fed." Austin picked up his pack, threw over the sack of bands for me to catch, and headed back to the truck. "That's two," he yelled at me over his shoulder. "Only a hundred fifty more to go!"

Left holding the bag, pliers, record books, and backpack, and running behind him, I felt like a coolie and I didn't enjoy it, nor did I appreciate his teaching methods. But I also was keenly aware of how much I was going to need his help. Plus, I sensed that underneath Austin's diatribes and pessimism there existed a fine individual who suffered for lost causes. I suspected that Austin, like the owlets, hid a gentle heart under a big bluff of feathers.

We jammed inside the truck, and the remaining fifteen rough miles were even more uncomfortable, with all the gear spread out across our laps and at our feet. Eric and Austin were making quips now and again, and posing pointed questions to Ben about his ranch, to which he responded calmly, objectively, and without apology. Unable to get his goat, they tried for mine, enjoying making jabs about the sheer lunacy of trying to band buteos within a 200-square-mile radius and all in a short nesting period.

"Your study area should be about twenty square miles," said Eric, speaking like a professor, to which Austin nodded his head.

"The whole objective, though, is to cover the entire Zumwalt because statistically speaking, twenty square miles would be too small to tell you much of anything."

"It'd tell one thing," Austin said glibly. "That you aren't nuts."

Approaching the back side of Findley Buttes, Austin stopped to lock the wheel hubs into four-wheel drive. The truck rocked and rolled over the same ruts, while Austin's handling of it made it impossible to stay in one position. I seemed to be trading laps, first reeling into Ben's, then Austin's, who was complaining vociferously. But I could tell that Austin was actually immensely enjoying wrestling with the rig, acting out some kind of fantasy of a television commercial for Chevy trucks.

"Holy moly," Austin cried, turning the corner to spy Ben's truck, wheels neatly submerged, in the swampy mess. He threw on his brakes.

"It didn't look like that yesterday," I maintained. "Well, at least at first."

"It's a floating barge! What in hell were you thinking of, McPherson, taking your truck through there?"

"I said, it didn't look like that, Austin," I repeated. "After we drove in it, the whole thing kind of filled up with water."

Austin put his hand up above his eyes to peer at it as if he were an Indian scout.

"Well, let's not just sit here talking about it; let's get it unstuck," I continued, growing tired of Austin's ribbing.

"Aye, aye, sir!" Eric said to me, saluting.

We got shovels to begin digging, while Austin maneuvered his vehicle around to face Ben's, and carefully position the winch— trying to find the best spot for traction yet at the same time avoid getting stuck himself. Ben then spent out the winch hook and chain and secured it to the front of his rig. Austin was out with a second chain, which he attached to the side of Ben's truck that was listing most deeply in the quagmire.

"Okay!" yelled Austin. "Get ready." Ben climbed into the driver's side of his ailing truck and tried to start it. "I'm going to need a push from you guys to get this thing rolling."

The two trucks spewed exhaust and the electric winch whined. But nothing budged.

Austin leaped out. "Hold it!" he bellowed. "Let's set a better grip."

Everyone was at the front of Ben's rig, securing chains, and I shoveled a few more loads of dirt. The winch groaned even more pathetically this time; Ben spun the tires, while Eric and I pushed with everything we had, eating Ben's mud.

"Push like hell!" roared Austin, his head hanging out the window. Ever so slightly, there was a lessening of resistance from the stalled truck. Ben, carefully accelerating, trying not to dig a deeper hole, began to inch forward.

Suddenly the weary truck was freed from its oozing coffin, face to face with the Forest Service vehicle, headlight to headlight.

"You see, all it takes is a little finesse," Austin shouted grandiosely, shutting off his truck. The chains were unhitched, the shovels thrown back in the flatbed, and the winch turned off. "Now, let's get out of here," he said, getting back into his truck and trying to start it, while Ben climbed into his. I was wondering whose truck to ride in, when Austin's rig suddenly died. No one paid much attention; Ben and Eric joked, while I tried unsuccessfully to brush the mud off my clothes; but after a few moments Ben's and Eric's eyes turned to Austin.

We weren't hearing anything from Austin. Ben's engine was purring in neutral, but Austin's big rig sat silent and spent after its herculean effort.

Austin slammed the truck door. "Dammit!" he shouted.

"What's the deal?" said Eric.

"The damn truck won't turn over!"

For the next half hour, every mechanical trick the men tried, from jump-starting to knocking around the carburetor, met with failure. Nothing seemed able to resurrect the truck, and it sat on its haunches like a sleeping lion refusing to be awakened. Austin fumed, while Ben took charge, quietly retrieving the spare chain from his truck and driving his rig to park in front of Austin's.

"I'll be happy to tow you in," said Ben amicably, with a slightly superior tone. He hitched up the towline as Austin looked on, refusing comment. "I think we've got it here," said Ben. Sulking, Austin climbed with Eric into the impotent vehicle, which left me to ride with Ben, who for the first time today was smiling broadly. As he accelerated along the rutted road, hauling the government truck, he began to whistle some country tunes and reached over to put his arm around my shoulder. Not knowing quite what to do, I pulled away slightly. Still grinning, Ben dropped his arm, but began to sing out, in a surprisingly good, rich baritone voice, a song I had heard before called "Mexico Way."

The verses rang on, as all country western songs do, about a poor cowboy plucking his guitar in a small town bar, lamenting his tragic life after being done wrong by a pretty señorita. Ben's triumphant voice was accompanied by two hundred or more steel bird bands jingling in a brown paper bag on my lap. I thought again how these last two days had not turned out at all as I had planned. Everything was a mess. And after word of this got out, I would never get anyone to help me with anything.

I twisted around to check how Eric and Austin were proceeding. In the blur of billowing dust, I could just see their slumping shoulders and heads bobbing up and down, up and down, as they sat, powerless and dejected, being dragged down old Zumwalt Road.

Chapter Seventeen

THE DANCING SUNFLOWER HEADS of arrowleaf balsamroot that had strewn yellow carpets across the grassland in early May were faded and colorless by mid-June. Their green lancelike leaves were now as leathery percussion instruments, rattling in the wind, augmenting the chorus of crickets that seemed to sing from every square foot of the prairie. But where the balsamroot left off, the Indian paintbrush, pink sticky geranium, and purple lupine began.

In endless bouquets planted between the growing bunch-grasses, the colorful wildflowers grew and thrived. There were many different species of Indian paintbrush on the Zumwalt, each a striking hue, from fiery crimson to sulfur yellow. This plant was known to be partially parasitic on the roots of some of the grasses, but not to any detriment; the two had been associated with each other for thousands of years. I always found it hard to believe that the color of the paintbrush was actually given off from the sepals, not the bloom of the petals, which were greenish and tubelike and inconspicuous. Poems had been written about fields of paintbrush creating the illusion of running flame; on the Zumwalt, some rolling hills indeed looked like a wavering fire heated by crimson coals.

Wild lupine grew interspersed with the Indian paintbrush, like cool water to a blaze. Its small, sweet-smelling, pealike flowers, like the little beaks of birds, rose like jeweled crowns above leaves that spread in symmetrical green whorls—leaves that resembled fairy pinwheels catching the smallest sparkling drops of dew.

Lupine's name was a misnomer, really. Derived from lupus—wolf—the plant originally was thought to devour the fertility of the soil on which it grew. The truth was just the opposite. Lupine was a leguminous plant, which meant it was a soil builder; the nodules on its roots drew and fixed nitrogen, and left the soil in better, rather than worse, condition.

As I followed the ten-mile loop skirting Swamp Creek this morning, my mind turned over the facts again, trying to piece together clues to explain the growing mystery behind the unusual numbers of hawks. Several things were beginning to arise as possibilities.

Normally, two details govern the distribution of nesting birds: the availability of nest sites and food. Hawks, in fact, will not breed unless there are suitable nest sites and an adequate prey base present. In the Zumwalt grassland, nest sites were plentiful, and ranged from a motley assortment of scattered groves of aspen and pine trees, gallery shrubs and trees along the creek bottoms, and isolated erosional remnants of rocky outcrops. Their wide distribution throughout the Zumwalt seemed an added bonus. Scientific evidence suggested that the density of breeding raptors didn't fluctuate at random, but instead was regulated. Some scientists were finding that in areas where nest sites were plentiful, hawk nests were often separated from one another by roughly equal distances.

As for the Zumwalt having a sufficient prey base, anyone with eyes could see that there were thousands of little critters—mostly ground squirrels—on the rampage in the prairie. I wasn't sure why they were so plentiful; I hadn't yet begun my study of hawk food habits. But I could think of one explanation; the Zumwalt Prairie was not plowed annually.

Among the open plains, more small mammals live in natural grasslands than in habitats that each year or two fall under the plow and disk harrow. Annual plowing greatly reduces small mammal populations by taking away these animals' food and cover. As a corollary, highly cultivated areas are also of little use to predators—such as buteos—that depend on small mammals for food.

The tendency of modern land-use practices to simplify habitats, by cutting down diverse old-growth forests and replacing them with uniform stands of even-aged conifers, or turning over the soil each year to plant croplands, effectively takes away much that wildlife needs. Scientists are beginning to recognize that, as human influence on land intensifies, wildlife numbers decline.

To the west, just skimming a grove of aspen, a red-tailed hawk unknowingly revealed its nest location by dangling a limp ground squirrel to its mate, who flew nearly vertically from one of the small trees. Nearing the nest, I sat down in the grass to scan the situation with my binoculars. Now that the deciduous trees were fully leafed out, all nests were well camouflaged; only the commotion evoked from a protective raptor parent gave hint where nests were located. Every grove of standing trees had to be inspected for nests on foot, which was incredibly time consuming.

The red-tail had spotted me. Lying back in the itchy grass, I paused for a while just to watch its graceful movements. The thought that kept nagging me as I observed the buteos day after day was that the Zumwalt was not a wildlife refuge. It was not a national park. It wasn't even a national forest. The Zumwalt Prairie was privately owned land, and more important, a working range. Something in the way it had been managed allowed for a diversity of wildlife that was highly uncommon. What was the secret to this management? Something told me that if I could only find the key to this system, and discover the role that cattle played, for good or bad, I might unlock an essential part of the mystery.

The cows now being loosed on the grassland were another issue adding complexity to the prairie picture. By mid-June they were dispersing over the rolling rangeland like brown and black fleas on the back of a giant green dog. More and more were appearing each day, although I rarely saw a rancher. The wild chorus

I had become accustomed to over the last several months reverberated with a new sound: the baritone lowing of range cattle. And all the roles played by the prairie plants and animals were having to readjust to a new level of coexistence.

At first the buteos seemed unruffled by the intrusion of the large, slow-moving creatures that rested in the shade of their nest trees while grazing the waist-high grasses. I suspected that the hawks were too busy securing food for their growing nestlings and defending their territories from other invading raptors to be overconcerned with much else, especially something that apparently held little threat. To them, I was far more menacing than any cow. Both red-tails now were circling me, arcing high, then low, in a desperate attempt to drive me away. The nest was not high; I could easily climb the tree. Snatching my pack with the bird bands, I hurried to get the job done quickly and leave the family to return to their business.

Only fifteen feet off the ground, the stick nest held three thriving nestlings, about five weeks old. One youngster, terrified by my presence, leaped out from the nest, and paddling both wings in frantic motion but losing altitude like a popped balloon, crashed unhurt on the ground 150 feet away. He sat there upright, unmoving, looking both humiliated and scared.

I was still clumsy at banding, especially when perched in a tree like this, leaning against an aspen branch that gouged into my back, while trying to grab squirming masses of feathers. One of the young in the nest had baling twine inextricably wrapped around its foot—a potentially serious problem when it came time for the bird to leave the nest and to hunt. I cut it free with my pocket knife after a wrestling match, for the petrified nestling tried to claw me in self-defense with sharp, powerful talons.

After both birds were banded and their new numbers noted, I concentrated on the third sibling, who was screaming on the ground. Both parents, circling overhead, were beside themselves. I walked toward the nestling, who, seeing me coming at him, hopped like a range hare in the opposite direction. I spoke gently, edging closer; the bird hopped along even faster. Finally, it became a running match as both parents frantically screeched from above.

With a long jump I was on top of it and scooped it up off the ground. This will take only a minute, I crooned soothingly, trying to calm it down, but the bird was nonplussed. Inexpertly, I tried to put the band on its leg while holding it still, but my sweaty palms made working with the pliers difficult. The poor bird resigned itself to my ineptitude, while my pliers kept slipping and the band twice dropped into my lap. At last finishing the job, and feeling like a bungling quack trying to pass as a doctor, I apologized to the brave little thing, climbed back up the tree, and placed it back in the nest with its overwrought siblings, numbers 7a-877-55262 and 7b-877-55258. I began to wonder, as the female redtail drove me off in disgrace, if the benefits of banding really exceeded the mayhem I had caused this little family.

A mile upstream, I nearly missed seeing the lopsided stick nest woven with twigs, weeds, and grasses, cloistered in a thorny hawthorn bush. When I was within thirty feet, the female launched and was immediately joined by her mate, who lumbered with heavy, sluggish wing beats, typical of a Swainson's hawk takeoff. Soon, however, the pair was sailing upward in oscillating spirals, their flight strong and graceful.

The slightly upturned wings, longer than almost any other buteo, are the hallmark of the Swainson's, and they catch the eye more quickly than their rather unobtrusive coloration. With a blackish brown back, dull white belly and throat, and chestnut breast, the Swainson's beauty is subtle, like that of an attractive person whose full charm is hidden at first glance under a full-length rain coat and brimmed hat.

The birds remained silent but would not leave the vicinity of the nest. Their nonaggressive defense was indicative of the species, for of all buteos, they are known to be the gentlest. Their relationship with their neighbors reflects this; sparrows, robins, orioles, and bluebirds sing and nest in bold proximity to Swainson's hawks, and at times even beneath them in the same tree, unafraid of this large bird. But for all their peacefulness, Swainson's hawks are not weak spirited. Their annual migrations to and from the pampas of Argentina are the longest of any North American hawk, and when they travel in immense flocks—like locusts, thousands squeezing together in between narrow corridors through Central American mountains—their flights are most spectacular. This particular nest held two pale blue eggs, probably laid within the last week. I retreated as quickly as possible, not wanting to interfere at this critical point in the nesting cycle.

At last I came upon the headwaters of Swamp Creek, where the ground leveled out and flaxen meadows waved flags of bright flowers. As occasionally happened on my prairie explorations, I saw at the far end of Swamp Creek meadow a curious, weatherbeaten building, long abandoned, that appeared to be an old schoolhouse. These skeletons of the past were a reminder of what the Zumwalt had been early in this century, when ranchers had homesteaded much of the prairie and divided it into 160-acre parcels. They had raised cattle and horses, and had lived in and amid this grassland. Now they were gone, having forsaken the prairie to live in town. The entire county had fewer inhabitants than one hundred years ago. These tumbledown structures, the few that had survived the harsh effects of wind and winter and time, spoke as ghosts of a history now gone.

Listing to one side, with wooden walls reflecting in the sun a patina silvery as driftwood, the schoolhouse still seemed to possess an air of dignity. Its rattling frame told of persistence under adversity, a will to hold on to the very last. Moving closer, I read a faded inscription just above the door frame: SCHOOL DISTRICT #8. WALLOWA COUNTY.

Peering in, I could see a giant blackboard running the length of one side of the room. No desks or chairs remained. An old chimney pipe stood in one corner of the room, but the woodstove was gone.

For several minutes I looked at the dark, decrepit room, visited now only by spiders and old ghosts. I wished I could know the history of this old abandoned schoolhouse—one of only a handful that remained on the prairie. Who had come to school here? What had life been like for them so many long decades ago? What had the Zumwalt been like then, when homesteads may have outnumbered hawks and people used horses and buggies to travel long-forgotten roads to town?

I climbed back outside through the slanting door frame, and the bright sun hurt my eyes for a moment. Five Hereford steers that had followed behind me across the meadow to the schoolhouse stared in bewilderment when I reemerged, as if I were an apparition. "Boo!" I shouted firmly. For once I was able to scatter the animals, who took off in every direction.

As I walked away, I turned to gaze once more at the frail building. It stood silent, pathetic yet proud, a reminder that people had always been a tightly woven part of the tapestry of the prairie spirit.

Chapter Eighteen

THE FIGURES WERE OVERWHELMING. By the third week of June, I had found a staggering 118 buteo nests. That was the good news. The bad news was that most of the nests required another visit to band the nestlings and to check on the raptors' productivity: how many nesting pairs had successfully raised their young, and how many nestlings had survived to fledge from each nest. These numbers would cast the real verdict as to the Zumwalt's capability as a prime raptor area.

From perusing the maps and aerials, I concluded that at least seven days of lengthy hikes remained if I was to explore the majority of the prairie. I was nearing the end, or was it the beginning? Flinging the topos from my lap, I realized I had to face it: I could not possibly retrace all my steps of the last several months in a mere week's time and come up with the necessary productivity figures. And without them, all I had was a substantial arrangement of hawk nest locations, but little else. The work would have little explanatory value, like doing a detailed experiment but walking away before obtaining the results.

None of us, from the scientists at the U.S. Fish and Wildlife Service who were funding the project to the professors I was working with at graduate school, had suspected the Zumwalt's prolificacy. Even if I worked from dawn until dark, with Austin and Eric's help, the sheer size of the study area, the difficulty of getting around because of lack of roads into the interior, and the time involved to climb even one tree would preclude rechecking all the nests. The irony gnawed at my mind: the Zumwalt's success would be my failure.

Day after day I continued to hike, uncovering one or two new nests. The sun-tipped beauty of Baker Canyon, which lay deep in the interior of the prairie, drove some of the discouragement from my mind as I explored the area early one morning with the melody of western meadowlarks echoing off rimrock walls. It was an easy area to cover, for a little-used, grooved dirt road coursed the bottom of the canyon, following an intermittent stream that was now mostly dried up. Escarpments rose up on either side of the canyon; few trees punctuated the veldt of bluebunch wheatgrass and Idaho fescue, and those that did stood out starkly, easily visible. Hiking was pleasant and quiet, for no cows had yet been let out here to graze. Savannah sparrows hopped rather than flew over the grasses, up and down again, as if playing a private little game of hide-and-seek, all the time scratching out their droll call, which sounded like a tiny, whining child entreating "pleeeeeeze daddy." Their streaky coloration blended well with the grasses, which waved in unison, going in and out of shadows thrown from billowy, cumulus clouds skillfully orchestrating the morning sunlight. A sienna-coated coyote padded stealthily along the ridgeline, almost paralleling my movements, his erect, pointed ears on the alert. The bristling mane on the back of his neck was tipped with black and highlighted his already glossy coat. From high above, the "kree-a" of a ferruginous hawk reverberated in the canyon, its agitated cry sounding more like the harsh notes of a herring gull. Was the hawk's aggression directed at me or the coyote, I wondered, or both? I knew as well as the ferruginous hawk that coyotes were opportunists, good hunters as well as scavengers. They would eat any small mammal they could capture, as well as porcupines, snakes and lizards, grasshoppers and berries, domestic poultry and livestock, and native birds. This one seemed intent on something. Hungry.

The canyon deepened and the rock walls, which lined the top

of the draw like a brush stroke, became more precipitous. I began to wonder if I had made the best choice by walking along the bottom of the canyon as I craned my neck farther and farther back to scope the cliffs; if I continued much farther it would be difficult or even impossible to climb out. The coyote, as well as the hawk, had vanished over the hill. Electing to change course, I clambered up the side of the canyon, negotiating crumbling rock and crusty soil, to arrive at last at the windswept mesa above Baker Canyon.

The flatland that stretched for many miles made for exceptional visibility. Although I couldn't locate the coyote, within close range was an ongoing drama that I sat down to quietly observe. Three buteo hawks, each of a different species, were in the throes of battle. The smallest of the three, a dark phase Swainson's hawk, almost completely sooty black except for its gray, banded tail, had fully extended its lethal talons to rip at the air only inches above the rusty back of a red-tail. The red-tail twisted over deftly, raising its own talons in retaliation and momentarily flying upside down, leaving itself vulnerable from below. As if in alliance with the Swainson's, a large ferruginous came up at the red-tail from underneath, which left the red-tail little else to do but again roll over and be swiped at from both directions. Finding itself in such a compromising position, the red-tail shot off like an arrow between its two pursuants, and then, with a characteristic scream, retaliated by stooping at the Swainson's and reaching out to grasp the narrow-winged hawk's talons with its own. In a flurry of feathers the two spiraled earthward, while the ferruginous entered the fray from the rear. Before touching ground, the two locked buteos unlatched talons and tried to outdo one another in pumping up in the air to regain lost height.

It was a losing battle for the red-tail—two against one—but the hawk had probably gotten itself into this mess in the first place by invading the nesting territories of the Swainson's and ferruginous hawks. Sensing imminent defeat, the red-tailed hawk conceded;

closing its feathers tightly, a gesture not unlike pulling on a cloak to leave, the bird bulleted out and over the canyon, finally escaping the lasso of the two buteo victors.

While scratching out some notes, I thought how observing wild creatures was at times like watching a rodeo, with a similar sense of excitement and anticipation, cavorting and danger, winners and losers. This was especially true during the summertime explosion of courtship displays, breeding activities, and the raising of young. It was a rodeo, replete with its own set of clowns and wild horses and crazy cowboys: cowboys clutching the necks of Brahma bulls like a tenacious kestrel riding the back of an invasive eagle; clowns like the silly ground squirrels squeaking and scurrying all the time, taunting frustrated pursuers like hawks with comical antics and daring escapes.

I watched as two yellow goldfinches rhythmically undulated through the air toward the canyon's willows with the single goal of joining the rest of their noisy flock. Alone, the goldfinches were easily vulnerable; within their large group, however, they could ward off predators by the force of their numbers.

Of course. That was it. It was numbers I needed. Not just Austin and Eric and me, but Ben McPherson and other ranchers; Glenn Smith and those from Fish and Game; people from the BLM; volunteers from the Forest Service. One person alone couldn't cover nearly two hundred square miles in a week's time, climb trees, and band birds. But twenty could—twenty people, divided into groups of two, hiking ten or so miles a day, for three or four days.

I needed to check the maps first, to look at routes, geographic areas, numbers of nests, and distances apart. Volunteers would need to be equipped; I would have to get copies of maps, data sheets, a supply of tree spurs and climbing ropes, bird bands, and pliers. People would need simple instructions on what to record, as well as some cursory training in buteo identification and how to read the nestlings' ages by the development of their feathers. I could pair inexperienced people with knowledgeable birders.

Of course it could work. In a cowboy county that prided itself on its rodeos, it was perfectly right and natural; a new kind of roundup. A buteo rodeo!

Stopping to take a swig of tepid water from the water bottle, I sat down to jot some notes at the canyon's edge and carelessly dangle my feet over the side. The harsh "kree-ah, kree-ah" of a disturbed ferruginous echoed up the canyon. Less than a half mile away was the overflowing stick nest gripping precariously the steep rimrock wall, and beyond that another nest, far larger, with what looked to be a rounded form settled on top. Brushing the brown loamy soil from my pants, I tossed on my pack and proceeded on.

Two adult ferruginous hawks circled above, screaming weakly as I closed in, then soon took off down the canyon, leaving me a minute to stare down into the tumbled bowl of sticks that was their nest. It was empty. Directly below it, however, before the cliff wall dropped off and plunged into the canyon, was an eroded ledge on which lay the clear remains of two ferruginous eggs. They were broken; the white and yolk gone; and toothmarks etched the creamy white and brown smooth sides. Undoubtedly the work of a coyote.

Within five minutes the female ferruginous hawk returned to circle above me again, soon joined by her mate. The halfhearted cries and large, slow movements seemed somewhat pitiful, dispirited in comparison with those of birds whose nests still had something left in them to defend. The vision of the lean and graceful coyote with the black fringe around his neck came to mind. I wondered if this canyon, these ground-nesting birds, were part of his seasonal hunting ground.

Less than a quarter mile from the first nest, a completely different story was being acted out by another two, but fiercely aggressive, birds of prey. Before I even had a chance to scope their nest, the hostile birds charged, winging eye level with the canyon rim, in my direction, and at first glance, from their large size and powerful flight, I nearly mistook them for golden eagles.

But the broad wings and feathered tarsi soon identified the agitated pair as ferruginous hawks. The two birds were dissimilar in appearance. The female was a dark phase bird, one of only a handful I had seen on the Zumwalt. Unlike her mate, whose back and shoulders were typical of the coloration of the species—rufous, lightly streaked with brown—the dark bird's back was the color of deep clove, and even the underside of her wings and her belly, which in her mate were seagull white with a faint tinge of red on the legs, were deep chocolate brown without any signs of streaking. The two birds' only similarity was in their mutual white tails, which were ruddering side to side as they flip-flopped directions through the air.

I could see their prominent stick nest through the binoculars, and it rivaled the size of any eagle's, crafted on the top of rock pinnacle just at the canyon's rim. Considering the fate of the previous nest, it looked dangerously accessible. Nest violations by roving mammalian predators was always a problem for this species, choosing as they did to nest in low, open places reached easily by foot. Nature had equipped them, though, with an intense will to defend their nests against all intruders, and armed them with powerful weapons of skillful flight and potent talons.

The abject, threatening behavior of this particular pair of hawks seemed unusual, however. Something was setting them off; and then I saw it. Stopping in my tracks, I fell to the ground to take cover. My traveling companion of the morning, the trotting coyote, was stalking their nest.

I had seen coyotes hunt only a few times in my life. Their style, though, was predictable. When pursuing small mammals or birds, coyotes pad along stealthily and then, at an appropriate moment, pounce on and secure their prey. The ferruginous hawks, aware of the danger to their nest, were flying in full regalia.

Three still-downy heads slunk down in their nest while their two parents prepared to defend them to the death. The coyote, lunging up on powerful legs, attempted to nip the birds as they repeatedly dove at him from above. His glossy, burnished coat reflected health and strength. The birds' talons were not actually striking him, and the birds' attacks appeared more as warnings, which he ignored. He edged closer.

In the nest one youngster, either braver or dumber than the others, stood up to see what was going on. The young bird looked like a small checkerboard, black primary feathers interspersed between patches of white down. His yellow beak was open and his brown eyes, shiny as smooth, wet pebbles, were round and wide. This bird, scarcely three weeks old, would be unequipped to fly for a week or two longer.

As the coyote continued to close in on the nest, the adult ferruginous hawks' flight grew more wild. Now the talons actually scraped the sides of the coyote, but still he refused to be intimidated. The silly young nestling, in his innocence becoming a target, turned to stare at the coyote and opened his feathers wide, in a motion of fear and bluffed bravery.

The coyote leaned back on his haunches, only a few feet from the cliff's edge and the nestling, and prepared to pounce. The female ferruginous hawk suddenly careened at full velocity toward the predator from behind. With the force of an unleashed eagle, she struck the coyote, knocking him off his footing and sending him through the air, an unwilling projectile, over the lip of the cliff.

I sat stunned, breathless, not believing. Two birds, unconcerned for their own safety, had fearlessly and successfully defended their young from a powerful, cunning predator three times their size. It wasn't possible.

But it was possible. The proof now lay at the bottom of Baker Canyon, motionless, with a broken neck.

Chapter Nineteen

AT FIRST, MRS. DELACY'S cryptic note, "You can stay," failed to fully register when I arrived home that evening, still wrapped up in the drama I had witnessed earlier. I read the line again, then let my eyes continue down the note's graceful, practiced penmanship, with a growing sense of deep relief.

You can stay, but please move your things to the room across the hall, the little orange one, and keep your foodstuffs in the refrigerator in the mudroom. I moved some of your food out today. I'll be needing all the space in the kitchen refrigerator when my family comes to visit later this summer.

I'll be gone for a week taking classes at the University. Donald will be in and out, sometimes staying with friends. He knows what to do. I appreciate your looking after the house. Please clean up after yourself, and continue doing your laundry down the street.

Best ever,
Dorothy

"Hallelujah!" I shouted to the empty hallway, with a second glance at the dining room table, which, if cleared of the eclectic assortment of knickknacks, would be a splendid place to lay out all the maps and sort out routes for the "roundup." I threw my pack and scope on the floor and dashed upstairs to see my new room, which was indeed far smaller—small and linear—than the spacious one with the broad windows I had been using. The view of the mountains I had come to love would be gone. I would leave the antique double bed, the fine chinoiserie chest, the large closet and

Chinese rug, and have instead an orange area rug, a soft twin bed covered with an old orange floral spread and pushed up against two white plastered walls, a tiny closet, and two small windows that looked out over the street. But I could also see the sunset and, anyway, what did it matter? I was outdoors most of the time and needed only a place to hang my hat. And even though I detest orange, its vibrancy would only help to shock me from bed in the morning. All that mattered was that I could stay.

Someone was banging at the front door. Leaping down the stairs three at a time in my exuberance, I ran to the door to find Austin and Eric standing typically stonefaced on the other side of the screen. "Come in," I said cheerily. "I can't wait to tell you my idea."

"Oh God, what now," said Austin, tiredly.

"But first say you'll both stay for dinner. I can dig up something. I've been wanting to thank you anyway for helping me out of the mess on Findley Buttes."

"Do we have to take our boots off again to come inside?" Eric asked cynically.

"Indeed you do," I retorted. "I've just been accepted into this household, and I'm not going to risk getting my invitation rescinded. Why don't you make yourselves at home in the living room while I get dinner. What brings you here, anyway?"

"Two things," answered Austin. "I'm thirsty and want a beer and also wanted to see how the banding was coming along."

I arranged their boots, caked with mud from the forests, on the front doorstep, put my pack and scope in the closet, and led them to the couch near the television. "The banding's going great, but I'm sorry to have to disappoint you about the beer. None of us drink it around here. I can offer you some orange juice, though."

"Crimeny," groaned Austin, settling into the couch and putting up his stockinged feet on the coffee table. "I should have known. You're everything Sparkey says and more."

I darted into the kitchen to get three glasses of juice and

momentarily was chagrined to find all my food removed from the refrigerator and most of it stacked on the shelf in the mudroom, as if Mrs. DeLacy had begun the job but not had time to finish it. The orange juice and milk, however, were in the fridge, although my leftovers weren't. Rapidly stuffing food and covered bowls into the refrigerator, I grabbed glasses and ice and poured the juice.

"Are you a Mormon or a Christian Scientist?" asked Austin when I handed him and Eric a glass.

"Neither. I just don't like beer. Alcohol puts me to sleep."

"Such a live wire," commented Eric, disparagingly. "Remind me to never ask you out to the Gold Room."

"What's the Gold Room?" I asked, getting comfortable in the chair and trying to think of the best way to break the news of the upcoming rodeo.

"Dancing and liquor and more fun than sitting around all night looking at maps. Oops, I almost forgot who I'm talking to," said Austin, who all of a sudden broke into a singsong voice. "Oh she's a smooth-talking, slow-walking, slick, silver-tongued, good-looking, cold-hearted, Bible-totin' goody-two-shoes."

"Whaat?"

"Sparkey's song. He sings it about you. Everybody knows it."

"Sparkey's a fool," I said hotly.

"Everybody knows that too. But the song's true. Now what are you going to try to rope us into this time with that slick, silver tongue of yours?"

This didn't seem the appropriate time to bring up my plan, for it did depend on how smoothly I could sell it to a disparate group of people—too many with big egos—and briefly I felt sorely deflated. Did everyone feel about me as Sparkey did?

"Ahem," coughed Austin, with a pat to my knee. "You also mentioned something about dinner. Don't worry about Sparkey. He just knows you're competent and he's not. You're a burr in the Fish and Game's craw. They'll never forgive you for taking away the job from one of their guys."

Dinner was a strange, makeshift medley of leftovers and canned soup. While I tried to find something to eat in the mudroom, Eric helped in the kitchen as Austin set the table, opening and shutting drawers and cabinets at random, muttering "Not here; not here; not here. Where does that woman hide her damn plates?"

I hurriedly put together a green salad, cut up some fresh broccoli, and found just enough leftover potato salad sitting on the counter that I decided should go to them, since I wasn't very hungry. We sat around the table, eating, and talking raptors, and I knew the moment had come to spring my idea on them when Austin's mouth was momentarily occupied, full of potato salad.

"I know how we can get the productivity figures," I said lightly, and then continued before either had a chance to comment. "I'm going to ask everyone I know, and hopefully you know, around here to help us—hike to all the nests, band the nestlings, take down data. We just need to enlist twenty or so people and we can cover the entire area in three or four days."

"You're crazy," said Eric.

"No I'm not," I replied objectively. "There's you two, me, and Ben McPherson. That's four. We can get Glenn and other people at the Fish and Game, ranching friends of Ben's, Donald DeLacy maybe, resource specialists at the Soil Conservation Service, buddies of yours from the Forest Service, even maybe the owner of the bookstore, who told me he adores hawks. It will be a community event."

Austin shook his head. "You'll never, in a thousand years, get those people together. A lot of them hate each other's guts."

"You'll do it, though, won't you?" I entreated, handing over the last of the potato salad as a peace offering. "Ask your friends, help me round up some spurs and pliers. If we don't get this information, the study won't mean anything. You know that better than I do."

"Dumb idea," said Eric, but Austin was at least mulling it over in his mind.

"We'd have a great time," I continued. "A bird banding round-up. A buteo rodeo! Everybody with one common goal."

"Buteo rodeo?" scorned Eric, leveling his gaze at me. "What in hell is a buteo rodeo? And just why do you think they'd want to help you?"

"Because—" I suddenly felt hit in the stomach. Reveling in the warm glow of my plan, I had not considered that to many people, what hawks did was of little or no interest. Eric was right. Why would anyone care about helping me with this esoteric study? What could it offer them?

"Because, hell, it could be fun!" shouted Austin. "A buteo rodeo. The idea's so absurd, it just might work. Just when were you thinking of beginning?"

"This next Saturday."

"Less than a week away?" said Eric. "You're insane."

"If you can find most of the people, we'll take care of the equipment," Austin offered, with Eric scowling. "The problem is, you won't find them. These folks won't work together. The ranchers hate the government, the Fish and Game hate the Soil Conservation Service, the Forest Service despises the Bureau of Land Management, and the Park Service wants to come in and take over and has made an enemy of every cowboy in the county. It's one big bureaucratic mess. Everyone holds everyone else responsible for the problems we have."

"The hawks don't know that," I said, smiling, knowing I had them, however tentatively, on my side. "All I ask is four days. Three days. Three days of people putting aside their differences and coming together for the good of the Zumwalt."

"You forgot one faction," interrupted Eric. "Lawyers. Get the lawyers out there and they'll bring any chance for success to a screeching halt."

"I disagree," replied Austin. "That's the surefire way to unify all these groups. *Everybody* hates lawyers."

After a day at home to carefully peruse the maps and come up with forty different round-trip routes, which covered a major portion of the Zumwalt, I turned my attention to convincing people of the value of taking part in this wild scheme. My first call was to Ben McPherson, who did not laugh at me and once again generously offered his time, and even said he would find some other ranchers to take part. Donald DeLacy, whom I spoke with at breakfast the next morning, said yes. His girlfriend liked birds. I wasn't sure how much help I would get from them. Austin and Eric had reluctantly said they would see who they could come up with at the Forest Service and the BLM. That left Phil, the owner of the bookstore; biologists from the Fish and Game; and those at the Soil Conservation Service. I decided to swing by the Soil Conservation Service first, for I had been meaning to take some time to talk with the regional director, whom I had met briefly once or twice before and liked right away.

Something about Don Baldwin made one feel immediately comfortable. His eyes twinkled, and his easy smile and hearty laugh came often. From his close-cropped gray hair and lined, sunbronzed face, I guessed him to be about fifty-five, but his fit form made Don appear younger. He listened enthusiastically to the idea and instantly bought the concept. As he talked about the ranchers and the Zumwalt, Don, unlike many other government workers, referred to them with sincere respect, which, as I knew from Ben, they gave back to him in equal measure. Don was highly educated but did not flaunt it; he was well versed in all the new data on soil, grazing, livestock, wildlife, and biodiversity but did not force his knowledge on anyone. He had overseen the range of the entire county for the last thirty years, and had developed an amazing rapport with most of the ranchers.

In a quiet, easy way, he merely showed examples—examples that apparently worked. From the rancher's view, as I again learned from Ben, Don was a breed apart from the standard government worker. He cared little for government formalities or the political two-step; he was independent and savvy and ethical in his doings, and cared more for the grassland than for any reward from his superiors. He sometimes was rebuked for not participating in all the bureaucratic nonsense, but this didn't trouble him at all. As long as the range and soil conditions were improving under his stewardship, that was all that mattered.

Don was easy to query, for he talked freely, especially about the range, and what he offered was knowledgeable and perceptive. In less than a month's time, I would be depending on him to help me learn about range conditions and also to design a strategy to investigate, in depth, the true quality of the Zumwalt's grassland, not merely its face value. Today, however, my focus was on rounding up volunteers, and although Don declined to climb trees, citing his age with a laugh, he said he would be happy to go along and would proffer his two hardy assistants, giving them some days off work.

I left the SCS feeling optimistic that my plan could be pulled off. That made seven now, or maybe nine, if Donald DeLacy was serious about helping. I didn't relish the idea of seeing Sparkey at the Fish and Game, but I needed Glenn's help and that of several others in his employ. On reaching the Fish and Game office, I found Glenn still poring over papers. So much of a biologist's work was paperwork, I thought sadly.

Glenn was at first as cynically disparaging as Austin and Eric had been; but as I continued to smooth-talk, to use Sparkey's phrase, he slowly warmed to the idea, finally agreeing to spare four men for three days, if, in turn, I would agree to hand over to him a complete copy of all my information. Glenn wanted maps of all the hawk nest locations, data on all the productivity figures, and the band numbers. I saw no problem with this, and we shook hands. Glenn then called in two biologists I didn't know—a dark-haired man in his mid-thirties named Walt, and a tall, curly-haired, mustached fellow, who looked only slightly older than I, named Peter, to tell them of the plan and their part in it.

"Okay," said Glenn, turning again to me. "We'll give you, Marcy, your three days. But don't, under any conditions, team us up with any rancher. Walt here would probably be sorely tempted to take his shotgun along just to show what he thought about their damn cows."

"I truly appreciate your help," I said sincerely. "So it will be you, Walt, and Peter, and who else? Did you say four, Glenn?"

"Not me!" Sparkey suddenly yelled from the doorway. "You aren't getting me, Glenn, not on your life! Not after the way she treated those guys who helped her get that truck out of the ditch."

"What are you talking about now, Sparkey?" said Glenn.

"She poisoned them!"

Walt and Peter stared at me, as I turned to face Sparkey. "What are you saying?" I gasped.

"I just talked to Austin an hour ago," Sparkey said knowingly. "I had a question for the Forest Circus and they put him on. Seems he and Eric were sick as dogs yesterday after eating what you fed them the other night."

"I don't have the slightest idea what you're talking about," I retorted.

"Potato salad. They said they thought it was the potato salad. You was real careful not to not eat any, Austin said. But just kept piling it on them. He said it was spoiled."

Oh no! How long had Mrs. DeLacy left that salad sitting on the counter when she cleaned out the refrigerator? I'd never thought it might have gone bad.

"Austin told me about all you're plotting. And somehow you bewitched him and now even these guys here into going in on it. Let me tell you straight, no one with brains should be mixed up in this rodeo thing."

"Oh, shut up, Sparkey," said Glenn, laughing. "We're going to need your help. You're our bird man, remember? We'll get our hands on all that data we've been wanting for a long time."

"I'm warning you," said Sparkey ominously. "First, potato salad. Just what could she do next?"

Chapter Twenty

A FLOTILLA OF TRUCKS converged at the Fish and Game at precisely half past eight on Saturday morning, the fourth week of June. Some were inscribed with government insignias, others were not. Some were beat up, like mine; others, like Ben's, were freshly washed. A group of men, many of whom didn't know each other, stood around in awkward silence, talking now and then among those they did know and smiling rarely. Out of a company of nearly twenty, only three were women: Donald DeLacy's girl-friend, the wife of a BLM worker, and me. Several of the men were examining the heap of climbing spurs and ropes piled in the gravel driveway.

Reviewing the collage of disparate people, I saw among them the faces of ranchers, tanned and skeptical; of Austin and Eric, with several compatriots I didn't recognize from the Forest Service and the BLM; the four Fish and Game guys, including, much to my chagrin, Sparkey, all of them garbed in their drab, skin-tight uniforms; the bespectacled bookstore owner, who looked entirely out of place in this setting; and several people I had met at one time but couldn't readily identify. Many of the nineteen pairs of eyes were trained my way, looking for some direction. With a sigh, I also noticed that the people had already naturally grouped themselves into alignments as if they had been instructed: ranchers here, Fish and Game here, Forest Service here. I began to wonder if this was going to turn out to be a disaster.

"I'm so glad you all could make it to Wallowa County's first buteo rodeo," I began. "I can't tell you how much I really appreciate your help. Why don't we all go inside and I'll explain some things, give you equipment you'll need, and describe some different routes you might take. Then we can divide up into pairs," I added, but trailed off, seeing looks shooting between the different faces, looks that could be easily read: "Like hell am I going to be paired off with that sucker from the Forest Service."

The sound of clumping boots followed me to Glenn Smith's office, where I had assembled all my topographic maps on the wall to give a full overview of the land that needed covering. People crowded around the room, mindful, however, not to stand too close to each other.

This isn't going to work, I thought abruptly. *This isn't going to work at all.*

Nervously, I picked up in my arms the collection of additional topo maps for the volunteers to use. "I have organized ten hikes for today, each one four or five miles long. All of them have about two to four hawk nests, which I've marked on your maps. If you have any preference as to where to go, please let me know after I describe all the options." I slowly drew my finger across the dotted lines I had outlined on the wall map, and called out the names I had invented: Pine Creek Loop; East Salmon Creek; West Salmon Creek; O.K. Gulch, Beaver Creek; Aspen Creek Spurs; Carol Creek, among others.

I had been careful to change one name: "Bennett's Yuck."

Bennett's Yuck had been one of my least favorite hikes. The area—badly overgrazed, crawling with Black Angus cattle, and almost completely devoid of hawk nests—was a "corporate ranch," owned by an out-of-state conglomerate and run by a hired manager. As I pointed it out to the group, referring to it mildly as Bennett's Draw, the significance of the fact that few ranches on the Zumwalt Prairie were corporately owned began to dawn on me. Wallowa County was an anomaly in today's ranching world. The vast majority of the land was held by individual families. Melanie Deane had spoken for most of the ranchers she knew when she had argued to me that the new, restrictive regulations and higher fees imposed by the government were forcing the smaller operators— the family ranches—out of business. Large landholdings and extensive public grazing permits were increasingly being acquired by giant corporations that often cared less for the condition of the range than for making a short-term buck. With this changeover in ownership, the husbandry and condition of the land were invariably changing. If Bennett's Yuck was any indication of the new order of things, I wasn't sure the change was for the better.

The dead silence in the room led me to switch my tack, which convinced Austin, as he told me later, that I had a far better future as a cruise director than as a biologist. "Why don't we stop and take a moment to introduce ourselves to each other," I said, trying to ignore Austin's rolling eyes and frown as he shook his head at me. "What you're about to do today," I continued, "will benefit the Fish and Wildlife Service whom I work for, and other agencies concerned with this region, as well as the ranchers, who own this land we'll be covering. I'd like to introduce Austin Scott and Eric Peterson, from the Forest Service, who have been so helpful, Glenn Smith from the Fish and Game—most of you know Glenn, I think—and Ben McPherson, standing at the door, who has already helped me out and taught me a lot about ranching, and, well, maybe the rest of you can introduce yourselves and tell what you do."

At first no one spoke. I felt the old sinking sensation again, realizing I was coming across as an eighteen-year-old camp counselor squawking at a covey of campers. Around the room the proud, quiet men were looking down at their boots, embarrassed and uncomfortable, unwilling to be the first to speak, and in my heart I knew this buteo rodeo idea was possibly the stupidest thing I had ever thought up. Only one person looked perfectly at ease, as he stood wearing a huge grin. Sparkey was delighted.

Ben's blue eyes caught mine; he smiled and tipped up his chin; the gesture gave me the shot of confidence I desperately needed. "I'd like to introduce my friends and fellow ranchers Rex Gray, Pat Trupp, Bill Woolbright, and Tip and Brad Hadley," Ben announced. "I think I can say this for all of us, we enjoy having hawks on our land to take care of the red-digger problem, and look forward to these next few days of getting out and doing some banding."

"Bless you, Ben," I wanted to shout. Taking his lead, the other people rattled off their names, and I thought I saw a faint flicker of interest in their expressions, probably precipitated by their eagerness to get out of there. "Each of you will need a few items, which I've collected for you here," I continued. "You'll find data sheets to write down all the information you collect, a sackful of bird bands, and a pair of pliers, and, of course, you'll be carrying your topo map, to keep track of where you are."

"It's easy to get lost out there," called Sparkey from the back. "Bad country with all those badger holes and cow pies."

Ignoring his outburst, I went on. "I'm going to pass around some bands so you can see how they go together; they squeeze around the birds' legs real easy. Each band has a different number. There's a place on the data sheet to write it down."

Phil from the bookstore raised his hand, as if he were in a classroom. I nodded at him. "What are the plastic bags for?" he asked, pointing a long finger at the stack of plastic bags, each with an index card inside, sitting on the end of Glenn's desk. I cleared my throat.

"For collecting castings. Castings are, um, undigested material, like bones and fur, spit out by the hawks. When examined under a microscope, we can tell just what the hawks are eating."

"They eat red diggers," said Brad Hadley, to which Sparkey replied cynically, "Naw, they eat newborn lambs."

"Gross!" blurted Janelle, Donald DeLacy's pretty, petite girl-friend, and leaned up to nuzzle closer to him. "I'm not going to touch hawk barf!" Everyone laughed, and signaled to her their agreement.

"I'll leave picking up the castings to your discretion," I added, trying to speak above the din, "but really, they are helpful." No one was paying the slightest bit of attention to me, so I waited a minute. The room finally quieted. "Lastly," I continued, "you probably saw outside the pile of spurs and ropes. For those of you who are experienced and want to climb trees, they're useful in getting to the higher nests. But please don't feel you have to use them. If the nest is too high, forget it. I don't want anyone to get hurt."

Austin then came forward to demonstrate how to use the spurs, whispering in my ear, "You just don't want to get sued," then called out the suggestion to everyone in the room that those with tree-climbing experience should pair up with those who had none.

"Okay," he said, taking charge. "Who has used these before?" A few hands slowly went up. Most of the government biologists had had experience with the equipment, whereas none of the ranchers had, having little need to climb trees out on the range.

"Gotcha," said Austin. "You guys, split yourselves up. Those with experience pair off with those who haven't any. Those with the most experience need to take the cultivated lands near town, where the biggest cottonwoods are. The trees on the prairie are pretty scrawny."

No one moved. A palpable tension mounted in the room. "Split up, dammit!" Austin said, obnoxiously. "We don't have all day to mull around."

"Since we're neighbors, let's be friends," sang Sparkey.

"Ah, shut up, Sparkey," said Austin. "I'll go with Joe Blow here," he said, and like a grizzly bear walked over to Ben McPherson and placed an outstretched paw on his shoulder; Ben met Austin with something close to a smile. Their strange chemistry fueled a reaction between other men in the room, who began to mix together like oil shaken together with water. Not waiting for the centrifuge to stop spinning, I handed out equipment in rapid succession to ranchers oddly paired with federal government workers, Fish and Game biologists with those from the BLM, agency with agency, in motley combinations of two. Routes were chosen, and spurs and ropes and extra binoculars were grabbed up, as people made their way to their trucks. There was talking, even joking, mingled with the sound of rattling spurs, plastic bags stuffed into backpacks, and paper being shuffled and snapped to clipboards. A few people stopped to ask me more questions, and to say they couldn't be here tomorrow. That was a problem I had already considered. Speculating that interest in this rodeo would probably wane on consecutive days, I had strategized to hit the most productive areas on the first day. "Never thought I'd live to see the day Barney Lewis and Les Fischer would ride together in the same pickup," Glenn Smith chuckled to me as he looked over his route.

"Why?" I asked, even though it was none of my business. He turned and spoke quietly. "The Forest Service, for the last four years, has been blaming the BLM for what they think was a lousy riprap job they did on Lucy Creek. Convinced they could have done it better. You know how it is. People spilling over on each other's turf. We've got too many policy makers for the same pie."

A biologist I had met the other day—one with an easy smile and curly brown hair that looked a little too unruly and Chaplinesque for the Fish and Game—came over to talk to Glenn. For some reason I found myself wishing he would be my partner, but then, overhearing Austin's bellowing voice raging, I excused myself and ran outside to the parking lot.

"Lady Stetson! Get out here!" Austin ranted.

"I'm here!" I shouted back, standing in the exhaust of the running vehicles circling together like a wagon train.

"Just where you want us to round up after the rodeo?" he said, leaning halfway out the window of his truck.

"Oh, I'm glad you asked!" I shouted so everyone could hear. "If I'm not here when you finish, just leave everything in Glenn's office. I hope I'll see you this same time tomorrow."

"Slave driver!" yelled Sparkey, riding as a passenger in a Fish and Game truck, having paired himself with a buddy from work.

"Just who came up with these data sheets anyway?" he added, shaking a stack of them out the window.

"Thank you all again," I continued. "And for your help, I'm planning, day after tomorrow, to host a barbecue at Hurricane Creek. Please come and bring your families."

Weaving through the lot as if his truck were a race car, Austin piloted up beside me and whispered, "No way in hell will I trust *your* food," then gunned out of the lot, kicking up rocks. The curious convoy of utility vehicles began filing out behind him, one after the other, and I wondered, feeling personally responsible, how these unlikely marriages between such seemingly opposed partners would fare alone out on the prairie.

"So where's that leave us?" said a deep, quiet voice behind me, and I turned to face the biologist who had been with Glenn inside. "I think we're the last ones left."

A sketch of smile lines emanated from the sides of eyes that held both warmth and humor. "Let's go find out," I said, smiling in return, and noticing he was very tall, with the muscular lankiness of a runner or cyclist, his long face finely chiseled, with high cheekbones, a straight nose, holding an air of refinement that seemed amusingly juxtaposed with his funny, bushy brown mustache. "You're Peter, aren't you?"

He nodded, picking up a pile of the castings bags and putting them in his backpack. "Think they'll kill each other?" he asked, grinning, looking out after all the trucks.

"Oh, I hope not," I said tiredly, then scanned the map for the route not yet chosen by anyone today. Carol Creek. One of the farthest out on old Zumwalt Road. It was a pretty hike, and interesting in that along the creek, within a half mile of each other, were three buteo nests, each of a different species. The red, blue, and yellow marks made it evident.

"One of each," said Peter, immediately picking up the fact. "Is that common, to have the different species nesting so close to each other?"

"More common than the other way around," I answered, wondering if I should pick up the spurs and act like a tree climber. I was sure, though, that he had heard from Sparkey that I wasn't. "I've been finding that hawks of the same species prefer to build their nests farther apart from each other, at least a mile away, as a general rule. But, on the other hand, they seem to allow hawks of a different species to nest closer."

"Intraspecific aggression," Peter said, then added with a laugh, "similar to what happens here."

The trip with Peter was a pleasant one, slow going along the deeply rutted road, which allowed us time to get to know each other and to watch the subtle, changing landscape of the Zumwalt. The grassland stretched warm and broad in the bright sunshine, and the lush green bluebunch wheatgrass and Idaho fescue furnished the high steppe with a velvet vibrancy. Wildflowers were changing color and shape once again, with a new chorus of summer species. Prolific lupine and an array of yellow composites made quilts of purple and yellow. When we stopped along the way to watch drifting hawks, I noticed the fine feathering of purple avens in the strong wind, and clumps of summer blue triteleia lilies looking as if their balloonlike corollas were going to pop. I never could quit marveling at all the color of the prairie, which was just now accented with sprinkles of white from yarrow flowers like drops from a dripping paintbrush.

Two hours from the Fish and Game headquarters, we arrived at Carol Creek, now, in midsummer, a trickling, ephemeral stream. A wary red-tail took off from a fence post not two hundred yards away, flying nearly perpendicular and screaming his characteristic call that was immediately answered by the running notes of a flaming orange kestrel.

"You do some incantations to get these raptors to come to you like that?" said Peter, stretching after the drive in the warm air, which threatened to become increasingly hot.

"No magic; they just know me," I replied, teasing, and hopped the fence post that the red-tail had previously occupied. To reach the nests, we first crossed a half-mile strip of dry-farmed, cultivated land that paralleled the road. Once again I made note that this habitat seemed shunned by nesting hawks, used only for an occasional hunting sortie. All trees and shrubs had been cut down, rendering them nearly useless for many nesting species. Once we had crossed out onto the native prairie, however, with its rich diversity of plants and grasses and stock ponds providing more wetland habitat, the land exhibited more nesting wildlife.

We walked through the grasses along Carol Creek, grasses that had not been grazed yet, some reaching thigh high, interspersed with similarly tall flowers. "Look out for badger holes!" said Peter, mimicking Sparkey, when I tripped in one. I seemed to have a knack for falling into the stupid things that lay as hidden mines every five feet or so on the prairie. Crossing meadowland and Kentucky bluegrass habitat for nearly a mile, we finally saw the first of the three buteo nests, which was well exposed in a hawthorn tree along the winding waters of the creek.

The two adult ferruginous hawks spotted us at almost the same moment. From their immediate and aggressive response, I knew the nest was still active. "Ready to go banding?" I asked, and Peter took the spurs from my hands.

"I've heard all about you from Sparkey and Austin. I know you're the best tree climber around. Let me try, just this once," he remarked with a teasing smile, and walked on ahead, quietly padding through the tall grass like a cheetah toward its prey. With both parents circling above, Peter reached the tree and scaled it quickly with facile agility.

"Three young, nearly ready to fledge, and an addled egg," Peter called down, and I hastily got out my pencil and clipboard, spilling all the castings bags out on the ground in the process. "Female, band number 877-55347." He paused to band another. "Male, number 877-55348. There's also a Belding's ground squirrel, a pocket gopher, and wings of a magpie in the nest." The sun was in my eyes as I looked, but I could see he was having a time with the last nestling, who kept trying to bolt from the nest. "This last female's number is 877-55349," he said, slightly triumphant, when he succeeded in banding the bird.

"I'm going to drop some castings to you, so be ready to catch them," he said, lightly tossing them down into my waiting hands.

"You want what else is in the nest?" he asked cryptically. "I can toss it too."

"What is it?"

"Cow pies," he called down, laughing.

"Good grief, no!" I yelled, thinking how odd a habit it was that ferruginous hawks liked to line their nests with cow dung. Perhaps it had insulating qualities.

Peter climbed down and handed me the spurs. "Next time, it's all yours. Those little beggars are feisty little devils."

I smiled. "Sure thing," I answered, knowing that the next two nests were only about eight feet off the ground. We walked along the creek, spending, to my surprise, more time laughing than talking, pointing out wildflowers and skittish sparrows, admiring the healthy growth of the grasses.

Coming up out of Carol Creek to the rolling mesa that over-looked the majestic Wallowa Mountains far to the south, we paused, without saying a word, to take in the wild scene. The sin-gular fragrance of the prairie was pungent in late June. Whether from the decay of remnant arrowleaf balsamroot and other spring-time flowers, or the ripening seeds of grasses dispersing, or from the luxuriant growth of summer flowers, the air had a sweetness, I thought, like no other. I had known mountain air, and the rich, loamy air of old-growth forests, and the salty air washed clean by the sea; each held a special spot in my heart, and yet something about the air of the Zumwalt stood out above them all, having a life all its own, recharging and pure and heady, swept clean by miles of unobstructed winds.

Peter inhaled deeply and finally spoke. "There's nothing like a prairie," he said thoughtfully, anticipating my agreement. This I was fully prepared to give, and was about to, when his next words caught me off guard and suddenly filled me with strange perplexity.

"The sad thing," he began, looking me in the eyes, "the real pity of it, is that it's privately owned."

Chapter Twenty-One

I FOUND MYSELF staring after Peter as he walked on down the draw. His words for some reason shook me.

The pity of the prairie being privately owned—so much more was wrapped up in that simple statement than I had previously assumed. Just what did it mean, what were the implications and the ramifications of everything that depended on this land for sustenance? There was a great difference, of course, between public and private lands. But how to ferret out the benefits or drawbacks, or was it a complex combination of the two? What would be the difference between the management regimens, and how would they affect the grassland, the wildlife, the people of this rural landscape?

I thought about these things overnight but came to no conclusion. The clear vision didn't come back, only left me unsettled. All I could make of it was that there was more to this question, and there were more significant consequences, than I had once thought, and somehow it would make a great difference to the future of wildlife management. But the effects, the answers, eluded me.

Most of the same volunteers showed up for the second day of the rodeo, with the exception of two ranchers, the BLM biologists, one Fish and Game official, and Donald DeLacy and Janelle. I had expected attrition, and the schedule wouldn't be adversely affected. In general, the volunteers stayed in their same pairs and seemed to have developed at least a minimal form of communication between each other. And, most valuable to me, the data sheets continued to pile up, rich with information, on the high shelf in Glenn's office.

I handed out more bird bands, more data sheets, and maps marked with new routes, and watched again the same strange procession of vehicles, all with contrasting insignias, leaving the Fish and Game lot. Ben and Peter hung around looking at the maps, and for a moment I thought the three of us might go together, until Austin intervened. "Let's go, McPherson," he said, slapping his big hand on Ben's tall shoulder. "For a cow man you're not a bad climber. Today I'm going to convince you to get rid of all those damned cattle and do something better with your life."

Ben smiled at me, whispering, "See you later." For some reason I found myself blushing—the old, inane habit, over which I had no control—and looked to see Peter staring at me quizzically.

"Well," I said, embarrassed, "so it leaves us again?"

"Where to today?" he asked, his mouth turning up in a quirky smile, and I noticed, not for the first time, that Peter's eyelashes were as long as a girl's, which was unusual yet also attractive on his masculine face. He was not handsome, the features didn't really all go together, yet there was something appealing and fun and youthful about his looks that made me glad for the chance to go banding together.

Glancing over the board, I was surprised to find Findley Buttes left; of course, the area was expansive and ought to have been separated into two parts to make a feasible outing. Looking over my shoulder, Peter etched the map with his long finger.

"Seems to me we could cover it better on horseback. All those canyons and the back side along Little Sheep Creek could be scanned on the rim for nests. Would you be up for it if I could rally up the horse trailer?"

"But what about horses?"

"The department has them; the guys often use them in the back-country, especially in Hell's Canyon."

"Sure," I said enthusiastically. "I'd love to go riding."

"All right then. Let me see what I can do."

In little over an hour, Peter and I were rattling down Zumwalt

Road pulling a horse trailer with two department horses, a bay gelding named Coco, and a chestnut mare named Buttons. Buttons had not wanted to get in the trailer. She had tried to nip and had reared at the door. Peter had to convince me she was gentle and an experienced trail horse who was familiar with the country. Reaching the trailhead on the east side of the buttes, within a crow's flight of the site of the truck fiasco, we parked the trailer and Peter led the horses off the ramp. Working together, we saddled and bridled them. Coco was easy, but Buttons wasn't keen on the cinch; she laid back her ears and whirled around to bite me. Peter caught her head just in time.

"Cool it, Buttons!" he yelled. I knew instantly that Buttons and I wouldn't be best friends. The tall mare also had the habit, Peter told me too late, of bloating out her stomach when the cinch was tightened, then sucking it in again, so when I swung up into the saddle it slipped down her side, with me in it.

Peter laughed so hard there were tears in his eyes. I was humiliated.

"Ever ridden before?" he teased, and came over to give me a hand. He kneed Buttons in the belly and tightened her cinch. "Now try it, and use this on the old girl if she misbehaves," he said, handing me a stick from the ground to wield as a crop.

For the first few minutes, Buttons held her ears back flat against her head, signaling her cantankerous mood this morning, but after a few quick slaps with the stick, she straightened up and relaxed and pricked up her ears with interest. Her gait was short and choppy, but she stepped out quickly, not at all like tired old rental horses so common in recreation areas. She seemed a rather intelligent horse, watchful and curious about the wildlife around her. Spread out before us, rimmed in the east by the toothy Seven Devils Mountains, were the grand vistas of the Imnaha River Canyon, Little Sheep Creek, and countless other minor drainages running into the Snake River Canyon. I liked the feel of the wind patting my face and the rhythmic sound of hoof beats as the horses tramped through the grass. We were alone. We were free. The wild beauty was staggering in its reach and breadth. I had longed for this: to feel the rolling gait of a horse, to soar like a hawk over the flat mesas.

Kicking Buttons once in the sides, I whispered, "Let's go," and, forgetting all about Peter and the task at hand, I let Buttons have her head to trot, to canter, at last to gallop, with speed to challenge the hawk's flight, and a magic carpet beneath her hooves. All the long months of plodding footsteps, of watching hawks, but flying with them only in my mind, were gone as the fleet quarter horse mare continued to pick up speed, delighted to take her freedom, to feel the lifting off from the earth, in wings of movement.

Peter was galloping Coco beside me, with a look of fury on his face. He was shouting, and I reined in a reluctant Buttons, who fought to be given her head again, tossing it side to side as if wanting to spit out the bridle of captivity. I understood.

"What the hell do you think you're doing?" bellowed Peter, pairing up beside me.

"What's wrong?" I said, unaware of having committed any heinous crime.

"These are trail horses, not thoroughbreds," he said, calming down slightly. "They're only used for pack trips and trail riding. Not racing."

"I'm sorry," I said. "I didn't mean to tire her out, or get her too hot. It's just something I've longed to do for a long time. I wasn't thinking."

"That's not it. These horses have lots of stamina. It's that they have to be perfectly steady, and sure footed, and never have the tendency to bolt if they're to be used in these canyons," he explained with a look down at the cavernous dropoffs before us. "One misstep on those canyon trails, and they're gone, and so is the rider. Horses and mules are lost every year; we're lucky more riders aren't killed."

"You mean they fall over these cliffs?"

"Some of the trails are only as wide as a big man's shoulders," he continued. "It's hairy business going in and out of these canyons. A person has to trust his horse completely. Our horses are well trained and experienced. And they never, ever run with a rider on their backs."

Buttons was prancing about with her newfound freedom, and I had to work to calm her down. I felt foolish and inexperienced, and we rode in silence, stopping now and then to chart our course on the maps and scope the cliff faces for hawks and falcons. Peter discovered a red-tail nest I hadn't found before; it held three active young. A mile down the canyon, recognizing again the pencil-thin white markings on the walls, I told Peter there was probably a falcon eyrie. Coming up on it, we left our horses to graze and proceeded on foot, to discover a family of prairie falcons. "My God, look at that flight," said Peter, watching the tiercel arc and spin over our heads. Its call was distinctive, a higher-pitched cry than that of a peregrine, but just as wild and evocative. For an instant I was thrown back to all my years in Colorado, when I had lived with and studied wild falcons. Hawks were glorious, but there could never be anything as wonderfully wild as a stooping falcon.

We stopped for a bite to eat after that, not as elaborate as the lunch I had with Ben, but the typical tunafish sandwiches, peaches, M&M candies for energy, and warm stale canteen water. We parked under the spreading arms of a small aspen grove, sharing our spot with a group of cows, who were also trying to avoid the afternoon heat. They brought little black flies and a stench of manure with them.

"I don't know about you, but I'm getting in from the sun, away from these stupid animals before they trample my lunch," Peter said. "They're not welcome to my sandwich."

"You don't like cows," I said, laughing, and moving out with him.

"No, I don't. Especially here, considering all the plant and animal diversity. Grazing is completely incompatible in areas where wildlife is considered of primary value. Livestock grazing denudes the range, causes it to become a desert—it's happened all over Oregon, all over the West."

The cows, I noticed, were nibbling the new shoots of aspen coming up, as well as mowing the grass under the trees to almost bare ground. "What about elk?" I asked. "Don't they do the same thing?"

"They never congregate in one place for long, so they can't do the damage. The problem is with the ranchers. They resist government regulations and think they can do whatever they want on their land. Graze when and where they so please, and pile on as many animals as can be squeezed in. They call it their right. They say it's nobody else's business. But that's going to change."

"Change? How's it going to change?"

"Well, there's growing agreement among all the agencies that when agricultural practices pollute rivers and destroy fish spawning grounds and squander topsoil, that's the public's business. There's got to be regulations, you'll agree to that, and if that means higher costs for the ranchers, then that's the price they'll have to pay. Otherwise, they shouldn't be allowed to manage it. Ranching operations occupy great expanses of public land. That land doesn't belong just to them. It belongs just as much to you and me."

"I agree with you there," I said. But, remembering Ben's statement about privately owned land, I added, "Do you think the two can ever be compatible? Ranching and wildlife diversity?"

"Nope."

"So, in your experienced opinion, you think the best, the highest, use for this land, this prairie, would be to turn it over to public ownership?"

"Unquestionably."

"But what about all the ranchers? Their families?"

"Get the ranchers *off*, that's the only way. Take away grazing permits, and let it return to what it was. Let it get back to its former productivity. Then you'd really see wildlife."

A flicker of doubt passed through my mind like the shadow of a cloud on a field. If we weren't seeing wildlife now, what were we seeing?

Peter stood up and wiped his mustache clean with a napkin. "If we want to cover the rest of this ground before nightfall, we'd best get going. I'll tighten the horses' cinches up if you pack up the gear. Or, I can leave Buttons for you."

Buttons stopped grazing and looked up. Seeing that her lunch-time was to be shortly curtailed as Peter headed to her side, she flattened her ears against her head in the old style and lifted up her hind leg as if preparing to kick. "I can see you and Buttons are pals," I said, laughing. "*I'll* collect the lunch."

We rode for several more hours, until the shadows grew long and the lowering sun began to flood the earth with an orange glow. One of the nests I had discovered three weeks earlier was empty— the young had already fledged—but the three ferruginous young were still close by, and protected by their parents, so I knew the nest had been successful. We banded four red-tails and two later-nesting Swainson's hawks, who were just large enough to keep the bands on.

Returning to the horse trailer just before sunset, I tried to help Peter with the tired horse by opening the loading door, but its weight, as it fell toward me, was too much and it crashed down, making a terrible racket and nearly breaking the pulley. Peter grimaced.

We arrived back in Enterprise at quarter to eleven, and I was home by midnight, hungry and sore.

The next day, the last of the buteo rodeo, began early—too early—and even fewer people showed up. Now we had lost Sparkey (whom I didn't consider a great loss); Phil, who unfortunately had stepped on his glasses while collecting hawk pellets; and the two SCS guys. The ranching contingent had dwindled down just to Ben.

There weren't enough people to cover the last of the hikes, but that was all right; I could do them myself. And the information everyone had gathered in only two days' time was invaluable. As I distributed maps, bands, plastic bags, and sheets one last time, I reiterated again for everyone to please come to a celebratory barbecue tonight at seven o'clock.

Austin swung over on his way out to whisper ominously in my ear, "Mirror, mirror on the wall, *she's* the one who'll poison us all!"

"I didn't know the potato salad was bad!" I shouted, and the few people remaining turned around to stare. "A little joke between us," I said, and went back to handing out equipment.

I found myself with Peter for the third time, and began to wonder if it were coincidence or if he felt obligated to stay with the same partner, or perhaps he enjoyed our working together. But he didn't bring up the horses again.

It didn't matter; most of today's excursions were along roads. I thought that after two days of strenuous hiking, the volunteers might appreciate a day off their feet, and there were plenty of nests, most red-tails, parked in the scattered little aspen and pine groves along the roadsides.

Peter and I drove Crow Creek Road and found a wealth of five nests, most of them low, within ten feet of the ground. We took turns climbing them. We discovered that three were not active anymore, and the birds had disappeared. Only a partially eaten egg remained in one. Another nest lay on the ground; the tree in which it had been built had blown over. The third had slumped out of the tree, as if it had been built by a shabby contractor.

The other two hawk nests had survived to produce six nestlings quite nicely, and with the last markings on the data sheets, I became anxious to tally all the figures over the last three days. Peter and I quit a bit early, so I could be at the Fish and Game when everyone began rolling in with data sheets covered with information.

Watching them arrive one by one, I suddenly felt strongly

indebted to these people. A simple barbecue in their honor did not seem at all sufficient, for all of their time, all of their willingness to waive differences and for a while come together to work for a common goal—a goal in which they may or may not see much benefit.

With people congregating in Glenn's office, sharing their adventures and trials with one another, putting back bands and hanging up spurs, I suddenly saw the rodeo for what it really was: it wasn't just a rodeo of hawks; it was a rodeo of people—people who had had a good time, people with different backgrounds and values but still coming together, being lassoed, perhaps against their will at first, to communicate, to walk together on a wild prairie, and to round up some crazy birds.

Seeing all the people, so different in many ways and yet the same, for an instant I considered their similarities to the hawks, who also were distinct species, yet alike. Perhaps we all were too quick to criticize. Maybe we needed to look where something was coming from, before we disparaged too much.

The culmination came later that night at the barbecue, when the people, many bringing their families, came together for one last time, to share in camaraderie. Somehow I knew it would be not only the first but the last buteo rodeo of Wallowa County. But the sense of satisfaction was real, shining on every face—faces of children and adults munching on hamburgers and potato chips, sipping beer and 7-Up and Cokes. I related to everyone what we had accomplished with all their obliging help. In a three-day period, we had successfully located fifty-six nests of red-tailed hawks, thirty-two nests of ferruginous hawks, and sixteen nests of Swainson's hawks. In addition, the vast majority of the nests were producing at least two or more healthy young, most of which were now banded.

These were astonishing figures, more, I think, than anyone realized. And their significance went far beyond the remoteness of Wallowa County, for they revealed a secret:

In a little-known native grassland of northeastern Oregon colloquially known as the Zumwalt Prairie, buteo hawks coexisted in one of the highest, if not *the* highest, nesting concentrations in North America.

Chapter Twenty-Two

THE BUTEO RODEO'S verification of the phenomenal density of buteo hawks on the Zumwalt only served to highlight more questions and make their answers all the more portentous. What were the mechanisms driving the structure of the hawk community? What was going on behind the scenes to produce their distribution, density, and productivity? Now that the bulk of the banding was done, except for the later-nesting Swainson's and several areas not covered by the roundup, I intended to find out.

Even in my elation at the success of the rodeo, one thing stuck in my mind. What we had found—the location of hawks' nests and their seasonal productivity—was simply a measurement of one performance, for one year. A single snapshot. It was a baseline, yes, but it had little explanatory value in itself; it did little to help illuminate how the hawks functioned in the ecosystem. What I needed now was to uncover the nature of the system within which the hawks were embedded—what my professor Dr. Warren called the "coextensive environment."

It was a stepping-stone procession, how these things worked together, what made them tick. The coextensive environment of the buteos revolved around what they ate and where they chose to nest. In other words, it was a trip down the hawk staircase. At the top level of the staircase were the hawks themselves. Down one level were the creatures that the hawks ate, such as ground squirrels and pocket gophers. Since these animals, too, had specific habitat requirements, one must progress down still another level of the staircase to discern: What do these animals eat? How does livestock grazing affect their habitat?

To figure out the key elements of the hawk's nesting habitat required heading down the hawk staircase in another direction. From the top level, step down one level: here are the hawk nests. But trees and shrubs and outcroppings also were a product of their environment. Therefore, one must go down to the next step to discern: What does it take to grow aspen, Douglas fir, and ponderosa pine in the prairie?

A variable factor in the equation was, of course, people— people such as ranchers and land managers who ran up and down the stairs all the time and affected the coextensive environment by doing such things as putting out cows to graze the shrubs and grasses and altering the habitat, for better or worse, of the ground squirrels and sprouting trees.

Hiking alone on the gently sloping hills leading up to the mouth of Baker Canyon, I pondered these things as I tried to identify the Zumwalt's different plant communities that fit together in irregular shapes and sizes like a thousand-piece puzzle. I needed to understand all these "microhabitats," as well as map them accurately, on the one inch to hundred scale aerial photographs.

A precise, yet holistic, method to classify all the rangeland vegetation was needed, and the Soil Conservation Service had devised a superb system. Their practical classification scheme took into account much more than plants. It also looked at an area's topography—where it occurred in the landscape, the degree and direction of slope, and its range in elevation; its microclimate—annual precipitation, beginning and ending dates of its growing season for native plants, and exposure to wind; as well as its soil characteristics. All of these things together defined what the SCS labeled an "ecological range site."

Each range site differed from all others in its ability to grow and support a characteristic assemblage of plants. That was the key. And the beauty of these ecological subdivisions was that they provided a common language for a grassland's study, evaluation, and management. By carefully studying aerial photographs of the Zumwalt through a stereoscope, and also by going over the soil maps and doing some field research with the help of Don Baldwin, I determined that the Zumwalt Prairie supported five distinct ecological ranges. Unfortunately for ease in mapping, the five sites did not occur in big, lumped pieces. Instead they were distributed throughout the Zumwalt in a random mosaic pattern covering the entire 200-square-mile radius.

The most plentiful range site in the Zumwalt Prairie was the Rolling Hills Range Site. This prairie habitat sported a lush growth of bunchgrasses, primarily Idaho fescue, and, very rarely, would support a tree or two. It occurred along the wide, flat mesas and gently rolling ridge tops of the prairie. Next in abundance was the strange-looking Biscuit Scabland Range Site, a landform phenomenon that had circular areas of bunchgrasses surrounded by shallow, stony, barren soil. From a distance, biscuit scabland habitat resembled little oatmeal cookies on a giant cookie sheet. No one had figured out the reason for the ecological oddity, although some suspected frost heaving played a part in it.

The South Exposure Range Site was also made up predominantly of grass, mostly native bluebunch wheatgrass, and, true to its namesake, generally appeared along drainages and moderately steep areas that faced south and southeast and west. Like the scabland habitat, its soils were shallow and couldn't support trees. But rocky outcroppings ranging from three to thirty feet tall were prominent in this range site.

The North Exposure Range Site didn't make up much of the Zumwalt, but where it did occur the land was lush and soils were deep. Its situation was the opposite of the south exposure sites, for it existed along moderately steep areas and drainages that faced north and northwest. Longer-lasting snowdrifts in these shadier areas made for rich soils with good water-holding capacity. Like most of the Zumwalt, it was primarily a grassland community, but, unlike the other sites, it was vulnerable to invasion by some forest species—ponderosa pine, Douglas fir, and, more rarely, aspen.

The fifth and last range site of the Zumwalt Prairie was found bordering the intermittent prairie streams. Dry Mountain Meadow Range Site had riparian characteristics, and, if not overgrazed, abounded with sod grasses growing like carpets in its deep loamy soils. Native hawthorn trees, willows, and cottonwoods occasionally occurred in these sites, which often stayed green far into the summer.

Mapping the range sites and their multitudinous distributions throughout the prairie on the USGS aerial photographs required hours of labor; but if my suspicions were right, the key to the unusual abundance of the Zumwalt buteos was hidden inside the quantity and quality of the five ecological sites. I guessed that the hawks were not placing their nests at random but, instead, were segregating themselves out along the different range sites, for reasons, at this point, I wasn't quite sure of.

My thoughts suddenly shifted from the immensity of the situation to anticipation at seeing again the brave and beautiful ferruginous hawks of Baker Canyon that had saved their brood from the menacing coyote. I had thought of them often over the last weeks. Reviewing it again in my mind, the episode still seemed more fantasy than fact, that two eagle-sized birds, whose flight at times seemed less finessed than lumbered, could skillfully outmatch a coyote while risking their lives for their three defenseless young. I had purposely excluded this area from the rodeo because I wanted to come back alone to admire again the proud, wild birds and band their nestlings. I estimated that the babies must be five weeks old, and near fledging.

Of all the birds I had painstakingly located and watched this summer, this was probably my favorite family. In some intrinsic sense, these birds epitomized the word *buteo*. Buteo: an open-country, wild hawk . . . highly efficient at soaring . . . a bird that feeds on a wide variety of prey, mostly deleterious rodents . . . a bird that mates for life and is devoted to its young.

Buteos offer much to the ecosystem, and are helpful to humans, but they are more than that, too. When they fly, they seem in a curious way to embody freedom and grace, and now, I realized too, an instinctive form of heroism.

The trip down the canyon was not as pleasurable as the last had been. The continual presence of cows, who had grazed down, almost to bare ground in places, the luxuriant bunchgrasses, marred it. The stream at the bottom of Baker Canyon was now a mere trickle, and, not being fenced, was trampled and stamped with the marks of multitudinous hooves.

This time I stayed along the bottom of Baker Canyon, where I could observe the rimrock from below. I was a bit surprised to find that the first pair of ferruginous hawks, which had nested nearer the mouth of the canyon, had disappeared completely; I thought it not very significant, however, remembering that they had lost their first clutch of eggs to coyotes. Many times a bird of prey will not renest if its first set of eggs is destroyed. Yet, something else in the canyon that hadn't been there before made me slightly apprehensive. The deep, scoring marks of oversized truck tires twisted along the edge of the meandering stream. The sign left over from the mud treads appeared fairly fresh and covered the cloven footprints.

Probably just some rancher out to check on his cows, I decided. However, the trail left by the truck was not a straight shot up the draw; the tracks wound all over the bottom of Baker Canyon and sometimes disappeared into the creek to reappear on the other side.

I picked up my pace, startling the cows along the way as if I were a specter they hadn't seen until I was right on them. Such unthinking animals, I thought crossly. My annoyance at the rancher who didn't fence off his stream, and allowed the destruction of such a lovely riparian area, continued to grow.

A half mile farther up the canyon I at last spotted the huge ferruginous nest that belonged to the courageous pair; I hadn't realized before how prominent it appeared. It was an architectural phenomenon of sticks, sitting like a beacon on the red canyon rim. And it looked easy to reach from below. A gentle grade wound up to it; I had overlooked that, too.

Sitting down on the muddy riverbank, careful not to position myself on a cow pie, I took out my data notebook. As I jotted down some information, I suddenly realized I wasn't hearing the telltale warning cry of any ferruginous hawks. Surely they had seen me. I was less than a quarter mile away from their nest.

I stood up promptly. There was no sign of movement from any living thing, except cows. I scanned the canyon from rim to stream through my binoculars. Something wasn't right.

Calming myself with the thought that at this stage of the nesting cycle, both parent birds were probably out hunting for food for their youngsters, who were undoubtedly ravenous and also required less round-the-clock protection now that they were fully grown and near fledging, I proceeded on. Maybe I had been mistaken on the nestlings' ages; perhaps they had already fledged from the nest. But even so, they should still be in the vicinity. The birds would remain a family unit for weeks longer, until fall migration.

The cows seemed to sense the new determination in my stride and, with frightened eyes, briskly bolted out of my way. Without knowing it, I was following the off-road vehicle's scarring imprints in the dirt. Here was a perfect example of how the misuse of ORVs could chew the landscape with an appetite as voracious as any herd of cows.

With my heart rising in my throat, I noticed that the tire tracks swung around, in an enlarging set of concentric circles, at the base of the canyon near the ferruginous hawk nest. They had stopped here. And from this point, no one could miss seeing the six-foot-high structure overlooking the canyon.

The weak scream of a bird surprised me from behind, and turning around, I searched the sky to see, with relief, a female ferruginous hawk beating the air with her wings in a rapid descent to the canyon's edge. The tone of the bird was atypical, however: not loud and harsh, but thin, stretched out. The hawk was in the first stages of molt and looked ragged, but that was normal for this time of year.

But she was not joined by her mate. Scrutinizing through binoculars from below, I couldn't see any fuzzy little heads topping the nest this time. But the birds could be hunkered down, of course, alerted by their mother's warning.

I inspected the tire tracks again and grew uneasy. These were not the imprints of a rancher out on the job; these were the markings of a joyride. I found myself strongly hoping that the nestlings, especially that silly, fearless one who nearly had gotten himself killed by challenging the coyote, had fledged before this. If so, they would be safe.

The female ferruginous took off and accelerated down the canyon. I scrambled up the side of canyon to the nest, passing evidence here and there of vibramed-soled shoes—not my own hiking boots. How old the prints were was impossible to know.

There was a bushel of scraps of ground squirrel castings littered below the nest. This nest obviously had been used for many, many generations. I carefully laid my backpack down so it wouldn't teeter and roll off the side, and freed my arms for the final ascent. The hawk wailed somewhere in the distance, which was encouraging. Getting closer, I could see that the nest was firmly held together by plant roots and cow pies.

But no expected peeps or squawks rose from the eyrie, which now was only a few yards above me. Catching my breath, I gazed around to see if I could spot any newly fledged birds rocking unsteadily anywhere along the canyon walls. They should be close by; they weren't old enough to be skilled fliers yet. But there was no sign of any of them.

A shadow fell across the nest—the shadow of a hawk. The ferruginous was directly over my head now, between me and the sun, and pealing out the same, bizarre whine, for some reason giving me goose flesh. I climbed more hastily.

A cry escaped my lips at the sight before me when I topped the nest. The three nestling ferruginous hawks—beautiful and fully feathered and on the verge of flying—had all been shot. They lay in a pool of broken wings and blood, all mounded together, as if they had fallen into each other. Their beaks were open, gaping; their eyes were rolled back.

I turned away, unable to look anymore. The distraught mother still circled in spiraling oscillations above the nest. But there was nothing in it for her to protect, except the dead, decaying bodies of her babies.

The scene filled me with outrage. Not *this* nest—the words kept repeating themselves in my mind—not *these* birds.

In my mind I saw again the little family that had risen to meet extraordinary circumstances. I saw the wily coyote at the bottom of the canyon and the triumphant flight of the victorious parents who had rescued their young from death. I saw their special vigor and spirit, now shattered by a senseless act.

Tears stung my eyes as I finished my work. I collected the castings, took the nest measurements, and compiled the required range data. But my heart wasn't in it. I tried to remind myself that there were other nests; the loss of one would not harm the prolific success of the prairie. Yet, on a deeper level, my mental picture of the Zumwalt was now tarnished. The dark side of ranching had been etched in my brain, and the sorrowful call of a ferruginous hawk would always stain the wind of Baker Canyon.

Chapter Twenty-Three

HARDLY PAUSING FOR BREATH, Mrs. DeLacy's agitated voice continued with nonstop details, explaining her plan to be away at school for another week; I was to be in charge of the house.

"My extra checkbook's in the top drawer of my desk in the den; the right-hand top drawer. Pay the bills as they come in, will you? Remind Donald under no circumstances is he to go on that trip with Janelle. It was a bad idea at the beginning and it's still a bad idea. He's to stay with his Aunt Gladys for a week in Medford, and she'll be by to pick him up sometime later today. Remember, don't let him fool you that he hasn't heard about this; he knows all about it. Donald needs time away from *that girl*. She's always fluttering, like some infectious mosquito, and with me here and them there, there's going to be mischief."

"Would you like to talk to Donald? I think he's still sleeping upstairs."

"No. We spoke yesterday. And he's not very happy with me. He doesn't get along well with Gladys. And he's determined to go on that raft trip. Hah! Over my dead body."

After hanging up the receiver, I stared at it for a while, my mind still fixed on yesterday. Donald was stomping around upstairs. Should I take time now to pay the stack of bills? Or head to the Forest Service to talk with Austin on my way out to the prairie? Donald had penned a message that Austin wanted me to meet at his office at half past nine, for some reason. I stood up and walked over to Mrs. DeLacy's desk to flip through the mail. Seeing all the utility bills, I decided to take care of them later.

After leaving a note for Donald, wishing him a pleasant week at his aunt's (although I strongly doubted it could compare to a raft trip down the Grande Ronde), I drove to the Forest Service building via the service station. The owner, Fred, knew me well by now, and he always teased with a slap to the hood: "This tank still runnin'?" "Hasn't conked out yet," I'd reply, although with the mileage edging near one hundred thousand, I wasn't sure how long it would last.

Austin's head was bent low over a stack of papers. He didn't bother to look up when I entered. "Sit down," he said, with as much interest as if I had been a chair. I noticed, for the first time, the sprinkling of white hairs that seemed to have recently sprouted along his hairline and down his sideburns, and wondered if his job was stressful.

"God, I hate poisons," he said, finally looking up to acknowledge me. He rubbed the bridge of his nose. "Pesticides. Herbicides. The Forest Service is like a little kid in a toy store when they get to bring out their little planes and spray the hell out of the landscape."

Pulling up a chair on rollers, I sat down next to Austin's desk. "Just look at this crap," he said, flinging an intra-agency memo in my face. Picking it up, I quickly perused a few paragraphs explaining a plan to spray the insecticide malathion over a 375,000-acre radius in Wallowa County.

"It's going to affect you, you know," warned Austin.

I laid the paper back on the messy desk. "What do you mean?"

"The Zumwalt. It's the grassland they're spraying. Keep yourself out of there the week or two those bozo dusters are applying it. They fling that stuff around without caution, like it's confetti. It probably wouldn't hurt you, but I don't trust that goddamn stuff."

"When are they—why are they doing this?"

"To control the grasshoppers, don't you know?" Austin said cynically.

"I haven't seen many grasshoppers."

"Oh, someone has determined this is going to be a bad grass-hopper year, and the ranchers have bellyached and whined and demanded the government to do something. Of course, the ranchers are 'independent,' quote unquote, and don't need government, but then when anything like this comes along they run along home with their tails between their legs, whimpering for us to save them."

Sometimes I didn't enjoy Austin's sarcasm, and it showed.

"Oh, I see, you're getting sympathetic with them," said Austin, leaning back and clasping his brown hands behind his wide neck. "You've spending too much time with that McPherson fellow, who is always mooning around your house. Don't think I haven't noticed. But don't let those cowboy blue eyes blind you from seeing what's really going on."

Leaning forward, I put my hands on the edge of his desk. "Austin, darn you, I'm not blind, and I don't like pesticides any better than you. But have you ever thought that maybe the ranchers are doing some things that might be, well, helping things out?"

"Yeah," he smiled, coolly, his brown eyes narrowed into slits. "Like what?"

I fought to think of something, but Austin interrupted. "Cool down, bird girl, cool down; this isn't the time to talk about the pros and cons of ranching. Your boyfriend and you can discuss it later over a glass of orange juice. But I wanted you to know about the spraying. They're planning it a month from now, and it's sure to have some effect on your birds."

"Ben is not my boyfriend," I exclaimed, but my anger quickly dissipated to a feeling of deflation as I considered the effects of the spraying. Swainson's hawks are known to subsist, at certain times of year, almost exclusively on grasshoppers and other insects, making them highly beneficial to farmers. Although they also prey on snakes and sometimes hares, and appear to be quite adaptable to changes in prey species diversity by virtue of being generalized hunters, they favor crickets and grasshoppers and hobble about in the grass, like half-grown turkeys, while trying to catch them. Parent birds teach their offspring to hunt the hopping insects with their feet. They constantly thrust their feet forward while they fly, and are expert at catching flying grasshoppers.

The malathion spraying, effectively killing off all the grasshoppers of the prairie, just at the time that the Swainson's families would be fledging their young, could have deleterious consequences that might not show up for several years.

"Between the use of malathion, 2-4D, and 2-4-5T, and the rest of that godawful stuff, your pretty Zumwalt Prairie and its contiguous cultivated lands around is really a toxic waste dump," offered Austin.

"I haven't noticed anyone spraying yet, except, I guess in the farmland nearer town."

"Well, it's legal. Perfectly legal. And ranchers and farmers do it openly, and still complain that they're overly restricted. They use 1080 and strychnine for rodent control as liberally as if they were irrigation water. God keep me from farmers."

"Where does that leave the hawks?" I wondered.

"We've documented some effects. Over the last few years I've personally handled three red-tailed hawks who were secondarily poisoned from 1080. Chuck Henny has the data. But most of these ranchers don't give a damn."

I left Austin's office feeling concerned about just how widespread and in what quantities herbicides and pesticides were used in the county. I changed my mind about spending the day in the field. Instead I opted to concentrate on learning what I could about the dates the Forest Service would be conducting its far-reaching spraying, and also about the agent malathion itself. The pesticide and herbicide specialist for the Forest Service was not in the Enterprise office but worked out of the town of Wallowa, and I took the extra half hour to drive there, hoping to catch him.

He was there, but the balding, lean man at first responded to my questions with reticence. I asked if he had any publications about malathion I could read. He glanced over his wire spectacles and eyed me suspiciously.

"You with the paper?"

"Oh no; I'm a biologist, working in the area. I'd just like to know more."

He slackened his sloping, thin shoulders. "All right. You'll find what you want in the second file drawer over there. You can help yourself. Just put everything back the way you found it."

For two and a half hours, I reviewed everything in the drawer, but most of it was innocuous. Malathion, I learned, was often referred to as the "safest" of the organic phosphates. It was one of the most widely accepted insecticides throughout the world, regarded as less toxic than most other widely used pesticides, and, purportedly, "relatively" safe in conjunction with humans and animals. When used as an insecticide, it was mixed with fuel oil. Up to 1956, there had been no confirmed reports of serious fish kills associated with its use, although there were several adverse reports of small-sized fish kills in shallow waters. (I wondered what happened *after* 1956.)

Malathion broke down rapidly in the soil and did not appear to move into underground water supplies. The government had judged it as posing "no risk of permanent effect on the natural environment."

Although there was no "risk," the specialist enjoined me, as had Austin, not to venture into the area for about a week after the spraying was completed. This was the last thing I wanted to hear, considering all the work that remained to be done. Running through the tasks in my mind, especially considering the time restriction now facing me, I felt as if I were drowning in a sea of impossible work.

I still needed to band all the Swainson's hawk nestlings. I still had to set up permanent photo plots of the range sites and nesting sites. I had to collect more castings, and I still hadn't begun the prey species research. And then there was analysis of the range condition.

The work had been progressing so well until now! Yet in little over two more months, most of the hawks would have left the prairie for their winter migration. The thousands of ground squirrels would have disappeared into their burrows to hibernate until spring.

Well, I couldn't do much about it. Sitting down at a conference table in the office, I arranged the set of maps I always carried with me, and went over again the remaining areas that still needed covering. Seeing them all spread out, I knew Austin had been right. I had bitten off more than I could chew. Already I could hear Sparkey's detestable cackle that meant "I told ya so." I could feel the pressure beginning to build at my temples. Reflecting on Sparkey always gave me a headache. And tonight, I thought to myself with an inward groan, I would be having dinner with him!

Peter, whom I had seen several times since the rodeo, for dinner and for hikes in the mountains, had been invited to the home of Sparkey and his wife, June, for dinner; thinking I might enjoy the evening, he had asked if I might come along.

Peter had laughed at my resistance when he told me. "You'll like June," he said, with a mischievous twinkle in his gray eyes. "She's a nice lady. She's a nurse." (*She must also be a saint*, I thought to myself, *to be married to him*.)

On my way out, the raspy call of an orange-crowned warbler cheered me somewhat; it was an amazing sound, like that of someone running a finger across a long comb. There were two birds calling back and forth in the grove of cottonwoods bordering a little stream behind the Forest Service. I found the spot of greenery refreshing after having been riveted for hours on the unknown hazards of chemical sprays.

It struck me again just how much I took the summer sounds of passerine birds for granted. The melodies of flycatchers and warblers, the kinglets and thrushes—they were the background noise of summer, of the outdoors. Without them the world would be unbearably still. How all the chemicals used—not only in this country but even more in developing countries where many native species overwintered—are affecting their numbers is unknown. But the growing supposition is that many indigenous songsters are declining, some rapidly, as a result of pesticide use. One has only to consider the peregrine falcon, nearly exterminated by the widespread use of the pesticide DDT before it was banned, to realize the potential disastrous effects of misuse, or overuse, of some chemicals.

I was not in a great mood when Peter picked me up in his Scout for dinner. Peter, too, had only today learned of the massive malathion treatment, but instead of blaming the ranchers only, he put the onus on the U.S. Forest Service. The subject arose again before dinner, and Sparkey agreed with Peter.

"The United States Forest Service and the BLM are both in bed with ranchers," proclaimed Sparkey, leaning back in a fuzzy gold recliner in their modest living room, decorated with wall mounts of deer and elk heads, and photographs of bighorn sheep. June had not yet arrived home from work, and Sparkey and Peter helped themselves to a beer, which Sparkey was flinging around in his hand to accentuate his words.

"The mission of both those government agencies should be to concern themselves with the health of the land," Sparkey continued, and for once I found myself agreeing with him. "The economic return to the ranchers shouldn't enter into the equation. Yet the Forest Service and BLM screw around and put ranching interests ahead of everything."

Peter, I noticed, was concurring with Sparkey, although not with the same vehemence. While Sparkey was ranting and waving his beer, a woman laden down with two sacks of groceries arrived at the screen door and said, in a small, entreating voice, "Can someone help me, please?"

Peter jumped up from his chair. He opened the door and lifted the groceries from her arms. A welcoming smile crossed the face of the tired-looking, middle-aged woman, with curly brunette hair framing her small, almost delicate face. "Thank you, Peter. I'm sorry I'm late but I had to stop at the store."

"June, Marcy; Marcy, June," Sparkey called, by way of an introduction, then continued on about the atrocities committed by every government agency except the one he worked for. Smiling, I accompanied June into the kitchen, wondering if I could help her with dinner, since no one else was lifting a hand.

"I'd really love some help," she said genuinely. "It's been a long day."

"Peter tells me you're a nurse."

"On busy days like this one I think I'd prefer doing almost anything else, but generally it's a good job, and pays fair." With the back of her thin, birdlike hand, she wiped the hair from her eyes and smiled warmly. Her eyes were deep brown, almost black, and quite pretty, shining like little agates. But all around them were lines of exhaustion. I wondered who worked harder, she or Sparkey. The answer was simple to guess.

She apologized again. "You must be hungry."

"June!" yelled Sparkey from the recliner. "Get me a beer!"

I found the barking command revolting, as if June were nothing better than a dog. Surely she would yell back, "Get it yourself!" but she didn't. Instead she quietly stopped what she was doing and went to the refrigerator to fetch a Henry's.

Without a word, she walked into the living room and handed the beer to Sparkey, then returned to the kitchen to work. Not once did Sparkey look at her, nor did he stop to say thank you. Peter glanced at me, reading my face. I was furious.

"Like I was saying," Sparkey droned, "the bill would give ranchers ten years to find a new lifestyle. That's *ten years*. If Congress would just get their act together, we'd be a whole lot better off."

"What bill?" I interjected, still seething inside. What in the world was that man talking about now? Sparkey looked up at me as if I had no right to join the male conversation, but Peter interceded.

"It's called, I believe, the High Desert Protection Act, isn't that right, Sparkey? Its purpose is to ban grazing from all wilderness areas. If I have my numbers right, there's about fifteen or so million acres of public lands designated wilderness that are being grazed by livestock. The bill proposes to take cows off six million of those acres in, like Sparkey says, ten years' time."

"Would that seriously impact the ranchers?" I asked.

"Damned right," Sparkey replied. "They'd have to get a real job, like the rest of us."

"Sparkey," June called from the kitchen, "could you please get the barbecue going?"

Sparkey took another swig of beer. "Like I was saying, Peter, there's no way in hell the conservation community should join in with the farmers. Getting citizens involved with ranchers and farmers will make them sympathetic and the whole resource will go straight to hell."

"Sparkey—"

"Your wife's calling you," I said directly. He ignored me.

"We've got to keep our priorities straight. We, as an agency, should be committed to the acquisition of land with fish and wildlife values."

"Could you please help me, Sparkey?" the voice from the kitchen pleaded pathetically.

Peter once again jumped up. "Come on. The girls want us to get the charcoal going."

I found myself annoyed with Peter, too, although all this really wasn't his fault. But Sparkey was detestable. As Peter walked by, he gave my shoulder a squeeze. I turned back into the kitchen.

"Do you always do all the cooking?" I asked June, curious about how this strange home situation worked. "I mean, after a hard day at work?"

"We don't have any children, so that makes my job easier," she responded, her narrow shoulders bent as she chopped vegetables over the cutting board. I couldn't tell whether childlessness made her sad. "Sparkey's an okay guy, and luckily, for the most part, I like my work. You know, men will be men," she said, turning around to reach for a salad bowl.

Although I had never considered myself a feminist, something about June's resignation and subservience to a man like Sparkey so appalled me that I suddenly felt like the fiercest woman's-libber alive. Yet this was not just an issue of men versus women. It had to do more with human dignity—treating one another with respect. That I was in the kitchen with June while the men were chatting by the barbecue didn't bother me. In fact, I much preferred being with June to being with that awful man. But his treatment of her was upsetting, as if she were worthless. I thought again of Austin's words about all the "good ol' boys" in the agency. I didn't have a problem with ranchers, per se, I decided; I had a problem with "good ol' boys."

"So, you're the girl studying hawks Sparkey has told me about," she said, to be friendly, as she finished putting away all the groceries and continued to whip together a salad. "How are you liking it here?"

I could only imagine what Sparkey had told her. "Oh, I enjoy the work, but I've got a long way to go before the summer's over."

"Sparkey tells me you're working all alone. Do you ever get nervous about, you know, being all by yourself way out there? Or does Peter go with you a lot?"

It amazed me how quickly word had spread about Peter asking me out occasionally. "He's gone a few times, but mostly I'm by myself. I don't mind it."

"*June*! Another beer!" Sparkey yelled from outside. June obediently went to the refrigerator.

"Here, let me take it to him," I said, smiling.

"Oh, would you? Thanks. I'll finish chopping the broccoli."

Picking up the cold beer, I walked toward the patio, but put the can behind my back. "How's it coming?" I asked Peter. "Smells good."

"Great," said Peter. "Why don't you join us?"

"Where's the beer, June!" yelled Sparkey.

I glared at him. "Why don't you go and get it yourself?"

He scowled back. "'Cause she's getting it for me."

Peter, looking uneasy, stepped in. "Why don't I go see if—"

"No, here it is," I said, thrusting the beer at Sparkey.

Sparkey smiled like the Cheshire cat. "There's a good girl," he crooned, and before I could respond, Peter had whisked me back toward the kitchen.

"Cool down," he whispered. "Just ignore him."

"How can I?" I exclaimed. "I can't get over the way he treats his wife."

"Relax. He's from the old school. She probably enjoys it. We're ready to grill the steaks. Just bite your tongue for a little longer."

"Enjoys it!" I stammered, but seeing June walking from the kitchen carrying napkins, knives, forks, and glasses, I swallowed my words and left Peter to help her. I felt my anger at Sparkey transferring to Peter—that Peter could put up with this, stand aside, and let it go on without interjecting a word.

Dinner was uncomfortable, with June repeatedly up and down to serve food, remove plates, refill drinks, pick up after everyone, but rarely entering into the conversation except when Peter or I directed a question specifically to her. Sparkey continued firing off orders and opinions, some of which had some merit, I had to admit, although he seemed always to take things to their extreme. He despised ranchers and their livestock, was 100 percent in favor of elk and other wildlife usage of the grassland, and had no qualms about sharing his uncompromising solutions.

"Take the ranchers off, goddamit!" he said, on his third or fourth beer; I had lost count. It was difficult to look at Sparkey as he talked, for the more vehement he grew, the more he harangued while openly masticating his steak. "That's the only way to solve our problems, Peter. Evict the goddamned cattle, and the cattle rancher, from public lands."

Peter agreed, up to a point, but I was still not completely convinced.

"I notice you haven't eliminated red meat from your diet, Sparkey," I threw out, but he ignored me.

"You've seen what they do out there, Peter. Look at those over-grazed areas on the Zumwalt. Even *she* has to have noticed 'em."

As usual, Sparkey refused to call me by name. Trying to have a meaningful, two-way conversation with this man was a waste of energy, I decided. His mind was entirely made up. When Peter tried to bring up my hawk study several times during the evening, Sparkey merely rolled his eyes and sighed. Over and over he alluded to his incredulity that the U.S. Fish and Wildlife Service actually hired a *woman* who couldn't climb her own *trees*.

This was unfair; there were plenty of trees I could and did climb, and Peter defended me, but after a while he gave up. June ate like a bird and did not enter into the conversation, probably because she was so weary, and it was strenuous for anyone to talk above Sparkey's voice.

"What about those ranchers on private lands, Sparkey?" asked Peter, referring, I supposed, to the Zumwalt Prairie.

"Lest ranchers continue to damage their own property, then that too should be bought up by a public agency."

"Whoa!" said Peter. "They'll never agree to that!"

"They won't have to. It'll be forced on them. And should be, if they're poor managers."

"I thought in some cases the range was in better condition than it was a hundred years ago," I said.

"Postage stamps," Sparkey replied coolly. "Mere postage stamp areas."

"I'll allow there needs to be better control over the grazing issue in some areas, but you have to admit there has been some improvement," I pressed.

"Hell, the land is so bad now it's easy to improve!"

"Isn't there another grazing bill pending, Sparkey?" asked

Peter. "By the way, June," he paused, glancing her way as she cleared his place, "the steak was just delicious."

"Thanks to the chef," said Sparkey, patting his own chest. "What bill you talking about?"

"Something proposed by the BLM—like phasing out several million acres of their grazing lands, turning them into a network of wilderness areas, national parks, and wildlife refuges? Have you heard anything about it?"

"Yeah, there's something like that. June, dear, dessert better be strawberry shortcake or *you* know whose head will roll!" Sparkey hollered to the kitchen, with a wink at Peter. This man was utterly repulsive! I rose to help June in the kitchen.

June was in the midst of drenching the shortcake with Cool Whip. I helped her serve up the plates and sat down, anxious for the evening to be over. I couldn't bear to look at June, whose face appeared more fatigued as dinner wore on. I tried to pass some subliminal messages to Peter that it was time to go, but Sparkey was in his element and dominated Peter's attention. Eventually Peter got my hint, and made a plausible excuse to Sparkey and June about having to get up very early in the morning to do a game bird count. June surprised me by reaching out to hold one of my hands in hers as we were leaving. "I enjoyed meeting you," she said. "Please come again sometime."

"Thank you. Dinner was delicious," I said in all honesty, but knowing I might never step across their threshold again.

"I hear some of the gophers may have tested positive for plague this summer," Sparkey called out to me, on an encouraging note, as we turned to walk down the driveway. "Aren't you starting those counts soon?"

Driving me home in his Scout, Peter rolled down the window to let in the fresh evening air that was sweeping down from the mountains—and into my bruised soul. The sweetness felt like a balm. "You're awful quiet," said Peter.

"Just thinking."

"Aw, just forget about Sparkey. He's just a big bag of wind."

"I wasn't thinking about Sparkey, Peter. I was thinking about June."

"She sure packs a good meal. And that shortcake."

"But to put up with *him*—"

"Oh, I don't know. I think, really, they have a good marriage." In the dark, I turned my face to stare at Peter in wonder. "I don't believe it!" I cried.

"No, I really do. I think she's happy."

"But the way he treated her, ordered her."

"Marriage, Marcy, is like a basketball game," Peter said reflectively. "It's a game of percentages."

"You really believe that?"

"Sure. If you win a few more games than you lose, then that's a good marriage." Peter reached out to put his arm around my shoulder, but I drew closer to the window. What Sparkey and June shared was not my idea of marriage, not even close. Nor did I consider winning a few more games than you lost something I wished to aspire to.

"You know, you're awfully peculiar," Peter said coolly, withdrawing his arm.

We continued on a while in strained silence, but at last my curiosity got the better of me. "Just why do you think I'm peculiar? Because I wouldn't want to be married to someone like Sparkey? There's got to be more to marriage than that."

"You know what I think? I think what you want is someone who brings you flowers every day and lives to serve you. You want some poor guy to put you on a pedestal," Peter responded. "Well, you oughta know, I'm not that kind of guy."

"I didn't say that."

"Those types don't exist anymore, Marcy. There's no such things as knights in shining armor. For God's sake, get *real*."

I was relieved to see Mrs. DeLacy's house looming darkly just ahead. Peter pulled in quickly, swiveling the wheel and kicking up gravel, reminiscent of Austin.

"Thank you for the evening," I said hoarsely while jumping out, longing to flee this awful conversation.

"I think you live in some sort of fantasy world, some olden days nonsense," said Peter with surprising passion. "You're wrong, you know, about Sparkey. He's really a great guy. But maybe he's right; maybe he's right what he says about you."

I ran up the porch steps as Peter took off, and with a shaking hand I reached for the doorknob. Once inside, I quietly closed the door behind me and turned around to rest my weary head against its solid frame.

Tonight it seemed to me that I had no friends and was fully incapable of doing my job. And I had mistakenly put my hopes and dreams where they had no right to be.

My dreams didn't include keeping score in a relationship. Love should encompass so much more—shouldn't it?—and be built on trust, honesty, encouragement, respect. Yes, *respect*. Perhaps Peter was right; I *was* looking for that knight in shining armor.

Tonight I knew I'd never find him. In silent misery, with my eyes still squeezed closed, I fumbled to flick on the light. Opening my eyes, I found the entryway still dark. Obviously a blown fuse; I would deal with it tomorrow. Shuffling my way to the stairs, I hobbled up and tried the second floor light. It didn't even flicker.

With Mrs. DeLacy and Donald gone, the darkness veiling the house made it an alien spirit. Feeling my way around, I tried turning on the lights in the bathroom and my bedroom. No luck.

I didn't care at this point. I flung myself on my bed in exhaustion. But lying in the dark, the house perfectly still, the reason for the outage suddenly dawned on me. I bolted upright.

The problem wasn't a blown fuse. Of course not. The entire power to the house had been disconnected.

I had forgotten to pay the bills.

Chapter Twenty-Four

I HAD LITTLE TIME over the next two weeks to feel sorry for myself or worry much about Peter's words; work was too all-consuming. Peter had called the next day, apologizing for his "abominable behavior" and for calling me peculiar, but I suspected that he still secretly thought as much. Oddly, his reaction didn't trouble me as much as did Sparkey's passionate dislike of, well, everything—ranchers, the Forest Service, BLM, every agency, both state and feds.

Our problems with managing natural resources were clearly correlated as much with the behavior of people as with the biological behavior of an ecosystem. Everyone, from every different agency or private consortium, had a different strategy for the resource. The Forest Service, the BLM, the Fish and Game, SCS, and the ranchers each had a separate management plan in mind for an area. There were plans for farming, for grazing and wildlife, for forestry and watershed protection and recreation; but few, if any, of these designs dovetailed. The plethora of agendas effectively bogged down all forms of communication. There were too many egos involved, too many chiefs.

And too much hearsay, I decided. Just what was the condition of the Zumwalt? Was it really in foul shape, as the Fish and Game believed, or was it well managed, as claimed by Ben and Don Baldwin? Wandering across square mile after square mile of prairie, I saw that most of the land was munched on by livestock; yet I observed crowding of cattle, patches of bare soil, and denuding of the grasses in only a few places. And even in early July, I still found wildflowers exploding in profusion, intermixed with the wealth of bunchgrasses. With the coming of hot weather, I had expected to see wilting flowers, a brown haze washing a short, stubby prairie like dirty water. Instead, lupine colored entire hillsides purple; cinquefoil lined fields like a citron blanket; red and deep scarlet Indian paintbrush still accented the mesas, intermingling with thousands of wild pink roses. Some grasses, yet ungrazed, grew so tall that my hands and arms brushed against their stalks as I walked across the fields.

Where the grasses were lower, armies of Belding's ground squirrels lurched pell-mell from hole to hole, popping up and down, always with a characteristic startled expression on their whiskered faces. Badgers still held vigil for the unsuspecting squirrel, while young hawks ornamented the sky with wild and crazy loops as they learned the art of hunting from their overworked parents.

Now that the mapping of all range sites was nearly done, which was gratifying, I was ready to begin one of the most exciting aspects of my research: the determination of the true state of the Zumwalt's rangeland health: its "range condition." The range condition of an area of grassland is truly the pulse beat of the health of the ecosystem. The range site classification system looks at a range habitat's *quantity*, but the determination of the area's range condition reveals that habitat's present *quality*.

A plant community is not a static entity. Many things can and do affect it. Vegetation, of forest or grassland, passes through a predictable sequence of vegetative structures as it ages over time, referred to by botanists as "successional stages." Successional stages generally follow a natural, progressive order, but outside influences can set back a landscape to an earlier structure. If the factors are severe enough—such as too many years of overgrazing, logging, or irreversible soil erosion—the natural plant community can deteriorate so much as to change its potential forever.

The SCS range classification system looks at these factors and determines what was the climax vegetation—the original plant community—for each range site; in other words, what would grow on the site if it were in its old-growth state. With this as the standard, the range condition, or health, of a site can be determined by comparing the kinds, proportions, and amounts of plants presently growing on a site with the climax plant community. Generally, the range condition of an area reflects the longtime grazing pattern of livestock and indicates to what degree range improvements are needed. For ease in explanation, range scientists have identified four different condition classes within which a plant community can fall: excellent, good, fair, and poor.

Excellent range condition means that 75 percent or more of the makeup of the present plant community is still like the original climax for the range site. In addition, to achieve this rating, a site must be experiencing no current erosion. *Good range condition* requires that 50 to 75 percent of the present plant assemblage be like the original. Here, current erosion can be no more than slightly active. *Fair range condition* means that only 25 to 50 percent of the complexion of a site is still like the original, and erosion is possibly moderately active. *Poor range condition* means that the present plant community resembles less than 25 percent of a climax community. Also in these sites, erosion can be and often is severely active.

Most people assume that little to no public or private rangeland still exists in excellent condition, and that grasslands can be found in good condition only rarely. The general consensus seems to be that most of the rangeland of the West falls into the poor-condition class, with some edging up to fair, but not much.

I would need to sample a variety of places, and come up with an overall picture of the health of each range site, to determine the range condition of the Zumwalt Prairie. Of course, range condition varied throughout the prairie and among different ranches; a wide spectrum of conditions would likely be apparent within each range site. But a random sampling taken over the Zumwalt's entirety could help shed light on the prairie's efficacy for native wildlife.

Don Baldwin spent a full day in the field with me, explaining the technique used to derive range condition. It was a complex method, based on the dry weight of plants. The weights of the major plant species that grew on an acre were determined and then compared with the weights that should be there were the acre in a climax state.

The technique consisted of five steps, and at first I found them all equally confusing. I had to read them repeatedly and carefully until I had them memorized:

STEP ONE: "Weigh several representative clumps of each of the major plant species in an area and come up with an average unit in dry weight for each species."

For this step I carried a little scale with me.

STEP TWO: "Run sample transects. Do at least five, better yet ten transects in the given area, and calculate the average number of units (weight) per plot."

For each transect I laid a meter circular ring on the ground and counted how many plants occurred in each, every five, seven, or ten paces (this was to be varied). Then I translated this number to unit weight. Finally, the ten transects were averaged.

STEP THREE: "Calculate the following formula: the average number of units per plot, multiplied by their unit weight. This equals the grams per plot. Next, multiply this answer by 10 to give you the correct pounds per acre."

(By this point I was always really confused.)

STEP FOUR: "Add up all the pounds per acre and get a percentage of each species of the total."

STEP FIVE: "Transfer these results to the data sheets [which are standardized forms for each range site] and compare *these* figures with the *climax*. This percentage will give you the *range condition rating*."

Once these transects started to render results, which took hours from dawn till dusk, I began to recognize certain things that earlier I had given only cursory attention. I was learning that some plants, more than others, were actually hallmarks of a grassland's health. Particular plants meant particular things.

There were the *decreasers*: those plants that started to reduce in the stand as the prairie health began to deteriorate. Generally, the first plants to decrease with overgrazing were the native bunchgrasses—primarily Idaho fescue, and then bluebunch wheatgrass, and also some native species of wildflowers. Some plants were *invaders*: those that came in to take the place of long-lived natives, and often of poor quality—the starlings and English sparrows of the plant world. Rattlesnake grass, cheatgrass, annual bromegrass, and rabbitbrush are examples of invaders.

Some plants, I discovered, were *despicable*, and showing up when the original plant community was so badly deteriorated that it could no longer command the site, for its potential capacity had been destroyed by years of abuse. I recognized some of these plants, such as gumweed and tarweed and cheatgrass, easily, for their nasty little seeds often worked their way into my socks. Gumweed and tarweed also had the unfortunate ability to drive away other plants.

It is discouraging that, once lost, seed stocks for plants that had adapted over thousands of years to a specific slope or valley or soil condition often cannot be restored. Replacement seeds for native plants in similar regions are usually very hard to come by. Also, knowledge about effective methods of returning native species to disturbed arid soils is limited.

I remembered the words of an old-timer, grassland scientist, Ed Faulkner, who wrote the haunting message that "many of the ills of the soil are those which we humans have induced."

In our mad rush to plant monocultures, or spray herbicides to drive out everything but grass for livestock, we often forget that it is the diversity of species in a landscape that creates the dependable, sustaining chemistry of an ecosystem. And there is aboveground and belowground diversity; the two are related, of course. Aboveground diversity of a prairie means that there is also a teeming diversity below, abundant with fungi, invertebrates, and bacteria, all of which enrich the soil.

When a farmer raises a monoculture crop, a decline in the range of microbial forms as well as aboveground diversity invariably results. Unfortunately, this produces a welcome invitation for epidemics, by pathogens or insect infestations. On a prairie rich in diversity, however, insects are naturally controlled, because they are forced to spend much of their energy budget flying around hunting for food among many plant species.

Don Baldwin said it best. If we correctly managed only the top millimeter of our soil, keeping a diverse wealth of decaying organic matter—or keeping its "voltage hot"—we could avoid nearly all the trouble we have with soil, including erosion and sterility. Immaculately clean soil, by virtue of extreme tidiness by a disk harrow or too many grazing mouths ripping away at all vegetation, has caused the disappearance of diverse organic matter. The only option left is the use of pesticides, herbicides, and fertilizers, for, unwittingly, we have created our own desert.

But the Zumwalt was not a desert—not even close. Trying to maximize my time in the field, I put off tallying my results until late in the week. Sitting down one evening on Mrs. DeLacy's living-room floor, calculator in hand, I worked steadily into the wee hours of the morning, trying to determine the actual range condition for transect after transect. By midnight I had literally hundreds of the standardized data sheets, filled with numbers, spread at my feet.

After collating all the results for my first week's work, I tabulated the conclusions, and then reread them—and reread them again. Although not yet fully complete, they clearly showed a distinct and startling trend.

Sparkey was wrong. And Austin and Eric. And Peter and Glenn and all the rest.

Oh, there were some poors, all right. A number of them. And a good share of fair conditions. That I expected. But far and away, the results showed that area after area of the Zumwalt's range sites were in *good* condition; and a number of them even came out with *excellent* ratings. That the Zumwalt Prairie truly was different was clearly evident now, not only in numbers of hawks or other wildlife but in the condition of its range. That this land combined both cattle and wildlife—that it is, to the chagrin of some, *privately owned*—made the results even more amazing.

Lying back on my hands, I sighed. Before studying the Zumwalt, I had supposed, like many people, that wildlife could not subsist with livestock. I had supposed that ranchers, as a whole, mismanaged their lands. But the facts now stared out at me like beacons to light understanding. The Zumwalt Prairie, with its beauty and teeming diversity, was a kind of rangeland that most of the West had not seen for decades. Intuitively, I had recognized this from my first day of work. I knew, on a deep, aesthetic level, that something most of the ranchers were doing here was *right*, although I couldn't give the reasons.

Pulchritudo splendor veritatis: Beauty is the splendor of truth.

Now there was only one problem: No one would believe me.

Chapter Twenty-Five

"I'M AFRAID YOU'RE COMPLETELY mistaken," said the voice on the other end of the phone, with a distinctly chastising tone. "An abundance of Belding's ground squirrels means the landscape is in poor condition. Better go back and do your homework."

Dave Phillips, chief range ecologist for Oregon's Soil Conservation Service, was adamant. When I called him to discuss the condition of the Zumwalt Prairie, which he had never seen, his position was unmovable. The same thing happened when I spoke with the head ornithologist of the Birds of Prey refuge in Idaho. "If you've got squirrels, you've got overgrazed range," he stated. "If the range is in okay shape, no squirrels. Ya can't have both."

Things were not adding up. Just when I thought the pieces of the puzzle were at last coming together, everyone else seemed to think I was off base. And after several such conversations, I began to doubt myself, too. Perhaps I had miscalculated, or run transects in the wrong places.

But the results of my second week's work only confirmed more strongly the conclusions of the first. Almost subconsciously, I found myself seeking the visibly poor areas, where Herefords and Black Angus hung out around stock ponds, to add some "validity" to the findings. But these places were the exceptions, not the rule.

Unquestionably, I needed to begin in depth the third tier of my research: the study of the hawk's food resource. But I needed help. I called a good friend from my peregrine working days at Chimney Rock, John Houle. John was conducting engineering research at Oregon State University, and had access to the immense school research library. I knew that he, with his clever research and computer skills, could unearth any existing bit of random, esoteric information on Belding's ground squirrels and northern pocket gophers. I needed facts; I could not deal anymore with mere speculation.

John and I had stayed in touch ever since my time in Colorado, although we had gone separate educational and research ways in the last few years. But I still considered him one of the finest individuals I had ever met. He was bright, solid, and caring, with unimpeachable integrity. Several friends were amazed that I couldn't seem to think of him as more than a friend. But what they didn't understand was that I needed—or thought I needed—more passion in my life. After watching spirited hawks and falcons wrapped in their wildness, I wanted something, or someone, to make me feel that way—always aloft, unsettled, a little carried away on the wings of romance, whatever that meant. John was dependable and trustworthy and kind. What did a twenty-five-year old raptor biologist need of that? At least, I told myself that when I saw him with other women who continually seemed to be buzzing around him. I would never stoop to be one of those. To his credit, he never seemed interested in all of their frivolities; he was always a bit removed. In any case, we were both much too busy with our research and our studies to have much time for anything else.

When I called him, John assured me that he would do all he could to uncover information on the rodents and get it to me. And he didn't laugh, which pleased me; he didn't say I was wrong when I told him about the contradictions I was finding on the Zumwalt.

"Believe in yourself, Mar," John said. "You can't do science to satisfy others. Remember, it's always been the person who broke the rules that made the advances." He laughed then. "And one thing about you, you've never been afraid to be an outcast."

But I didn't always want to be an outcast. I liked fitting in. Why did I never seem able to? If only I wouldn't keep getting myself into such silly scrapes, like this one about rodents. I didn't even care about rodents. But now it was vital to identify exactly what the hawks were feasting on and make a thorough inventory of the little animal's habitat needs.

Throughout July, I spent my days in the field and my nights bent over a microscope, which I had lugged with me from Oregon State. It was lucky, in a way, that Mrs. DeLacy was still away, for I didn't think she would be overjoyed that her dining-room table was littered with the remains of bird castings. Donald didn't care. He had returned from his week at Aunt Gladys's sullen and quiet, and was about to go visit his mother for another week. Then they would both be home for a break.

I suspected I had better get this part of the project over and done with before she arrived.

The food habits of the three hawk species could be determined on the basis of pellet analysis and by evaluating prey remains found in the nests. With painstaking care and documentation, I soaked each casting in water to remove fur and other debris, and dried all the little bones—leg bones and mandibles and skulls—which I then examined under the microscope. The remains from hawk pellets were more difficult to identify than those from, say, owl pellets, for hawks digested what they ate more completely. Another problem, which potentially could skew the data, was that pellet analysis could considerably underestimate the role of insects in the diet of the hawks. Insects were nearly always completely digested. This, of course, could especially bias the food preferences of the Swainson's hawk.

But I discovered that, by and large, the analyses came fairly easily. Although the three different hawks ate a variety of foods, from field mice to western meadowlarks (a few) to partridges and pheasants and snakes, the vast majority of their diet centered around only two prey species: the Belding's ground squirrel and northern pocket gopher.

Belding's ground squirrels appeared to make up more than 77

percent of the total biomass in the diets of all three species of hawk. Birds were constituting less than 5 percent of the biomass, and pocket gophers made up 12 to 20 percent of the diets. Zumwalt hawks were eating thousands and thousands of the injurious rodents. As I had learned over my years of falcon study, the total weight of food that a raptor population required is so enormous that predation by birds of prey is an effective, inexpensive, and important biological control. One well-known study had concluded that a raptor population of only twenty-nine birds had consumed *thirty-one thousand rodents* in one spring and summer. If one multiplied that by the hundreds of Zumwalt buteos, the results were staggering. And, as an added bonus, these thousands of rodents taken naturally by hawks didn't need to be killed with poisons.

So, Mr. Hadley and your horrid bull, you're right to say that hawks are a mighty force in the containment of red diggers. But this didn't help to explain why so many ground squirrels and gophers thrive in the Zumwalt, especially if they prefer poor-condition rangeland. I now had to determine the rodents' habitat preference, and after several consultations with mammalogists, we had come up with a method. I would run standardized counts of the numbers of ground squirrel burrows and pocket gopher mounds, and correlate these to their preference for range sites and range condition. It was simple: more burrows meant more squirrels, or gophers. It would be a relative index, but it would give me the necessary information.

There was a minor problem. Anyone who saw me running a transect would instantly conclude that I had lost my mind. I needed to count every blasted little hole, and ground squirrels make not nicely rounded, clearly observable mounds but small, inch-diameter punch holes in the ground, which are easy to overlook. I had to get down on my hands and knees, like a dog on a scent, and for each transect shuffle through the grass to count every hole that fell within an invisible three-yard width for two hundred yards.

Sometimes there were only a few holes; at other times, dozens. Therefore, my total concentration had to be on the ground, from an eye distance of two feet.

The worst part, of course, was that I had to do the same maniacal thing in the cultivated areas near town. Few ground squirrels inhabited this area, but the pocket gophers seemed to prefer it. I would be a visible target for all the ranchers and passersby. I hoped they would just mistake me for a small heifer.

But they didn't, as I soon found out. When Mrs. DeLacy arrived home—the day the telephone company disconnected her phone service, for I had put off paying that bill too, sure she would be home in time—she asked why I was spending time crawling about on all fours sniffing at alfalfa.

"Where did you hear that?" I asked, knowing full well that Sparkey was making me a laughingstock among the Fish and Game by telling everyone of my seemingly absurd behavior.

"Just why must you perpetuate such oddities?" said Mrs. DeLacy. Taking a breath, I explained about the rodent counts.

"Why, that's utterly fascinating," she exclaimed, the curious teacher in her coming out. "Next time I see Bill Beuford I'm going to tell him what you told me face to face. Bill is all for chemicals and poisons and that nonsense. That's the reason there's so much cancer today."

"Yes, that's one hypothesis."

"You know, for an environmentalist, dear, you're a rather smart girl."

"But Mrs. DeLacy, why would you think I'm an environmentalist?" Donald burst out laughing.

"I've raised eight children, and understand them. Each of them has grown up to be a good citizen and a person I can be proud of. Donald," she said, with a grimace his way, "will too. And by the way, I am pleased that you thought to have the phone disconnected. I quite enjoy the quiet not having one affords. No Janelle always ringing at all hours."

"You're not going to reconnect the phone?" I asked. Donald blanched.

"No. I'm not."

I smiled, but secretly wondered about the inconvenience of not having a phone. Mrs. DeLacy certainly had a flair about her. But I had come to understand that behind her unusual ways was a tender, highly intelligent woman.

"Yes, I've raised eight children, four girls, four boys. Make that five girls," she said, with a warm smile at me, seconded with a confounded look by Donald. "You may be a little different, dear, but variety is what gives spice to families. And with all you've done," she said, with a squeeze to my hand, "you're family now."

Chapter Twenty-Six

MRS. DELACY'S SHRILL VOICE yelling for me couldn't have come at a less opportune time. I felt in my bones that I was on the verge of experiencing one of those "eureka" moments rare in science, but her unwelcome pronouncement that someone was at the door for me had spoiled it. My statistical calculations spread out in disarray before me looked just that: a mess, hardly a revelation. Yet before I went downstairs, I jotted one or two quick thoughts to come back to later.

The measurements I had collected all spring and summer on the placement and characteristics of hawk nests were falling out into intriguing categories. Although all three buteos were dining on the same food, and living on the same prairie, they were dividing it up among themselves by choosing to nest in different places.

In a statistical sense (all biologists live and breathe under a statistical god), the three buteos were not so alike after all. Red-tailed hawks, the most abundant buteo of the three, had a definite bent for nesting in the large old cottonwood trees that grace the cultivated areas, and also, in the prairie, held exclusive title to the random groves of ponderosa pines. Ferruginous hawks, however, disdained such areas; never would they nest in the cultivated farmlands. Cultivation apparently had a detrimental impact on their nesting habitat. They claimed, instead, the isolated, rocky outcroppings for their throne. The gentle, complacent Swainson's hawk preferred the smaller sized aspen and pine trees that grew by themselves in irregular spots on the Zumwalt; they also were partial to the overgrown shrubs lining the Zumwalt stream banks.

"Home Sweet Home" was a very particular place. This meant that even though the Zumwalt looked like just one big sprawling grassland, its subtle mosaic of individual ecological range sites made for a diversity that each of the three species could and did use. For example, the south exposure range sites, with their abundance of outcroppings, made a home for ferruginous hawks. And as long as there were enough cottonwood trees, red-tails usurped the cultivated areas. They and their cousin the Swainson's both used the north exposure sites, which grew groves of aspen and fir and pine.

This partitioning of the prairie resource could explain why three such closely related species, such as red-tails, ferruginous, and Swainson's hawks, were able to peaceably coexist in such high numbers yet with so little observable competition among them. The small, microhabitat differences on the prairie provided a wealth of diversity. It also starkly showed how closely tied everything was to everything else—the plants, the rocks, the mammals, the birds, the watershed. Together they constituted a working ecosystem. It was pure folly to try to "manage" for one of the separate parts at the exclusion of the rest; clearly, any management action on one would have a rippling effect on everything else. From the lowly pocket gopher to the giant cottonwood, all had to be viewed in a holistic scheme.

Mrs. DeLacy sounded agitated; I leaped up and, without looking back, tore down the stairs. Standing there in the hallway, holding a foot-high stack of papers, was John Houle. I had forgotten how tall he was, and how good-looking, but most of all, how warm and genuine was his smile. It was an easy smile, full of good humor, reflected also in his twinkling, dark eyes.

"Your guest from Corvallis has been standing here for nearly five minutes," Mrs. DeLacy scolded. "Aren't you going to offer him some lemonade?"

Sometimes Mrs. DeLacy made me feel like a fifteen-year-old, and I momentarily regretted the decision to ever come and live here. But John, in his relaxed way, broke in with a hearty "Sounds good."

He put the stack of research papers he was holding into my waiting hands. "They're all I could dig up on short notice, but I think you'll find them interesting," he said, and then explained why he was here. "My professor asked me to pick up some equipment at University of Idaho, and I decided, kind of spur of the moment, you weren't too far out of the way and probably wanted this stuff as soon as possible. I tried calling, but the operator told me the phone was disconnected."

"Uh-huh," I mumbled, unable to think of anything clever to say, I was so taken by surprise. Mrs. DeLacy, however, had everything under control; already she had prepared three glasses of lemonade.

"I know that drive from Corvallis well," she said. "Six and a half hours. You must have got up terribly early to get here by ten."

"It's going to be a hot day; thought I'd get an early start."

"In the high nineties, I heard," I said.

"You better not go out in that prairie," warned Mrs. DeLacy. "There's no shade at all in that forsaken land. You'll surely get heat prostration. Edwin James's father died of it several years ago riding around in that tractor, when he had no business being out there in that heat. Even when Edwin took over the ranch, his father refused to give up his old unairconditioned tractor; he'd go over his soil 'til it was gritty like sand and still be out riding around. He'd probably be there yet, just him and his tractor, if Dr. Blackburn had been able to save him."

"I'll be careful," I said, with a look at John, who was enjoying his lemonade. "I need to band a nest of ferruginous hawks not too far out. Are you straight off to Idaho, John, or would you like to see the Zumwalt?" I asked.

"I don't have to be in Idaho until tomorrow afternoon," he replied. "I'd like to see this grassland you've been studying."

"And there's a bed in the basement you can use," added Mrs.

DeLacy, as an invitation. "But you better get out hiking soon; remember Mr. James and his tractor."

After all the times in Colorado when I had made a mess of things, I welcomed this opportunity to demonstrate to John my professionalism and honed skills in field biology. It was probably unnecessary for me to feel this way, for I knew that John valued what I was trying to do. He, too, was idealistic and appreciative of learning new things, and would never hold a grudge that a woman was, in Sparkey's terms, "trying to do a man's job." John, although well versed in a variety of subjects, knew nothing about banding birds, especially large birds such as raptors, and I was about to show him how it was done.

We left in my truck for the dry, south-exposure hillside leading to O.K. Gulch. Once there, we began our walk to the nest, and found that the elevation as well as the heat seemed to rise significantly. The landmark overlooking O.K. Gulch was a steep rocky bluff that seemed to rise straight from the ground like an ancient Egyptian pyramid. Scatterings of rocks peppered the shallow soil within several square miles of it, making the whole area seem like an eerie moonscape. Yet, because of the wealth of outcroppings and the area's remoteness, ferruginous hawks loved the spot; I had been meaning to return to one such nest when the nestlings were the right age for banding. With the malathion spraying right around the corner, the time was now.

Swinging my arms as we walked, I found myself, as I always did, talking freely to John about anything that came to mind. I could pour out my summer's worth of frustrations with Austin and Sparkey, and in the next breath exclaim over the beauty of a wild-flower; he always seemed able to understand, making not value judgments but illuminating comments that often revealed the humor in a situation. John had a rollicking good sense of humor, which, when mixed with his insight, made me profoundly glad for his comradeship.

"Sounds like you and Sparkey have really hit it off, have a lot in common," he said, laughing when I told him of the dreadful evening I had spent at his house. For some reason I said nothing about Peter.

"We certainly don't; we don't even speak the same language," I said.

John's eyes took in the Zumwalt. Whereas I focused on birds and grass, he, a water resource specialist, focused on hydrology. "There sure are a lot of stock ponds on this prairie," he commented thoughtfully.

"Sure are."

"That's very interesting. I'll bet it has a lot to do with distributing the cattle, doesn't it?"

How could he see that in just fifteen minutes when it had taken me three or more months?

"You know," he continued, "you won't find ranchers building stock ponds now."

I looked at him, puzzled.

"Because of water rights," he explained. "It's often impossible now to procure a permit and obtain a right. It used to be there was more water to go around. But now, our land-use practices have altered the delivery of water, and more claims are being put on these dwindling resources."

"What kinds of claims? What do you mean?"

"Well, besides irrigation for agriculture, there are mandated minimum stream flows for fish, general water quality regulations, demands for hydro power, and also just the requirements imposed by our growing population. Our supply of water is now cut into smaller and smaller pieces. Historically, water rights were issued based on the assumption of an unlimited water resource. But things, as you know, have changed. We have altered the landscape. We've created different watershed conditions."

"In what way?"

"Logging, for example, has a lot to do with it. When we take out all the big stuff—like the giant ponderosa pines—what results is a loss of what's called the 'sponge effect.' Now, we have a condition where, in springtime, water gushes forth, creating an erosion problem, and then dries up early in the summer."

"So, no sponge effect."

"That's right. Streams that come off watersheds today peter out when water demands are the most critical. These same streams used to run full-time. Water just isn't retained anymore, in a lot of cases. What we need to do is keep our focus on the watershed. Reduce logging to retain water longer in the streams, and let it out more slowly and all season long."

"So the Zumwalt is lucky, in a way, that it already has its stock ponds in place."

"You bet. It's too bad, really. People need to consider the consequences of their actions."

"In a holistic way," I interrupted. "That's just what I am finding, John."

The discussion buoyed my energy, but it soon waned under the wrath of the scorching afternoon sun. After an hour of hiking, I felt I had never before been so hot. Perhaps this was how Mr. James felt before he died. After two hours, I had already choked down all the water I had brought with me, which was to last the afternoon. Many animals, too, seemed affected by the heat, and most that we observed refrained from making any unnecessary movements. The red-winged blackbirds that usually skirted the ditches were now perched and still, as were the savannah sparrows. Yellow cinquefoil, with its hairy green leaves and bright petals, lay sadly drooping. Red soil and red rocks were everywhere, and hills were lined with badger holes.

We continued to climb, our conversation dwindling. Far below us, a few miles away but still visible, my truck was parked among roiling heat waves, and from this distance it looked ridiculously like a child's toy. Droppings from deer and coyote were easily visible in the bare soil patches, but their living representation was nowhere evident; they were probably hunkered down in any kind of shade, which was the only reasonable thing to do. The only sound, the only life, seemed to be the endless chirping of crickets, the sound of summer heat.

"Hey, look, over there," pointed John.

It was a ferruginous. Once again, he had seen the hawk first. John's powers of observation were uncanny and, I decided, vastly superior to mine—and always had been. It was a standing joke between us that *he* should have been the wildlife biologist. The hawk was sitting perfectly still on the ground between two big bull thistles. Spotting us, it took off, arising nearly perpendicular from the ground, and was joined by a dark phase ferruginous—the female.

"Their nest is right over there," I whispered to John. "Inside that large crevice in the rock. The last time I was here, there were four young."

Softly but quickly making our way, our boots stepping through clumps of daisies, bunchgrasses, senecio, and yarrow, we climbed up to the nest to find the four young still there, although much bigger than three weeks ago. The nest was well concealed in the cave, which stretched back nearly six feet deep and was comfortably shaded. Green lichen and moss clung to the rocks and, in the heat, emitted an appealing musty, woody fragrance.

Two of the nestlings were light phase, and two were dark; the birds were not completely developed, as evidenced by their remaining pinfeathers.

This should be easy, I thought; just grab them, band them, put them back in the nest. If only it weren't so unbearably hot.

When I reached down to unzip my backpack to grab the bands and clipboard, one nestling, a light phase female, hopped frantically out of the nest. John lurched over to grab it, but the bird was too fast. She flew, and hopped, flew and hopped, down and across the slope.

"Oh, don't worry," I said to John. "We'll catch her later, after we band these three. She can't go far."

After a hideous wrestling match, which undoubtedly was my worst banding job yet, John helped me with the next nestling. The heat was affecting my manual dexterity, which already was exceedingly sloppy with this rowdy trio. Feeling somewhat embarrassed, I read to John the band numbers to write down as I applied them.

"It's not usually quite so much of a production," I said, while the feisty birds nipped at and clawed me and their furious parents swooped over our heads. "Generally, it's quite easy. Ouch!"

The nasty thing placed his beak into the web of my right hand, between my thumb and index finger. *So much for you, little friend,* I thought, as I laid it none too gently back in the nest, amid a littering of ground squirrel mandibles, leg bones, and shed ferruginous feathers.

"We're done!" I said, to myself adding, "Thank God." With a quick look at my battle scar, which really wasn't much, I turned to John. "Now all we've got to do is just find the sister. We'll band her and put her back with her bad-tempered siblings."

But it wasn't that easy. In a heat wave that must have broken one hundred degrees, we scoured the hillside, searching for the little bird that seemed to have vanished into thin air. After two hours of fruitless looking, we decided to give up and return home, have a late lunch, and perhaps return later in the cool of the evening to find the nestling.

I wasn't overly concerned; after all, the bird was nearly fledged; she could get back to the nest.

Chapter Twenty-Seven

FOR THE SECOND TIME in one day, John, Mrs. DeLacy, and I were sipping lemonade on the back veranda when Austin charged into the driveway. After a brief round of introductions, which produced a rather subdued Mrs. DeLacy (I could tell instantly that she didn't approve of Austin), we began a harmless banter about raptors and the Zumwalt and the intolerable heat wave gripping Wallowa County. I lightheartedly related that day's experiences with the rabble-rousing ferruginous family, minus its lone sojourner.

Austin gulped his lemonade and banged his glass on the table with a thud. Liquid spilled from the glass; Mrs. DeLacy rushed to the kitchen to grab a sponge.

"Good God, girl!" Austin said, able to speak at last. His eyes were bugged. "You mean you left the area without finding the nestling? You left it out *unprotected?*"

I suddenly felt like a reprehensible mother. "We were planning to go back tonight," I stammered.

"I should say so!" he exclaimed. Mrs. DeLacy, wiping lemonade furiously from the table and floor, was all ears. "I should say so," he said again. "Lord above, don't you know you never, ever, leave a nestling out alone that can't defend itself, making easy pickin's for a coyote."

"You've done it, with that owl," I reminded him.

"That was different," he said objectively. "That bird could nearly fly."

"Well, this one hopped."

"On the *ground*. The owl, you remember, I put back in the tree. I'd never leave a baby bird out *on the ground*."

My heart was stuck in my throat, and I was speechless. John, Austin, and I left our lemonade and Mrs. DeLacy's cool veranda and piled into Austin's truck. Mrs. DeLacy's sympathetic "I'll have dinner waiting" didn't assuage any of the pain I felt —pain and embarrassment over my own stupidity. Of course, I should have known not to leave O.K. Gulch with a defenseless bird still out hopping about somewhere. I had worked with raptors long enough to know that. But this bird had seemed fairly mature.

I had little to say on our drive to the trailhead and once there, the breeze that picked up in the evening couldn't seem to fan the hotness of my face. Austin and John, talking together, took long strides straight up the slope; I followed quickly behind, trying to raise my spirits with the hope that the bird had already found her way back to the nest. Anyway, if she were anything like her spirited brothers and sister, she would be far too ornery and tough for the likes of any coyote.

As we approached the nest, I saw her. Indeed she had nearly made it back, and her anguished parent, on seeing us, was now torn between flying over her nestling and swooping over us. The adult ferruginous hawk made swift, powerful loops that began far over our heads and catapulted almost to the ground.

The nestling, as we could see instantly, was dying. Obviously, a coyote or fox had found her before she had reached the safety of her nest. The nestling's wings were broken; the feathers on her back were torn; her skin lay exposed and bleeding.

Tears filled my eyes; I couldn't stop them, even in front of John and Austin. Both men were quiet.

"What can we do?" I entreated.

Austin moved slowly and gently toward the bird. "She's got to be destroyed, Marcy. There's nothing anyone can do."

"Destroyed? Can't we rehab her? Take her to the Fish and Game?"

"Gangrene's already set in," Austin said softly. "It's the only thing to do."

Tears streamed down my face as Austin, in one swift, humane movement, wrung the neck of the agonized bird, while her two wailing parents swung overhead. Laying the bird down in the soft, sweet-smelling bunchgrass, Austin glanced at John, then at me.

"It's not your fault," he said kindly. "It happens, even to the best biologists. It's just the way of nature."

But this wasn't the way of nature; it was my fault. Austin was already halfway down the hill; John had stopped to wait for me, but then, intuitively realizing I needed some time alone, went on ahead.

I looked down at the sight one last time—another ferruginous hawk destroyed, but this time by my error. Once again, I asked myself: Is it worth it? Is it worth invading the lives of these wild creatures for the sake of science? To better understand how to "save" them? This bird, this little red nestling, would have been so beautiful.

I felt like a murderer and the very lowest slipshod biologist. And John had witnessed it all.

Chapter Twenty-Eight

MERCIFULLY, NEITHER AUSTIN nor John brought up the subject of the bird again for the rest of the evening. Austin invited himself to dinner and settled in at Mrs. DeLacy's to talk until midnight. John descended to the unfinished basement when Austin left, and departed early the next morning. Except for our walk in the wilting heat, John and I had had no time to talk alone. That was all right, of course; we were just good chums. I told myself that the disappointment that grew inside me as the evening wore on and Austin refused to leave had only to do with the terrible misfortune of the day.

The contrast of the cool air of the morning produced a renewed sense of optimism, and, alone again, I felt eager to continue the ground squirrel and pocket gopher counts. This required a lot of driving, for I wanted to place them at intervals throughout the entire prairie and touch on all five range sites as well as the cultivated lands, for a thorough sampling.

A quick statistical analysis of the data—looking at the variance of the count data I had already collected to determine if significant differences occurred in the densities of the critters among the sites—was revealing. It was only cursory at this point, but another pattern was indeed emerging.

Oddly enough, the cultivated area exhibited the densest populations of pocket gophers, although it had the fewest nesting pairs of two of the species of hawk. In the native prairie, the dry mountain meadow range site had significantly greater densities of Belding's ground squirrels and pocket gophers than the other habitats. The north-exposure range site also had a large number of ground squirrels. As I continued sampling, one other important fact emerged: The better the condition of the range, the greater the numbers of squirrels.

This information was vindicating but what it really meant, and just how I was going to make sense of all the disparate information I was gleaning, still eluded me. Austin had said as much last night, in his usual subtle manner, exclaiming, "You're wasting all your time barking up the wrong trees going after gophers and grass," but I didn't care. As I had learned long ago from Dr. Warren, before you embark on any scientific research, remember to always keep in mind your conceptual framework. And, in my hawk study, the North Star I always kept before me when considering all my options was this: *The capacity of a population* (in my case, *three* populations of three species of hawks) *has to incorporate the capacity of the parts of the population and their environments. The population gets its characteristics from the capacities of the parts.*

There was a distinct challenge to try to identify how all these parts worked, but beyond that lay the challenge of how to plan for future patterns of growth and modifications of land use to ensure that all members of this biodiversity puzzle survived. A group or agency couldn't possibly do this by rescuing specific endangered species one at a time; to protect intact, functioning ecosystems was far more cost effective and increased the probability of success.

If the Zumwalt indeed "worked," I wanted to identify how and why so that conditions here could be replicated in other places before it became too late.

The flat tire on the rear wheel of my truck was a disappointment, a silly inconvenience—I was anxious to be on my way before the day heated up. I knew I should be thankful that the tires hadn't blown before, considering the miles of back roads they had traveled.

Finding the jack in the bowels of the pickup, I was now faced with jury-rigging it to lift up the rear of the truck. The whole thing seemed heavy and unwieldy, and the jack was rusted and difficult to position properly. And, although I had just begun, I was already smeared with oil.

A shiny brown Forest Service vehicle drove up and parked beside mine, which lifted my spirits; some encouragement would be nice. Fully expecting to see Austin, I turned around ready for one of his disparaging comments, but stopped in my tracks. It wasn't Austin.

"What's goin' on?" said the slim, bearded fellow I had met once, through Austin and Eric, at the Forest Service headquarters. I remembered his name for some reason: Guy Hughes. He was the recreation specialist for the district.

I smiled wanly. "A stupid flat tire. But I guess I'm fortunate that it happened in my own driveway."

Leaving his truck running, Guy just stared. He was obviously not preparing to lift a finger to help. Oh well. This wasn't his charge anyway. I continued to jack up the truck.

"You know something?" he asked in a polished voice. "There's something infinitely attractive about seeing a woman change her own tire."

The words grated on me, and I ignored him. Guy only chuckled. "I suppose I could get out to help you, but it's much more pleasant to see a pretty young woman being so capable."

I decided instantly that I didn't care for this man. Peter had talked about him once, laughingly saying he was the Casanova of the Forest Service. His job was to talk and charm tourists into believing the Forest Service was doing a fine job.

Guy turned off the engine of his truck and got out. I could hear his booted footsteps crunching across the gravel behind me and feel his gaze burning at my back.

"There's oil on your clothes and on your face," he said, still chuckling.

"And on my hands, too," I replied, coolly.

"It's a pretty big job brandishing that jack, isn't it? You've got to have muscle power."

Guy laid his hairy arm across the rim of the pickup bed to rest. "You don't mind me watching, do you?"

I had little time or patience for this nonsense. Changing the tire required more concentration than I had expected. "Instead of watching, you could lend a hand."

"Ho ho!" he laughed, and stroked his red beard. "Oh, no. This is a dandy thing to see. A man doesn't often get such a chance close up." He stood back a step and crossed his arms. "You there, dressed in grease and so cleverly handling the job. Like I said, there's something almost sexy about a woman changing her own tire."

With disdain, I whirled around prepared to say, "Haven't you got anything better to do?" when a second truck swiftly pulled up alongside Guy Hughes's. Out sprang Ben McPherson, whom I hadn't seen for a few weeks. He was deeply tanned, as if he had been outdoors tending cattle or something, and when he removed his cowboy hat I saw a ring of white skin on his forehead that never saw the sun.

"Howdy, Ben," I said, thankful for the interruption.

"What's going on here?" he asked.

"Oh, not much," I answered. "Just changing a flat tire."

Ben glanced from me to Guy Hughes, then back to me again. "By yourself?"

I nodded. "It's okay. I've nearly got it now."

The look that Ben gave Guy quickly wiped the smug smile from Guy's face. "What kind of man are you?" Ben demanded.

"We were just in the midst of a nice chat before you drove up," Guy replied haughtily.

"What kind of man would just stand around and not help a girl change a flat tire, on a big truck, no less?" Ben shot a look of disgust at Guy, then squatted down next to me. "Here, give me that thing," he said, taking the jack from my hands. "I'll do this."

"Well, I must be going," Guy said cheerfully. "Before we were so rudely interrupted, I was planning to ask if I could go with you someday this week and see the Zumwalt. Very few Forest Service guys have seen it, and, considering my job responsibilities, I think it could be very important."

Ben kept his head bent to the tire, and I sighed. Why me?

"Austin said you shouldn't mind, and that you need help banding Swainson's hawks before the spraying next week."

Was the malathion shower really only a week away? I still had a dozen nests left to go. Caught off guard, I mumbled out loud, "I need to band the Swainson's then."

"Good; it's settled. I'll be here this time tomorrow morning. By then you should be, well, off and running." Guy jumped back into his truck and started it. "Good luck with the tire, cowboy," he called, backing out, with a flash of straight, orthodontically improved teeth.

Ben finished the job quickly, doing most of it himself. He worked silently, with a smile at me now and again, and at last permitted himself to ask, "Was that Guy Hughes, the recreation guy?"

"Yes. I met him once at the Forest Service; I remember then he asked if he could see the prairie. He said he enjoyed hawks."

"Yeah, sure," Ben muttered. "What a jerk."

"He certainly doesn't present himself well," I said, laughing, and I thanked Ben for helping with the tire. "Care to come in for a quick glass of lemonade before you go?" I asked, realizing, to my horror, that I was sounding more and more like Mrs. DeLacy each day.

He shook his head. "Naw, thanks though. I've got to check on some cattle and move them to a different range."

"And I must run more ground squirrel counts."

Ben finally laughed. "Yes, I've heard tell of those," he said, raising his brows with a smile.

"Would you believe that ground squirrels and pocket gophers appear to prefer good-condition range?" I asked enthusiastically, eager to discuss this with anyone who might be interested.

"Hadn't really given it much thought," he said, putting his cowboy hat back on. "Be careful around that Hughes guy; I don't trust him."

"Oh, don't worry; after he sees me collecting bird castings he'll never want anything to do with hawks again."

"Dinner, sometime?"

"Um, well, I guess so—maybe after this sampling period's over; it's a really busy time."

He smiled. "I've been awfully busy too. Call you next week."

I sat down in the driveway and sighed as he drove away. I looked at my dirty hands and then stood up to look at myself in the side mirror.

What a mess. It seemed that every time I saw Ben I had dirt or oil smeared all over my face.

Well, we'd see if he would really call. I wasn't sure how I felt about it, after seeing John yesterday. But in reality, I didn't need to worry about it. After all, Mrs. DeLacy no longer had a phone.

Chapter Twenty-Nine

TRUE TO HIS WORD, Guy Hughes was back in the driveway at precisely half past eight the next morning. I had decided on a relatively short trip, for my sake, but one that should reap some good fruit. Spaced along a five-mile round-trip hike that partially followed Deadman's Creek, three Swainson's hawks and one red-tail, too young to band during the rodeo, were lined up all in a row. The Swainson's hawks were each about a mile from the other, and the red-tail was sandwiched between them.

This kind of spacing occurred so regularly that I felt certain it couldn't be random. When dealing with two hawk families of the same species, "fences" (in this case, distance) make good neighbors. This bit of information could have useful management implications, I thought. Whenever, or for whatever reason, people tried to increase habitat suitability for hawks, it would be important to remember that hawks have an intrinsic and inviolate sense of spacing, no matter how many nesting sites or how much good food one provides.

Guy was wearing a spanking-new cowboy shirt with the pearl snap buttons and snap shirt pockets—not the usual Forest Service uniform. He smelled of aftershave, which struck me as odd, since he seemed obviously proud of his thick, neatly trimmed beard.

We took my truck, and, while driving, I waited for the comment, which never came, that he enjoyed watching women drive. He seemed better today, more reserved and less cocky. Trying to give him the benefit of the doubt, I thought perhaps he did have a true interest in birds and grasslands.

He seemed to enjoy the ride and didn't say much except to ask the names of the different birds he was seeing. Horned larks kept guard on the fence posts; their black breast mark, striking black facial design, and piquant little horns made a beautiful bird. Also sitting on fence posts were western kingbirds, which Guy first mistook for meadowlarks. The kingbirds, too, were arresting, with their canary yellow breast, contrasting white throat like a preacher's collar, and black eye patches that resembled designer sunglasses.

We parked the truck at the headwaters of Deadman's Creek and began our trek, bypassing another drainage that needed checking, Pine Creek, that I was saving for *me*. Ever since I had discovered it months ago, ripe with wildflowers and tall waving grasses, I considered it a special place of loveliness, and one I wanted to return to alone. I certainly didn't want to share it with Guy. It was among the few corporately owned ranches on the Zumwalt, and in this case, whatever corporation was stewarding it seemed to be doing a fine job. I didn't see any sign, from this vantage point at least, of cows in the watershed, and I respected their decision to keep their livestock well distributed, by virtue of cross fencing the range.

Cows were highly visible along Deadman's Creek, unlike at Pine Creek, but the transects I had done showed the land to be mostly in high-fair condition. The good sign apparent here was the *trend*. To determine trend, SCS scientists look at several things: Is the cover (kinds and amounts of vegetation) improving or going downhill? Is there a broad diversity of age classes among the native species, and a good number of new, young native plants coming in? Is there little erosion? All these mean an upward trend. Deadman's Creek was indeed experiencing an upward trend, although it wasn't perfect.

Guy and I saw different things as we watched the stream winding before us.

"This just goes to show that what the government studies say are true," he began. "Just look at all those cows."

"Yes, there are cows, all right."

"Like I said, the studies have shown so much land is in poor condition, and drastic action is needed to deal with the problems of overgrazing."

"There are lots of cows, but these aren't overgrazed conditions, Guy."

"Some of our guys in other parts of Oregon say that it's going to take fifty years or more to repair the damage."

"I'm sure that's true in some areas, but not here."

"It's the proverbial problem of eroded stream channels, lowered water tables, and invasion of sagebrush, all of it caused by grazing. Most of the stream headwater areas are deficient in aspen and willow cover that's needed by songbirds. The damn cows kill the stands of trees by rubbing against them and trampling the young saplings."

What Guy said was true unless, like here, the areas were cross fenced and cows were kept on the move.

Guy hiked in front of me, still watching the birds, and grew terribly excited at spying a mature golden eagle riding the lofty air currents. The bird was a grand specimen, with a head so gold as to appear white in the sun. Guy mistook it, in fact, for a bald eagle, which is easy to do.

"Its nest is in the giant ponderosa about a mile from here," I said, watching it also with my binoculars and admiring its casual sideslipping through the air. The old bird was a master, with no trace of instability, like the funny turkey vulture rocking even higher in the sky. The eagle maneuvered the wind easily, could accelerate buoyantly, then nose over spontaneously in a surge, as if playing a game with the air.

"Wow," Guy said in awe.

"Well, we'd better get going."

"Wow. You think that bird has young?"

"Probably," I guessed. "There were eggs, I remember. But I don't have bands big enough for eagles."

"I've never been close to a golden eagle's nest. Let's go and check it out."

"First I need to find my Swainson's nests," I reminded him. "Then, if there's time, we can swing over to the golden's eyrie on the way back."

The first Swainson's nest, snug and safe in a squatty, wide ponderosa growing by itself near the creek, was abandoned. On June 9 it had had two eggs, but today no sign of the adults or the eggs was evident—only one flimsy casting and a large porcupine asleep in the top of the tree! The base and sides of the tree showed damage and gnawings by porcupines, and I wondered if the little snoozing fellow had been responsible for the demise of the nest.

A meadowlark trilled as we came upon the nest of the red-tail. The nest was placed lower than some and was readily accessible. Guy, eager, climbed up and caught up the nestlings, one by one, for me to band. I tried not to think about the little female ferruginous I had abandoned two days ago.

He told me there was stuff in the nest and I should take a look. Inside were the remains of three pocket gophers, three ground squirrels, and one microtus.

"Pretty prolific hunters," said Guy, watching the parents sail by. Even though they were well above him, he respectfully ducked each time they made a pass.

When away and at a nonthreatening distance from the hawks, Guy and I sat down to have lunch before continuing. Always at a loss to come up with anything more creative, I had my stock peanut butter and honey sandwich; Guy, however, was enjoying a deli chicken sandwich.

"I could tell you wanted me to help you with that tire yesterday," Guy said, between bites. "That's one reason I thought I'd just stand and watch."

"I could do it perfectly well," I replied.

"Not saying you couldn't!" he said, wiping his mouth on his

cloth napkin. I saw him glancing down at my legs, which were clad in shorts today, in preparation for the hot weather. Really, I didn't care for this man. I pulled my legs under me, and he laughed.

"You know why I liked you from that first time I saw you at the Forest Service?" he asked, just when I had a mouth full of dry sandwich and couldn't respond. "You shave your legs. And I'll bet your underarms too. Most of the women I work with are so wildernessy, they don't believe in feminine things like that. I like the smoothness of a cleanly shaven leg."

I choked on my sandwich. "This is preposterous!"

"Tell me," he said, resting back on his arms and trying to catch some rays on his face, "to change the subject, is this private land we're on?"

I didn't know whether to stoop to answer this untoward individual or not. But anything was better than having him get personal. Curtailing lunch, I shoved the rest of it in my pack. "Forest Service land adjoins the Zumwalt," I answered coolly, "and some of this prairie is corporately owned."

"That's what I thought," he said, smiling in the sunshine. "And the Snake River's just east of us, isn't it?"

I nodded as I got up to go.

"It's amazing to think that the deepest river canyon in North America—a greater chasm than even the Grand Canyon—lies just a few short miles away. This Zumwalt of yours borders the Hell's Canyon NRA, doesn't it?"

The Hell's Canyon NRA, or National Recreation Area, is a stupendous wilderness attraction spanning about 650,000 acres, straddling the Snake River for over seventy miles. It is the Zumwalt's eastern border. The drop from the Seven Devil Mountains of Idaho to the bottom of Snake River is 8,043 feet, nearly 2,000 feet deeper than the greatest vertical drop of the Grand Canyon. Also directly bordering the NRA, the Wallowa Mountains and Eagle Cap Wilderness Area make a diverse and incredibly beautiful spot for the hikers who explore the area.

"I guess it will be affected, too," Guy said, with a yawn, getting ready to go on.

"What do you mean?"

"When it becomes a national park."

At first the words failed to register. I must not have heard correctly.

"National park?" I asked, rearranging my pack on my shoulders as we left the lunch spot. "What on earth are you talking about?"

"The Hell's Canyon Preservation Council has recommended study of a possible one-and-a-half-million-acre national park. I can't believe you haven't heard about it," said Guy. "It will include the Hell's Canyon NRA, the Wallowas, the wilderness area, and maybe this."

"That's huge," I said haltingly.

"Second only to Yellowstone in the lower 48," continued Guy. "It's a fabulous idea, whose time has come."

Guy didn't refer again to personal subjects; in fact, he became quiet and subdued as we finished banding the Swainson's nestlings. In the stillness, I couldn't help thinking about the national park venue for this area. What surprised me the most, as I went over it in my mind, was that I wasn't jumping for joy over the idea. I loved parks; one of my favorite places on earth was Olympic National Park in Washington. And, without a doubt, the beauty and grandeur of this area made it well suited to be a crown jewel in the park system.

Cresting over the rim of Deadman's Creek Canyon, the full glory of the Zumwalt spread out like a golden sea with flecks of rainbows. Seeing the loveliness, Guy became excited and expounded again on the greatness of the park idea. Proponents had already decided what to call it: "Hell's Canyon/Chief Joseph National Park."

The name was so completely politically correct that somehow it bothered me.

"Several members of Congress are already considering legislation," he recounted enthusiastically. "There's no question, I'm sure you'll agree, that this land should all be protected. This too," he added, with an arm's wave at the Zumwalt. "Like Ric Bailey said—"

"Who's that?" I interrupted.

"Of the Preservation Council. Like he said, using the deepest canyon in North America and these great mountains and even this prairie as a feedlot for livestock is like using the Mona Lisa to wrap hamburger."

I suddenly realized that I was living in a dream world with my research—such an idealistic, scientific dream world. So much impinged on this subject area, this Zumwalt that I had always thought to be so remote, with this perhaps being the greatest impact of all.

Guy wouldn't let me forget about seeing the eagle eyrie, so on the return trip we detoured to the nest I had found six weeks ago. I encouraged him to look from a distance; golden eagles are powerfully protective of their young. Guy, however, in his rapt enthusiasm, refused to listen.

"Mom and Dad eagle aren't here. Just one quick peek," he said, and went over and lithely scaled the big tree. I looked around nervously but didn't see the adult raptors. Guy reached the huge stick nest in short order and loudly whistled his amazement.

"Beautiful!" he cried down. "Just beautiful! One big guy, more feathered than those Swainson's hawks. He's all black and white —I could play a game of checkers on his back—"

At that moment, taking us both by surprise, the bold parent of the checkerboard collided into Guy and broke his hold of the tree. In what seemed like slow motion, Guy fell fifteen feet and landed in a heap on the ground, under the nest.

"Are you all right?" I cried, rushing over.

He was dazed but not hurt, except for his ankle and the tear in his new shirt.

"Goddamned bird," he said.

Wobbling, Guy stood up and tried to put weight on his foot. "Damn!"

"Would you like me to get some help? The truck's about a mile away."

"Oh no, even though it's probably sprained, or strained," he said, acting a little bit like a martyr. "I think I can manage. With your help."

"My help?"

"Let me just put my arm around you. There. That feels better. I think I can make it now."

Biting my tongue for what felt like the longest, most loathsome mile I had ever walked, I dragged Guy across the prairie. After the last few days of work—the turmoil of the lost fledgling, the revelation of Chief Joseph National Park, and now, a limping Guy— all the romance of being a wildlife biologist had safely been put to rest.

Chapter Thirty

THE RUSH WAS NOW ON to band the last of the Swainson's hawks. By the third week of July, red-tailed and ferruginous hawks had, for the most part, already fledged their young, and were well into the process of training their babies to be practiced fliers and adept hunters. But the Swainson's hawk nestlings were only now becoming fully feathered and on the verge of leaving the nest. And, being such late nesters, many Swainson's wouldn't be flying until the end of the month. But I would be confined to the office then, until the spraying was done. I needed to complete the banding now.

The Zumwalt, in midsummer, was bursting its seams with new animal life. Raptors of all kinds marked the skies, and their young teetered through the air as they learned control over their broad and beautiful wings. Unlike their accomplished parents, newly fledged birds generally announced their growing talents by squawking each time they tried something new, which only added to all the new sounds of the prairie. Later, when they became more self-assured and accomplished hunters, much of the constant wailing would cease, and with it much of the playfulness I was now seeing.

Newborn ground squirrels, emerging from their protective burrows, scampered like little windup toys in every direction through the Zumwalt. Like the hawks, they also squealed over their newfound freedom, which could be dangerous for them since it often made them an easy meal for a fox or hawk or coyote.

In every direction all things seemed to be burgeoning now—

multiplying, moving, growing in the short summer season. One could almost feel the vibrancy of life, the sense of omnipotence shared by all young things, the bold feeling of confidence that anything was possible.

There was even the hint of a possibility that I might be right about the ground squirrels after all. After carefully going through all the research papers John had found on Belding's ground squirrels, I began to detect a definite pattern—a consensus that seemed to be the antithesis of commonly held thought: *Belding's ground squirrels prefer succulent vegetation*. That simple statement, seemingly so innocuous, held the key to the Zumwalt's prolificacy. *Moist grass was the Belding's ground squirrels' staple food*. In other words, the more succulent the grass, the better the habitat for the squirrels. This being the case, everything the ranchers were doing to improve their rangeland was, in effect, improving the conditions for the little rodent. Better range condition meant more succulent grasses. Therefore, every time ranchers improved the holding capacity of the watershed, or protected soil quality by halting overgrazing, or worked to protect native, perennial species, they unknowingly produced a more favorable habitat for the Belding's, and, as a corollary, for birds of prey.

The same was true of the northern pocket gopher. The better the condition of the rangeland, the more beneficial for the gopher.

These data agreed with the results I was finding, and seeing, every day during my hikes on the prairie. The range that was clothed with perennial species and a large component of flowers supported large populations of the two prey items. In the drainages that were green with moisture, with deeper soils, or in the sod grass thickets in riparian areas, the squirrels were abundant. These were the same places the buteos were congregating to hunt.

I thought again of Dr. Warren's conceptual framework, for here it seemed to make such perfect sense: To understand something is to be able to see it as being essentially a system of simple parts and their relationships forming a whole—a whole essentially simple, ordered, unified, harmonious in role, and beautiful. The Zumwalt, certainly, was all of these things. And the hike over the softly rolling hills leading to Pine Creek was especially glorious in July. Even in the heat of summer, the colors of the landscape were still vivid, with a springtime freshness.

As was typical whenever I walked on the prairie, I couldn't decide whether to look up or down: to the sky, at the cavorting hawks and falcons playing tag with the elfish wind; or to the ground, with its widespread, still-blossoming wildflowers shaken up all together with the eaten-down bunchgrasses.

My joy took a slight dip, however, when I found a red-tailed hawk nesting in a basin adjacent to Pine Creek, sitting on two unhatched eggs. The female bird was still protective of her nest, and didn't appear to realize yet that these eggs would never hatch; they were addled.

Addled eggs occur occasionally among all birds, and I had already found several in nests across the Zumwalt. Of course, their regularity was nowhere near the extreme that had been documented in the endangered peregrine falcon when it had suffered from DDT. Scientists usually couldn't pinpoint exactly why an egg became addled; sometimes it was the weather, sometimes the parent was flushed from the nest for too long—generally, we just didn't know.

This bird's devotion to two lifeless eggs was both noble and sad. I left her to head directly for a Swainson's hawk nest that I knew would have hatched three young by now. Along the ridge top, I watched a Swainson's and ferruginous hawk competing for ownership of a richly green drainage rife with squirrels. From the same vantage point, I could see the Swainson's nest. I recognized it immediately; it was still holding tight to a grotesquely shaped hawthorn bush, pruned unmercifully in its past by cows.

As I closed in, I noticed that neither adult Swainson's hawk bothered to defend the nest. The behavior was not atypical. Swainson's were the tamest of all hawks, and had rarely, if ever, been known to actually attack a human intruder. But when I was nearly on top of the nest, I still reaped no response. I saw the reason then; for the second time this day, I had come upon an unsuccessful nest.

The next drainage over, however, revealed a feisty bunch of four ferruginous nestlings who had already fledged from the nest. Three of the fledglings perched in small ponderosas within a quarter mile of the eyrie, but the fourth sibling, more timorous, clung to the branch the nest was on, sliding back and forth like a canary in a cage. He either hadn't seen me or was paying me scant heed. The bird's attention was focused instead on three vociferous blackbirds chirping at him from below.

Garnering his courage, the young bird, beautifully feathered but still incredibly awkward, flapped his heavy wings to fly to a different tree. Immediately he was attacked by the pestering blackbirds, who could easily outfly him. In an obnoxious group, they flew above him and below him, assailing him from all angles. Terrified, the ferruginous made a lumbered about-face and pumped as fast as he could back to the nest, where the blackbirds couldn't get him.

I decided to leave the poor, frightened big bird alone, and continued on, smiling, to explore all the windings of the interesting drainages that scored the grassland. I could never be sure what I would find around the next bend or up over the next hill. Sometimes it might be a marsh hawk swooping low over a wetland while ruddering his banded tail, or a savannah sparrow playing hide-and-seek with the tall prairie flowers.

Pine Creek, my favorite place, was just ahead, over the next big ridge. I couldn't remember the exact dimensions of the large, corporately owned ranch, but I knew it encompassed all of the drainage and several around it. Although some ranches and farms on the Zumwalt were owned by big out-of-state conglomerates, these were the exception. Austin had told me, however, that on Forest Service and BLM public lands, they were the rule, not the exception. Large corporations, many of them oil and insurance companies, controlled the majority of the public lands, said Austin, and small, family-owned ranches, while holding a majority of the permits, took up only a fraction of the land. Reports over who leased what were highly disparate, however, and no one seemed to understand the big picture well.

Pine Creek was a deeper, broader drainage than many on the Zumwalt. This time of year, I wasn't expecting the same rich assortment of wildflowers as I had seen in early June; but as I hiked up to the ridge, the hills were still awash with colorful flowers. Although most of the early spring species were gone, the nodding blue triteleia, which look like little blue jack-o'-lanterns with papery thin petals, was growing in large patches. Yellow sedum clung to exposed rocks. There were so many hues of yellow, from the delicate cinquefoil, to the brassy sunflower, to the pale crocus yellow of buckwheat. Miner's lettuce, a tasty, edible plant, grew in the understory of small groves of aspen.

Perhaps most pleasing of all was the riotous pink of the sticky geranium. Fields of the tall pink geranium, growing as high as my knees, lay spread across the prairie. Its name had derived from the very sticky leaves that easily stick to boots and legs; the flower itself had little pink blossoms about an inch wide that grew in an open cluster. Growing alongside it were purple prairie smoke and pink penstemon, and all the flowers together cast the landscape in a soft, rosy glow.

As I neared the crest, I suddenly realized that I was no longer hearing any sounds from birds. Even the meadowlarks were quiet, which was peculiar. Sometimes this phenomenon occurred when the sun disappeared completely behind a fluff of cumulus clouds and sent the prairie shuddering into momentary bleakness. But everything now was fully illuminated in bright sunlight; there wasn't a cloud in the sky. I walked on, climbing upward, the only cadence coming from the humming wind and some wayward crickets.

Upon reaching the top of the hill, I stopped abruptly, my

eyes riveted on the sight before me with total incomprehension. Beneath my feet and stretching into the heart of the canyon all the flowers were dead. Every shrub and tree and wildflower lay lifeless and brown and curled up. The only living thing seemed to be grass, growing unnaturally in clumps between the brown litter of dead balsamroot and geranium and paintbrush.

Herbicide. Damn it to hell.

Regaining my bearings, I tried to guess what agent had been used. From the effects—all the dead forbs—I suspected that the herbicide of choice had been 2-4D—all to make room for more grass.

Recent studies were revealing that the toxic chemical in 2-4D did not affect only plants; it was beginning to show up in the tissues of rodents where 2-4D had been applied. This meant it could affect, secondarily, all that fed on rodents, such as hawks. What it might do to animals was still debatable, but judging from the residual noxious fumes that still tinged the air, I guessed that its effect couldn't be altogether healthy.

The reasoning behind the ravage was clear: get rid of the forbs—flowers—and shrubs to make room for more grass. But it didn't work that way: I knew from recent studies that forbs played a role in keeping moisture trapped in the ground, and allowed for succulent grass to continue growing later into the season, which meant more food for livestock.

I debated walking down the drainage: The smell wafting up, however, was salty and unnatural, and I didn't relish exposing myself to the recently sprayed herbicide. The Creek seemed lifeless now. I saw no birds, including Swainson's hawks, convening over Pine Creek.

I knew it would be weeks before I could bring myself to come here again. With growing sadness, I turned away from Pine Creek. Four weeks ago, it had been incredibly diverse and rich and lovely. Now it was devastated.

All for the sake of "management."

Chapter Thirty-One

THE WEEKLONG MALATHION spraying during the last week of July, although inconvenient, gave me more time to reflect on the data and, perhaps even better, hours to talk everything over with Don Baldwin, who probably knew more about the inner workings of the Zumwalt than any other person alive. Don was an expert on grazing. He understood its effects on the vegetation and on many forms of wildlife. Discussing my findings with him, and listening to his thoughtful answers to my questions, gave me still another key to unlock the mystery of the Zumwalt.

Many days, as I lay prostrate over the aerial photographs in the SCS office, marking down the range sites and hawk nests and transect plots, I would mention something that was troubling me. Don, who had a full grasp of the history of the county, often shed light on what had been here before and the reason for the change seen today.

I learned that few stock ponds had existed before 1950 on the Zumwalt. Water was limited to the creek bottoms, and cattle hung around these places, overgrazing them terribly, while leaving perfectly good range alone, for want of water. Also, in the past, livestock was brought in from winter pasture to the grassland very early in the spring. The native bunchgrasses didn't have a chance to get established. This also contributed to much of the grassland's being overgrazed.

Lack of distribution, lack of movement of cattle, early spring grazing—these seemingly innocuous conditions, which were still being proliferated throughout the West, could produce disastrous effects on native rangeland.

But since 1950, Don explained, the Zumwalt had wrestled with a barrage of range improvements, which many ranchers willingly took part in. Thousands of stock ponds were dug in the Zumwalt. To protect the fragile riparian area, many of these were fenced off and the water moved through a pipe to a trough for use by cattle. Also, early spring grazing was eliminated.

I thought again of my surprise at not finding any cows on the prairie when I first arrived. This was the explanation. Cows, as Ben McPherson had told me on our hike through Findley Buttes, were not put out on the prairie until June 1. The native grasses had time to grow, which allowed for enough green material for adequate photosynthesis and time enough to go to seed, for ongoing propagation.

The grazing regime practiced on the Zumwalt, I learned, was known as "deferred rotation" grazing. A rancher's entire spread was cross fenced into a medley of four different pastures. Each quarter section was grazed during the late spring, summer, and early fall. And, each year, a different quarter section was used as the starting section, so the one used the previous year was allowed to rest for most of the summer. This plan allowed the entire range to be grazed, but no single part very heavily; animals were moved, and the same pasture was not grazed the same season for two years in a row. According to Don, wherever bluebunch wheatgrass or Idaho fescue was the dominant grass, this grazing system was preferred.

Don explained, too, that two other grazing systems were heavily used—"season-long" and "Savory's management"—but both presented problems. The first never gave the grasses time to rest; the second often crowded too many cows in one area, which compacted soil and created overgrazed conditions.

It was a lot of information for me to digest, but the pieces were fitting together. Still, one question nagged me. Like an annoying mosquito bite that itches more when you scratch it, I still wondered what the grassland would be like if, as Sparkey hoped, all the cows were removed. Would that improve the quality of the habitat for hawks and other wildlife?

I finally asked Don. Without answering at first, he dug through stacks of papers in filing cabinets and handed me a slew of scientific literature to read.

"Look at these," he said. "See what you think. Then we'll talk."

For the next three evenings, I read the literature and carefully went over the studies that had been done. And I was astonished—astonished at what my training had been lacking. I knew something about birds. I knew something about wildlife. I knew a bit about grasses. But I didn't understand—had never been taught—how wildlife reacted to grazing. Most wildlife biologists I knew, and most environmentalists, hadn't a clue. And yet here lay the vital link to understanding and to management.

And it all involved something most of us never thought about.

I brought back the papers and dumped them in a heap on Don's desk.

"Got what you were looking for?" Don asked casually.

"More than that. All right, Don. Now I want to hear it in your terms," I said.

"Hear what?"

"About the second and third order consequences we never consider when we advocate removing cows from the prairie."

Don sat back. "You hadn't thought of those?"

"No. Few, if any, of us have, I think. And I worry they might be crucial to wildlife. Maybe we've been wrong. Maybe we're advocating the worst thing possible for the species we're trying to save when we cry to make private lands public or remove all ranchers from public lands. I don't know."

Don smiled and then grew thoughtful. "Marcy, it is true that in the past, and still, unfortunately in some places today, there exist miserable, unacceptable range conditions. But I truly believe it's getting better. And my guess is, if you removed all livestock, or made the private land public, you'd probably end up losing a good portion of your wildlife communities too, especially your deer, and antelope, and some of your birds. People need to be cautioned as to the grave second and third order consequences that very likely will take place by removing all livestock, which could destroy the very objectives they hope to achieve."

"Such as —"

"You'll lose your secondary grazers."

Secondary grazers, I knew, meant animals that have small rumens—the first stomach in the digestive chamber of a cud-chewing, ruminating animal such as deer, elk, or cattle. Secondary grazers include deer and antelope, as well as sage grouse and geese, and my Belding's ground squirrels and pocket gophers. All of these animals are not capable of taking large volumes of low-quality forage and turning it into food for themselves. They need high-quality forage, tender and succulent, and, generally, regrowth.

Primary grazers are species that have a large rumen compared with their body weight—elk, bison, caribou, and cows. These animals can eat low-quality forage. The reasoning is that without primary grazers, plants would grow into "wolf plants"—overgrown, not succulent, and having excessive standing leached residues. It is widely recognized that as a plant matures, its nutritional value declines.

Since both wild and domestic grazing animals prefer regrowth forage, it is important to have some kind of grazing done by primary grazers (elk and cows) to allow for grasses and plants to sprout regrowth forage. Otherwise, there would be no available food for many species of wildlife, the "overmature plants" not being acceptable food.

I remembered reading that in historic times, in places where there were no bison, like the Zumwalt and much of Oregon, early settlers almost starved because there were so few deer and antelope and other animals.

"Unfortunately," Don continued, "I think if you remove all livestock, which means all the ranchers too, we'll probably go back to those old presettlement days, when Ogden got excited if he saw one raven or coyote or crow. I'm talking private ranchers now, not those ranchers operated by ranch managers working for corporations. Many of those, I think, can be poorly run."

Although I didn't say so at the time, I thought to myself, considering last week's experience on Pine Creek, how sadly true his words were.

"Probably this will happen if grazing is prohibited on public lands: You'll see a great increase of cattle on private lands," said Don. "This could have a real negative effect. In eastern Oregon, about 50 percent of big-game critical winter range and a sizable proportion of crucial riparian areas occur on private lands. So it's important to remember, all resource management decisions, whether on public or private lands, have wildlife habitat implications."

"So, what you're saying is that livestock can be used as a tool to enhance wildlife habitat?" I asked pointedly.

"If it's done right, if the health of the grass—its growth and reproduction—is given top priority, with as much or more consideration as the health of the grazing animal, then I'll answer a qualified yes."

"You say *qualified?*" I questioned.

"Yes, qualified," Don replied. "You know, you've seen with your own eyes what a challenge it is. The real art of it all, as my pal Bill Anderson says, is to combine use *with* preservation, not use *versus* preservation."

"You're right you know, Don," said a sprightly voice from a doorway. We turned to see a small, white-haired woman, wearing jeans and cowboy boots, leaning against the doorjamb.

"Why Cressie, what the devil are you doing here?"

"I was in the building and thought I'd come say hello to one of my favorite rangers." The woman's sunny blue eyes sparkled, and her small features gave her an elflike quality.

Don introduced us. "Draw up a chair, Cressie," he said jovially.

"Oh, I can't stay. I must get back to work. I've heard about your work with the hawks, dear," she said to me, with a pleasant lilting voice. "I've always been extremely fond of them."

"You may or may not have been on Cressie's ranch, Marcy. Weaver Ranch. It's out Elk Mountain way. Homesteaded in eighteen eighty, wasn't it, Cressie?"

"Eighteen seventy-nine," she corrected, "by my father. What a wonderful growing up we had."

"You still work the ranch?" I asked.

"Oh my heavens, yes, dear," she said quickly. "If I couldn't do that, I don't think I'd last a minute more. We have a number of hawks at the homestead; there seem to be more every year."

"Why don't you take Marcy on a visit to your ranch sometime, Cressie? I think she'd enjoy it. She could point out the hawks; you could tell her some of the things you've done over the years."

"Over nearly four score years," she replied. I found it difficult to believe that this spunky little lady was nearly eighty years old. "Oh, I'd love to show you Weaver Ranch, dear. Just let me know when you'd like to, and we'll go."

I knew that everything had to be postponed until after the spraying, but the idea of seeing this little woman again and having a tour of her ranch sounded intriguing. "Perhaps sometime in August," I suggested.

"You won't regret it," said Don. "I think we can all learn a lot from this old-timer here."

Driving home later that afternoon, I thought more about secondary and tertiary consequences—all the things that we couldn't readily see but were vital to consider. I looked out over the Zumwalt, feeling chagrined at being closed out by the spraying, which also probably would have some kind of secondary or tertiary effect that no one had thought about.

Who would have thought that cows, such as that repulsive Henry, could have such a range of impacts? In the past I had assumed that all the impacts were negative. Now I was beginning to see that some of the impacts—*if grazing is done properly*—can be positive.

No grazing resulted in no regrowth. No regrowth resulted in wolfy plants. Wolfy plants resulted in no ground squirrels. No ground squirrels meant fewer hawks.

It was cyclical, complex, confusing. But it reminded me of the holistic tie that binds all things together. The only problem was, of course, getting all the different parties involved in resource management to work together, without animosity.

I arrived home and was surprised at the number of cars parked in front of Mrs. DeLacy's. It looked as if she must be hosting a large party. Funny, she hadn't said anything this morning about a party.

TOURIST HOME—VACANCY: The hand-painted placard was placed solidly in the ground directly ahead of the front porch steps. Tourist home? A man and a woman were in the process of taking their luggage inside. Another single gentleman was walking out the front door.

This was crazy! What was going on?

Leaving my gear in the car, I ran inside to look for Mrs. DeLacy. I found her upstairs in my room, taking out the second twin bed, which I didn't use.

"Oh, hi," she said. "Could you help me for a moment? Just pick up the other end of this bed and we'll carry it down the hall to Donald's room."

Not knowing quite how to respond, I lifted the foot of the bed. Together we lugged it to Donald's large, dark room, with posters of motorcycles of every kind splashed across the walls. Putting it down beside one wall, I finally collected myself enough to ask her who all the people were.

"Renters," she answered calmly. "You have worked out so splendidly that I thought I should expand. Any little bit of extra cash helps. Don't worry, though," she added, sensing my concern. "These people won't be staying more than one or two nights. They're overflow from the motel. Those rooms are all taken. Did you see my sign outside?"

"Yes. . . ."

"It looks good, doesn't it? The varnished sheen on the wood makes it pretty eye-catching, don't you think? I'm only going to have it up on weekends. The rest of the week should be quiet."

"How many people are you considering having?" I asked, hearing another car drive up outside.

"Well, right now I have room for fourteen."

Fourteen strangers! What was this woman thinking of! "Are you—are you going to cook for all of them?"

"Oh, heavens no," she said, her muffled voice coming from the closet, where she was digging out a large mirror that had been stored there. "I'm planning on putting this in the basement, and that extra set of dressers in the back of your closet. Maybe you can help me. No, indeed, this won't be a bed and breakfast. Everyone will have to make do for themselves. But they all seem real grateful for the rooms. They won't bother you."

"*But just who are they?*" I wanted to scream. But Mrs. DeLacy was already gone, to answer the doorbell.

Annoyed and demoralized, I walked over to my window. Someone was taking luggage from his Volvo. Perhaps I should get all my equipment, and cameras, from my truck. They were just lying there out in the open; I should put them in my room. But what good would it do? If any of these people were thieves, they would have no problem coming right into my room.

This was ridiculous! First, shut out of the Zumwalt; now, shut out of my own house.

Mrs. DeLacy was chatting away in high spirits downstairs. Feeling overwhelmed by all the noise and activity swirling about the house, I limped down the hall to the bathroom in search of some privacy. I had to think about this. Suddenly I found myself feeling more like just another homeless character than a member of her "family." And what about Donald? Was he going to share his room with someone?

Trying the handle to the bathroom door, I was surprised to find it locked. I tried again, wondering if Donald perhaps had mistakenly thrown the lock. The strange voice from inside was so unexpected that I jumped back from the door as if I had been scalded.

"Just cool your heels out there!" it cried. "It's *taken!*"

Chapter Thirty-Two

The "tourist home" lasted all of two weekends. One night I returned home to find Mrs. DeLacy and all the renters gone, and a log, having rolled out from the fireplace, merrily ablaze on the Oriental rug in the living room. Grabbing the first thing I could find—a crocheted afghan draped on the back of the sofa—I beat at the flames until they were out, then kicked the still smoldering log back into the fireplace. One of the renters, apparently, had chosen to start a fire on this cool August day and forgotten to close the fire screen when leaving the house for the evening.

After that, the stream of strangers became a thing of the past, and a welcome peace settled back into the old Victorian farmhouse. Mrs. DeLacy cleverly turned around the rug and rearranged the living-room furniture to hide the most visible marks of the fire, but a charred section of blue carpet always peeked out from one end of the couch as a silent reminder of the night she nearly lost her house.

My room became a place of statistical analyses, charts, tables, and taped-together maps, with piles of research papers arranged by subject stacked along the walls. So many parts, so many interconnecting parts, but as the results kept coming in and the data accumulating, a rather strange hypothesis began to emerge.

The facts were there, and they were significant: The Zumwalt Prairie had one of the densest concentrations of buteos in all of North America. All three western species of buteo, from the red-tail to the ferruginous and Swainson's, occurred in good numbers and appeared to be thriving. Seventy-six percent of the nesting pairs had laid eggs, and of those, 73 percent were successful. These were encouraging figures.

As an added benefit, the mosaic of range sites, each with its different characteristics as a result of climate, soils, and geomorphology, allowed for a diversity of nesting sites pleasing to the tastes of hawks, as well as owls, falcons, and eagles. The birds could "partition" themselves as they wished, and thus reduce competition between them.

In general, the rangeland was in good condition, which benefited the ground squirrels and hawks, as well as the cows and elk. All told, what was happening here was positive, and advantageous to wildlife; and, what's more, it seemed to be in balance. Ranchers, squirrels, cows, grass, trees, water, hawks, in balance.

Austin didn't believe me. Neither did Peter or Glenn. Sparkey, of course, spread the rumor that I had been "bought off" by the SCS and the ranchers, and my results were biased by my sympathy for them. If only he had known: I had come to the Zumwalt determined to find almost the opposite of what my results were revealing. My "sympathy," if I were pressed to the wall, was with the hawks, with wildlife; certainly not with any rancher's cows. But what if, in that search for good conditions for birds of prey and other native species, it turned out that what ranchers were doing actually *benefited* those wild creatures I cared about? Was this a form of "selling out"?

I needed balance in my thinking. I needed new eyes, someone from the outside, someone objective, to come out and see this place, and examine the results I was obtaining. Besides Dr. Charles Henny, a nationally respected raptor biologist, I could think of one other scientist whose work I highly respected. Dr. Chris Maser was a profound thinker, author of numerous books and articles, and an expert in wildlife and the range science. At midnight, on August 3, I penned a letter to both of them, requesting that they look at this area that, in my view, was highly unusual in many respects.

To my delight, within a week Dr. Henny had phoned Austin

to tell him that both he and Dr. Maser were coming to observe the Zumwalt with me during the second week of August. The spraying would be well over by then.

Austin sat sprawled on the plastic chair of Mrs. DeLacy's patio, sipping a glass of lemonade, when he told me the news. Dr. Henny had not been able to reach me by phone, since Mrs. DeLacy's was still disconnected. Mrs. DeLacy was well pleased with herself that she had "solved" the problem of Janelle hounding Donald. Of course, she didn't know that Donald was spending most of his time at a pay phone down the street.

"I think Peter's coming with us when you take us on the Zumwalt tour," Austin said, stretching and helping himself to the box of gingersnaps. He really did seem like a powerful polar bear—big and awkward-looking, but inwardly lithe and quick, ready to strike if the occasion warranted. "We're all pretty curious to see this grassland, where you're coming up with such conflicting statements."

"But, Austin, they don't conflict," I said. "Don't you see—I thought they would, but now, as I am beginning to understand how the whole thing works, I'm realizing that what seemingly clashed really is the reason for the harmony of the Zumwalt."

"Maser will set you straight," said Austin encouragingly. "You're a little mixed up right now is all."

"But I'm not, Austin."

"Mixed up about guys, too. Let me give you some brotherly advice, okay? Stay clear of Peter; he's no good for you."

"First you're my professor; now Ann Landers?"

"Marcy, I've always been fond of you. I've felt about you like I do my kid sister. You're a little nutty at times, a little too pure and goody-two-shoes for my taste, but that's all right. It takes all kinds to make a world. Peter would ruin you."

Austin was getting entirely too personal, and I was annoyed. "It's none of your business, Austin."

"I think it is. I'm the one who found you that dark night,

remember, you and that gun, alone and frightened at the Deanes' ranch."

"I wasn't frightened. You and that rotten practical joke of yours just startled the daylights out of me."

"I've defended your name when Sparkey's disparaged it, risked my life numerous times climbing your trees for you, and killed a hawk you left to die, and I didn't tell anyone about it."

He shoved three more gingersnaps at once into his mouth. "Ben McPherson's a country boy, a nice boy, but you with your strong ways would run him over. Peter, on the other hand, would never give you the love and respect you need."

"I've heard quite enough, Austin. What makes you think you have the right to talk to me this way?"

"You know what Peter says about you at the Range Rider Tavern, after he's brought you home from a date?" Austin continued, utterly ignoring me. "I've heard him. He tells his buddies, 'She's as much fun as a poke in the eye with a sharp stick.'"

"I don't believe it."

"You with your love of beauty and all would be dragged through the mud of taverns and good ol' boys and stuff that would kill your spirit. Deep down you've got to know that."

"I don't know a thing about what you're saying."

"Yes you do. If you'd just quit flitting around like a moth to different candles, quit trying to be the belle of the ball, and look into yourself, you'd realize that John Houle is the one for you. He's a great guy. Good sense of humor, a lot like me. He'd make you happy. Peter'd murder you."

I stood up. "I've had enough of this, Austin. What do you know about any of this? I've got to get to work."

Austin stretched and leaned over to tighten the shoelaces of his black forest boots. "Ol' Lady DeLacy could tell you. She's got eyes like an owl. She's raised more kids than anyone else in the county. Why don't you ask her?"

"There's nothing to ask, and I'm perfectly aware of my feelings,"

I said, although this ridiculous conversation was giving me a peculiar feeling of doubt.

I didn't dare tell Austin that Mrs. DeLacy, after meeting John, was impressed with him and had not refrained from telling me so in blunt terms. She did not approve of Peter, nor Austin and Eric. The whole thing annoyed me because she was acting like my mother. She had said, at the conclusion of her monologue, that people should be with "the one they're peaceful with." Love life? Peaceful? I was surprised that I wasn't more shocked or disappointed over what Peter was saying about me. But it still was humiliating.

But John? What about him? My friend—the one man I respected above anyone else. Ever since I'd met him in Colorado three years ago, and after all the crazy things we'd been through together with the peregrine falcons, he was still the person I could always count on—one who inspired my complete trust. From somewhere deep inside, I knew that what both Austin and Mrs. DeLacy had said was true. Peter and I shared different values; Ben could make me impatient at times; Guy was, well—Guy. But John was the one man with whom I could always laugh—whom I felt peaceful with.

I fought these thoughts down instantly, and looked at my watch.

"See ya next Tuesday," Austin said, rising to go. "I'll be by early with Chuckles and Maser."

I watched Austin speed out of the driveway, then turned to collect my gear for the day. Leaning against the door frame were twenty posts and twenty little flags to mark the location of the ground squirrel counts I was running.

Perhaps the ground squirrels and I were fated to be friends after all. At least they were inquisitive and congenial—more so than some people I could name, and they didn't care if I was only as fun to be around as a poke in the eye with a sharp stick. Plus, they were cute little chattery beggars.

I sighed. With my luck, they would probably give me the plague.

Early the following Tuesday, Chris Maser and Chuck Henny arrived in the Chevy Suburban station wagon, driven by Austin. Peter was not with them, but Glenn Smith was. We almost had all the government bases covered: Dr. Maser with the Bureau of Land Management, Dr. Henny with the U.S. Fish and Wildlife Service, Austin of the U.S. Forest Service, and Glenn Smith with the Oregon Department of Fish and Game. Only the Soil Conservation Service and the National Park Service were missing. Ironically, not one of us who were to examine and potentially make decisions about the Zumwalt were private property owners.

It was obvious from the beginning that Dr. Maser was highly skeptical. Dr. Henny, too, had doubts about my findings, and seemed to be somewhat worried that perhaps he had hired the wrong person for the study. Dr. Henny climbed out of the car, leaving me to squeeze in between him and Austin, with Dr. Maser directly behind me. Trying to arrange my long legs around the stick shift in a car full of four very serious, unsmiling characters, I found the ordeal similar to a preliminary examination for one's Ph.D. or, even more, a courtroom investigation where I was the defendant.

It didn't matter; soon they would see the Zumwalt for themselves and understand my own perplexity over the last months. I turned around to say hello to Glenn and take a closer look at Chris Maser. He was, I knew, a guru of sorts in wildlife management, well known throughout the country, and highly thought of among scientists as well as environmentalists. The aviator sunglasses he wore kept me from seeing his eyes, making it difficult to get a "read" on him; but I could tell from his dark, closely cropped hair and fit physique that he was probably somewhere in his forties. I guessed that Dr. Henny was in his fifties. He was more of an administrator type, although also an extremely well respected and well published scientist. He too sported a crew cut, the style of choice by a surprising number of wildlife biologists, who probably give little thought to their appearance, preferring function over fashion. Also, a crew cut makes it easy to pull on those ugly, tight green visors they always seem to wear.

Dr. Maser set the tone, as we motored down the highway heading to old Zumwalt Road, by peppering us with bitter comments about ranchers in general. Maser had many years of experience with public rangelands all over the West, most of them in inadequate shape; obviously, he expected to find the same kind of condition here.

Maser made the statement, to which all the men nodded in agreement, that ranchers too often were a greedy lot. "The problem with them," he said, in the objective monotone of a scientist speaking from a podium, "is that they all manage for their damn livestock, not the range. They put as many cows as possible on their land to get as much of a product and profit as they can, and just let the land go to hell."

"Don't the Forest Service and BLM do that as well, manage for the product?" I said, playing devil's advocate. "Don't those agencies create just as many problems on public lands?"

"She's right there," agreed Austin.

Dr. Henny, leaning slightly forward on the lookout for hawks, asked, "You have Townsend's here?"

He was speaking of ground squirrels, I knew, and I also knew what he was getting at. Townsend's were an indication of poor range condition.

"Not Townsend's. Belding's. I think I mentioned that in my letter."

"Are the animals reddish or gray?" asked Dr. Maser.

The question irritated me, as if I didn't know how to recognize the difference between the two species of ground squirrel. But I answered cordially, well aware that I was being tested on the soundness of my reasoning.

"Reddish, Dr. Maser," I said, turning around to face myself in the reflective aviation glasses. "Basically gray, like the Townsend's, but tinged with red above and below, with a brown streak running down the middle of the back. They call them red diggers here."

"Yes, I know that," replied Maser.

We turned onto Zumwalt Road and began the long, winding, rough ride that I now knew so well that I could recognize every twist and turn with my eyes closed and know exactly where I was on the prairie. Hundreds of sprightly horned larks flitted along the fence posts and darted and flapped in front of the Suburban. Red-winged blackbirds, with their colorful arm bands, haunted the drainage ditches, while immature buteos of every species could be seen sitting on telephone poles, not moving until we were almost upon them. Sometimes they would only perch and watch the car go by; other times they would wait until the last minute to take off, and swoop down, always with their sharp eyes on us. Cheerful purple daisies and white yarrow blurred alongside the red dirt road.

Both Maser and Henny were quiet, observing. I had Austin stop at mile intervals to show everyone a sampling of the buteo nests, many of which were no longer occupied but were still considered part of a hawk family's territory. Most of the time we stayed in the car, but in several spots I had everyone climb out to get a feel for the land, the vegetation, the other small animals. We walked to some close nests; I showed them representatives of range condition and ground squirrel transects. We also ran a few of our own, coming up with the same, standard results, ranging from high-fair to good condition, and a range of two to eleven ground squirrel burrows per two-hundred-foot transect.

Halfway around the Zumwalt–Crow Creek Loop, Henny made a surprising observation, one that he must have guarded closely for a long time.

"You know," he began thoughtfully, "some of the current thinking by Lokemoen in Colorado is that perhaps the most important factor, in the absence of pesticides, which determines population levels of grassland raptors, is land use."

He went on to cite a new study, recently published by a well-respected scientist. I was familiar with it. But as Dr. Henny began to explain it to the rest of the men, I thought anew about its significance. The facts he was relating may indeed, I realized, have more to do with the future success of nesting hawks than any other single issue. And J.T. Lokemoen's conclusions were strikingly similar to what I had been observing all spring and summer on the Zumwalt.

Lokemoen had said, in so many words, that what he had learned from his raptor studies in Colorado may seem contrary to popular opinion. But he was finding, verified by statistical evaluation, that the large, most closely controlled private ranches made the best raptor nesting habitat. He also concluded something so startling that many wildlife biologists would find it difficult to believe until they thought about it carefully: "For decades, cattle ranchers have been managing raptor populations by keeping human disturbance at a minimum on their land."

The phrase "keeping disturbance at a minimum on their land" jumped out as the missing ingredient I had been searching for ever since I had arrived on the Zumwalt. Oh, there were cows, all right, and they could be obnoxious, I well knew. And a problem. But there weren't hordes of people here or activities going on. As many scientists had already confirmed, nesting raptors and lots of people just don't mix.

Another issue affects hawks—the condition of the rangeland. To benefit wildlife, private ranches must be in good condition. And this, I knew, was where the Zumwalt shone. As we continued our grassland tour, I sensed my companions' incredulity changing slowly to enthusiasm. Intermingling with cows were vast areas of still-green native bunchgrass, waving, shimmering like a hand stroking a pelt of exquisite fur. Driving hour after hour along the ruts, along the unpeopled expanse, I slowly watched Chris

Maser become converted, as did Dr. Henny and Glenn, and even Austin.

"You know, Chuck," began Dr. Maser, as we stood outside the truck, examining the soil for erosion, "if everybody took care of the range as the folks here do, our rangelands wouldn't have ninety percent of the problems that they have now."

Henny nodded, and Maser threw away a handful of ground he was holding. "This is the best-looking range I've seen in the West for years," he added. "You were right, Marcy; I didn't think it still existed."

The five of us directed our eyes to a Swainson's hawk swooping down on a red-tail that apparently had trespassed above a green swale, rife with squirrels, that the Swainson's considered his own. While we watched the short-lived confrontation, I knew without a doubt that although my knowledge and experience with rangelands was not as vast as that of these men—*that* I would eagerly concede—what I did know, and had grown to deeply love, was the Zumwalt. And now, at last vindicated in their eyes, I wanted to shout for joy.

My joy wasn't only for me, but for the existence of a place like this: a shining example for other rangelands across the country; a native grassland prairie where ranchers were managing first not for their livestock but for their range.

Here, I realized, was the key. Here, lay all the difference.

Chapter Thirty-Three

IN LESS THAN A MONTH'S TIME, a change more penetrating and widespread than any effect produced by cows, or by aerial sprays or random field cultivation, swept the prairie.

Fall was coming.

Nothing people could do could stop it. And although the feel of it was subtle—cooler mornings and nights, shorter days—the reaction of the animals of the Zumwalt was profound.

By mid-August, just when I expected things to be rolling full swing, the adult male ground squirrels began disappearing, not to be seen again. A week later, adult females and juvenile Belding's ground squirrels began to vanish.

I knew what was happening, but it seemed too early. Something inside me wasn't ready for this yet. We were just getting started.

But the ground squirrels and hawks and owls and all the rest of the wild things that lived in the quiet grassland knew exactly what they were doing. By the middle of July, the Belding's ground squirrels were getting ready for fall. They began to consume dramatically larger amounts of food, by mid-August doubling their weight and increasing their fat content fifteen times. Belding's have one of the longest hibernation periods of all North American animals. They don't cache food, like many of their relatives, but instead store as fat all the energy they need to survive the long winter months. Their short burst of activity—which had seemed to terrorize the prairie in the summer while they mated and scampered and raised their young—was now at its end. For eight long months it would be as if they never had existed on the prairie.

The hawks would feel the change. All the food they had depended on since arriving in spring would be gone. And so, with the fading of the squirrel, would come the withdrawal of the buteos from the prairie. The skies no longer would hear their cries or be decorated with their flight.

The ground squirrels of the Zumwalt had benefited from the range's good condition and had stayed aboveground far longer than in many places. For just as the Belding's ground squirrel's emergence from hibernation is timed with the availability of green vegetation, its disappearance coincides with the drying up of the grasses in midsummer. On the Zumwalt, with its good supply of native grasses, the Belding's enjoyed a longer season aboveground. Once again, here was a secondary consequence of responsible grazing practices: the better condition range produced a better food supply for the squirrels and hence the hawks.

Many of the adult buteos were already gone by early September. Some of the immature red-tails that had fledged in the summer, however, were still hanging around on fence posts and perching on cottonwoods in the cultivated areas near town, on the lookout for pocket gophers. Red-tailed hawks' family groups split up with the coming of fall migration. Parents departed together but left their young to go it alone. Swainson's hawks, however, are more social creatures, and right up until actual migration time, young fledglings remained very dependent on their parents to feed them, protect them, teach them. They hunted together as families, and presumably left together, grouping with larger associations as they began their long trip in late summer to South America.

In the weeks following the malathion spraying, I had been looking for any noticeable impacts on the prairie, and on the Swainson's hawks in particular. I had not been able to discern anything. The Swainson's hawk nests had all fledged their young with apparent success. The fate of those fledglings later in the season was hard to determine, though, and long-term results of the spraying would be difficult to judge, considering the complex range of factors impinging on the ecosystem.

My eyes still expectantly searched the skies, hoping to see life and flight, although it was vanishing daily. The rapidly overtaking stillness was haunting and disconcerting, and something inside me railed against it, not wanting to give up the exploding passion of summer, whereas Cressie Green, with whom I was driving today, seemed to take it all with calm acceptance, having seen it happen for seventy-eight years. The roll and sway of the seasons, the ebbs and flows, the riches and losses, the striking effect of fall and winter on every living thing on the prairie, were to her merely a fact of life.

I had been looking forward to this day for many weeks. Cressie had said she would take me to the ranch her father had homesteaded on the Zumwalt over a hundred years ago, and I hoped to learn from her more of the history of the remote grassland—things that could not be found in books or research reports. Few of the old-timers were left, and lifestyles were changing dramatically, although many of their sons and daughters and grandchildren still worked the prairie. Cressie still owned and operated the same ranch where she had been born nearly eighty years before, a rarity in this transient age. Many ranches on the Zumwalt, in fact, were owned by and passed down in the same family for generations.

As I drove along Swamp Creek Road heading for Gould Gulch, I stole glances at this tiny woman, no more than five feet tall, whose unlined face held an uncommon contentment. Yet for all her small stature and outward calm, I sensed almost a kinetic energy within, evidenced by her lively blue eyes and youthful zest. Something of the grandeur and strength of the Zumwalt seemed to be a part of her, and I was struck again by how much people are formed by the landscape in which they are brought up and live.

We are all products of landscape. That is the problem inherent in cities with little or no green spaces. Studies show that children brought up with frequent encounters with the natural world display enhanced physical, intellectual, and social development. Urban natural areas and wildlife are two important keys to protecting our quality of life. Yet too often, people have to travel to distant locations in order to view wildlife and inspiring scenery. And it is getting worse. Eighty percent of the United States population now live in highly developed areas. We are becoming a generation severed from the natural landscape.

"Right over there used to be the old Presbyterian church," said Cressie, pointing up toward a hill of aspen. Her eyes seemed to be reliving memories as we passed different places, and the pictures she spun conjured up a Zumwalt that had disappeared long ago. "It was always a bit of a mystery what really happened to it. After a few years people quit coming to church, and started having dances there instead. And it burned down, one day, just like that." Cressie's mischievous eyes twinkled. "Probably the wrath of God, don't you know."

"And right over there used to be the old McKinney homestead," she continued, indicating a ring of old trees. "To you, I suppose, it only looks like scattered prairie dust, but in the old days there was a beautiful big farmhouse there. Laura McKinney was a dear friend; she had seven brothers. They'd walk to school every day over that hill; it was only three miles away. I was always sorry we didn't go to the same school. There used to be a number of schoolhouses in the Zumwalt at the turn of the century."

I remembered the old one-room schoolhouse I had discovered on one of my long treks down Swamp Creek. Ever since then I had hoped to find someone who knew something about it.

"Might I know something about that old school?" replied Cressie to my question. "Why, of course I do. That, dear, was *my* school," she said, with a whimsical smile. "So, the old thing's still standing? I'd love to see it again."

"You would?"

"Only if you have the time," she responded. "We could drive

down Mark Taggart's livestock road; I know he wouldn't mind. I've brought my gate gloves with me."

She held the worn leather gloves out before her and slipped them on, in a smooth, well-practiced motion.

"Cressie," I said, as we approached a barbed-wire gate leading to the cutoff, "let me get the gates."

"Don't you dare," she adjured, raising her eyebrows. "I've been doing this for many, many more years than you. You just stick to the driving." She jumped out as soon as the truck had come to a halt, and, after a springing walk to the gate, deftly opened it. I was impressed. I well knew how difficult many of these ranch gates were to open; they required finesse as well as a good amount of strength.

After we passed through three gates, the road ended abruptly with a locked fence. I looked on as Cressie, unperturbed, got out of the truck, motioning for me to follow, and lithely scaled the five-tiered barbed-wire fence with ease. She moved as gracefully and quickly as a prairie rabbit; I had to walk at a brisk clip to keep up with her. At the top of the biscuit-scabland overlooking a gulch, we could see the tumbledown schoolhouse sitting like a forsaken, lone soldier in the middle of the meadow. A golden sheen, cast by the early morning sun, rippled against the old glass windows.

"It was a dear, wonderful place," said Cressie, hiking along without a trace of fatigue. I looked around for all the cows that I had shooed away when here a few months ago, but they were nowhere to be seen.

"How many years were you here?" I asked, still working to keep up, which was hard to believe, for my legs were half again as long as hers. This woman should be running marathons.

"I went to school here from kindergarten until eighth grade. It was quite a distance from home, but I didn't mind, for I rode my horse, Bonnie. In those days there was a barn next to the school, where schoolchildren tethered their horses during the day. I see the fence is gone too."

"What fence?"

"There used to be a fence all around the schoolhouse. With no gate. It was funny, you know. Church was held here on Sundays. The ladies would all come in their best long dresses and have to jump over the fence to get to church. We children found that very entertaining."

Walking inside on the creaking wood floor, I smelled the same musty odor I remembered filling my nostrils before. The room was dark except for streams of pale light licking in through the door and windows. "Do you remember anything special about your years here?" I asked, curious about a life I had never lived.

"Oh, many things," she mused, "but the storms, those winter storms, were really something. Every year the wind would blow so hard at times, and the place creaked and groaned so, we were all sure it was going to fall down all around us."

"Weren't you scared?"

"Oh no," she said spryly. "Why would I be?"

There was something very pleasing about the strong and sure quality of her voice.

"I think the hardest transition for me was when I left this old school and went to the big high school in Enterprise," she continued.

"So you liked going to school here."

"Oh yes, yes indeed. It gave me a lot of things. I learned good, old-fashioned practical living. It gave me self-reliance. It's too bad, in a way, this old place has been ransacked. Someone's taken it all, all the old chairs and desks. It happens these days, you know."

Leaving the school and continuing on to the ranch, Cressie slid on her gate gloves in preparation for all the fences. "Cressie, you must have been a tomboy," I said, laughing.

"Oh, a terrible one!" she said sprightly. "I never was, much to Mother's chagrin, a typical girl. I loved to ride too much. I loved the land, the solitude. Everything about the outdoor life and work I enjoyed. My poor father," she added. "I tagged after him everywhere, pestering him to death!"

A little before noon, we reached Weaver Ranch—or what remained of it. The house was nearly gone; I had expected to find it still standing. Three years before, vandals had come to the homestead and stolen what they could of old sleds, barn wood, horse tack, and old machinery, and then burned the rest to the ground. If anything was left unattended these days, Cressie said, bit by bit and part by part, it disappeared.

I ran my hands over what remained of an old sled and a hand-crafted wagon. The sun warmed the wood and gave it a singular smell; Cressie said proudly that her father had built all the sleighs and wagons. He had been quite a craftsman, as evidenced by the large old barn that still stood behind the ruins of the farmhouse. "My brother and I used to love to climb up on the very top of that old barn," she said. "We were naughty; we'd scamper up, hold onto the top for dear life, and peek over at my parents' house to see what they were up to. One day my mother discovered us hanging there, and had the fright of her life. We were quickly and suitably disciplined."

As much as I loved the Zumwalt, as I gazed on the miles of empty space stretching from the ghost farm I found it difficult to imagine living so far away from everything for year after year. I asked Cressie if she was ever lonely out here.

"Never lonely, dear," she answered with a gentle smile that lit up her face, revealing something of what she must have looked like in her youth. "In those days before the depression, every 160 acres on the Zumwalt had a farm. The road we were just driving on was alive with people then, going to and from town in their buggies and wagons in summer, and in winter tucked cozily in their sleds and sleighs. Because we were known to have the best spring water far and wide, not a buggy would go by and not stop to get some."

"It seems so hard to believe, seeing it now."

"Between people visiting, school and church, the ranch work, and the dances, we were a busy lot." She read the lack of comprehension on my face. "Dances are another thing that have disappeared," she explained, with a hint of sadness. "In the old days, you see, ranchers opened up their homes and people came from all around to dance. Seems like there was more time then. Everyone would get together, parents and children alike, and someone would play the fiddle and somebody else the organ, and we would dance and dance. I don't think there ever was a rancher that didn't love to dance."

Cressie handed me my sack lunch and, still grasping hers, plopped down on the ground in a spot around what must have been an old campfire ring. I smiled at the picture she made; small and sturdy and ageless, short legs clad in clean blue jeans and flexibly crossed Indian fashion. How many eighty-year-olds could do that? She seemed such a part of this ranch. I sat down beside her, feeling relaxed and glad for the chance to be here, to enjoy the sun, in these last days of August that felt just right—not too hot, not too chilly yet. The ponderosa pines surrounding the homestead were threading the wind like fingers stroking a cello. This music, however, was wild, and with it came a delicious upwelling of the fragrance of dying needles.

"Would you care for a cookie? How 'bout a banana," offered Cressie, handing them over from her sack. "I must admit, I'll never get over having to pack a lunch. I put in either too little, or too much. In the old days we never packed lunch when we were out riding. When we got hungry, we'd just stop at the nearest farmhouse and have lunch there. If the folks weren't home, that wasn't a problem. No doors were locked. You just went inside and helped yourself, but you were sure to always do the dishes, and leave things just as you found them," she said merrily.

I asked Cressie if she still rides.

"Of course I do. But I don't ride quite as much as I used to, for I have a little dog now, you see, that can't keep up with my horse. So I hike along with Higgins, and my husband, Paul, rides. But riding is still the love of my life. When I was growing up, I rode everywhere. I was familiar with every canyon, hill, creek, and gulch. Sometimes I'd go by the Indian camps; of course, that was a *long* time ago. There was one about a mile from here. There were mostly squaws and children, and they used to camp here a few days each year when I was little. I'd ride by and try to talk to them, but they would only laugh and laugh. Couldn't understand a word I was saying, I guess."

"I'll bet you're not afraid of anything, Cressie," I said, with genuine respect.

"Oh, I'm afraid of some things," she said matter-of-factly, "but nothing out here, on the Zumwalt. Cougars don't scare me and neither do bears. Nothing about the land. But I *am* afraid of people."

This surprised me. "Have you always been?"

"Oh no! I used to never be afraid of a single soul! No one was, out here, you know. But in the last years, people have changed." I leaned back on my hands and waited for her to go on. "Life has changed, even way out here. What you're seeing is not going to be around for much longer. You look surprised. Dear, ranchers are a dying breed. People from the city have moved in. And they don't know or care about the life we used to live. It's funny, you know, in a way. People blame us for so many things."

She stood up and smiled a secret, elfish smile to herself. "But you know? In those olden days, we had fun. We were happy. I've been blessed with a very happy life. I don't envy anyone anything."

For one piercing moment, as Cressie walked over to get something from the barn, I found myself strangely envious. Cressie Green's square, straight shoulders had not a flinch about them as she walked, although mine slumped.

We are losing something, I thought with regret. *We are losing a set of values just as surely as we are losing our native species.* But what could anyone do about it? I looked around at the wooden fences and unpainted barn and the aspen trees shaking their dancing leaves over my head. Maybe their stewardship wasn't perfect, and maybe there was room for improvement, but I wondered if perhaps some of these old-time family ranchers had a love and understanding of the land that went deeper than our government wisdom. There was a pride—I had seen it—in the families where ranches had been passed down. What would happen to the land if, through untenable laws and sky-high fees, ranchers were permanently evicted?

Cressie didn't seem to know anything about the national park plan for this area. But over the last weeks I had been hearing more and more about it, from various sources. Many talked about the creation of Hell's Canyon/Chief Joseph National Park as a very likely reality.

Guy, of course, was all for it: He would probably get a new job. Peter and Glenn were enthusiastic, thinking it would improve the area for wildlife because it would eliminate cows. Austin, however, after our day on the prairie with Maser and Henny, was beginning to vacillate.

As was I. How, exactly did I feel about it? I hadn't completely made up my mind, although some of the recent statistics I had read made me very uncomfortable. According to park rangers across the nation, tourists, coming in such numbers and bringing with them their four-wheel-drive off-road vehicles and mountain bikes and cars, were beginning to burst many of our national parks at their seams. Recreation had turned aggressive, and demands for the comforts of home followed the multitudes fleeing the cities. Serious environmental damage was being done at many of our parks, and many were in a profound state of disrepair, suffering abuses at the same time the manpower necessary to deal with the problems was shrinking. The whole purpose of our national parks had changed dramatically over the last decade. Originally, they had been set aside for their beauty, and for their value as a repository of biological and scenic diversity; they were now becoming, first and foremost, tourist attractions.

The face of the West was on the verge of changing. Espresso bars and modems and ORVs were beginning to take the place of the sweat, dirt, and tears of generations. With the elimination of ranchers, the floodgates could at last be opened wide and the proliferation of more and more Vail, Colorados, and Jackson Hole, Wyomings, made possible.

Seeing Cressie, all seventy-eight years of her, with a halter just now casually thrown over her shoulder and her gate gloves back on, I realized with sadness that something infinitely precious would disappear with her passing and the passing of people like her. Our working connection with the land would go with the departure of the farmers and ranchers.

Would the grasslands and wildlife be better off then?

Chapter Thirty-Four

BUCKHORN LOOKOUT is one of those places where the real seems to merge with the unreal. It is, literally, the end of the Zumwalt Prairie, for, from Buckhorn, the grassland drops precipitously down, to river canyon blending into river canyon, at last to plunge into the depths of the deepest gorge in the world. No bridge crosses these rivers; Hell's Canyon alone is ten miles across from rim to rim.

It is a land of gold and red, of changing shadows that flow in from far distances. Almost as if in defiance of the unbelievable depth of the gorge, on the eastern rim the Seven Devils Mountains rise to chew the skyline with the rugged beauty of young mountains.

It is also a land of unquestionable stillness, except for the wind, and of few roads and fewer people.

I had come to Buckhorn on this chilly late September day for a special reason: to look back. To look back over the Zumwalt that lay behind it and see at once the whole grassland gently swelling and rolling with soft curves that were no longer green but brown. From this vantage point, the Zumwalt, instead of the "island" it really is, seemed much more a sea—heaving grass for waves and sending up hawks for gulls.

The Wallowa Mountains, capped with an early snowfall, girded in a protective semicircle the southern and western border of this wild empire. It was easy to imagine these rings of mountains acting like a fortress to guard the hidden treasure that is the prairie.

I still couldn't get over the fact that my fieldwork was nearly completed now, although I did have two pairs of worn-out boots to prove it. Nor could I believe that all I had studied had disappeared; since September 8, I had not seen a ground squirrel or, although I constantly scanned the sky, a buteo.

I missed them, I realized, with a bit of a letdown. I missed watching them play on the wind—their dipping and darting, arcing low, then high, while the grass waved in sheets below them, and the shadows scalloped out the ground. I missed seeing them go after the squirrels, artfully hunting those silly red diggers.

I also missed the grazing herds of elk, the spotted mule deer fawns bounding after their mothers over the hills, and the sleepy porcupines with hardly enough energy to open their eyes when I would come upon them sleeping in a tree. Even the cows were gone, most of them brought in from summer range to be pastured on farms in town.

The rattling of the yarrow plants, once white but now brown and gone to seed, caught my attention. I scanned the prairie for color, for the waist-high grasses and sprinklings of wildflowers that had thrown bouquets fit for the gods, but they, too, were gone. Only a few scattered pockets of delicate pink clarkia, a white flower like a tiny button with rosy sepals, gave hint that the sepia-toned grazed hillsides once burned with a full palette of hues.

Standing on the brink of the canyon, feeling the warm sun caressing my face, I reflected on what lay before me with the end of my first field season in the Zumwalt. This winter I would return to the university to continue compiling and analyzing the data, and to pen some of the conclusions of my research. Next spring, with the arrival of the birds again, I would come back to the Zumwalt for another season or two of research. It felt good to know I was coming back.

The Findley Buttes stood out prominently in the autumnal colors of the grassland as my gaze swept south. Something in their starkness reminded me of my first impression of the Zumwalt. Then it had seemed forsaken and lonely. But now, a half year later, the prairie had revealed itself to be a place of unbelievable beauty and diversity, a rich land of incredible value for wildlife, plants, and people. The Zumwalt was a shining example of good stewardship over long generations, but would it stay this way, I wondered, with all the changes threatening it, all the factions pulling on it and desiring to be its keeper?

With sadness I saw the bitter war over the western grasslands being waged between two disparate cultures—environmentalists and ranchers—for what it really is: a tragic irony. It's a war that should never be. If the truth were only realized, these two archfoes would see they are actually allies in the fight to save rangelands from a future neither side wants.

Of course, before I came here, I was just as guilty. Like many others, I thought that ranchers and grazing and wildlife could not mix. But over the course of my research and my days and weeks and months in the field, I had come to discover that grazing is only a tool. I had observed that grazing, like fire management or riparian fencing or the replanting of native species, is a mechanism that can change vegetation composition, density, and structure, and as such, change small mammal and bird populations by altering these species' habitat.

In terms of its consequences, grazing could have varying results. Some, unquestionably, could be detrimental to the resource. These are usually the examples put in front of the public, and those on which decisions are made. But, as evidenced by my Zumwalt findings, when grazing is done with the top priority given to the native vegetation, when the phenology and physiology of the key plant species and the ecological capability of the resource are kept in mind, grazing can richly enhance wildlife habitat. I was coming to realize that these examples needed public exposure too.

In the final measure, it is our approach to stewardship, our focus and goals, that will determine the results. To reap any real lasting success, we must turn our eyes to a land-based philosophy, one where the second and third order consequences are always considered whenever something is done to the land. We need to try to save entire functioning ecosystems. The physical and biological capacities of all the parts need our protection, while keeping our focus on the whole.

The Zumwalt Prairie is a grassland, wild and free and beautiful. What will it look like in one hundred years? In the face of growing population and urbanization, it will take a new, unprecedented kind of cooperation and communication between the public and private sector for us to preserve biodiversity. With the myriad turf matches between agencies and people, this will be an overwhelming task. But if we don't try, if the sides continue to fortify the battle lines, we chance to lose rural places like the Zumwalt to the impending suburbanization of the West. The damage to the landscape resulting from a solely recreation-based economy—one without ranchers, without those people who work the land and deeply care—could potentially be more long lasting and avaricious than that wrought by any cow.

For an instant I thought I heard the gull-like cry of a ferruginous hawk. Whipping around, I saw to my surprise a lone reddish bird, about the size of an eagle, just disappearing over the stony canyon rim. I rushed over to the side of Buckhorn and ran along the rim, hoping to catch sight of it again—that splendid *Buteo regalis*—strong and swift and spirited, the most powerful and grand of all the buteos, and utterly dependent on wild, uncultivated native prairies and unpeopled places. But it was gone, blending somewhere into the walls of the endless canyon.

My heart in my throat, I knew I could not sit back and watch birds like this disappear because of our bitter feuding. Especially, I thought to myself, considering all I had been through.

In six months' time I had become personally acquainted with 2,478 ground squirrel holes, 874 pocket gopher burrows, 149 range transects, 176 baby raptors, and 138 raptor parents. I had learned how to climb trees with spurs, band baby birds, decipher topographic maps, and "read" the native grasses. I had nearly been killed by a bull, had put out a house fire, had found out something about love, and even had put on a rodeo—a buteo rodeo.

Undoubtedly, native prairies like the Zumwalt will need understanding and protection. I would work for that. But also needing appreciation and support are conscientious private ranchers who manage their lands with thoughtful stewardship and in ways beneficial to wildlife. To eliminate them from the land could very well eliminate those things we hope to save.

A lowering western sun was sending the first crimson blush of evening over the land. Something about its radiance brought to my mind the words of Johann Kepler, the famous astronomer, who, at the end of his work on the harmony of the universe, had written joyously: *"I thank thee, Lord God our Creator, that thou allowest me to see the beauty in thy work of creation."*

I had seen that beauty. I had seen it in the Zumwalt. Ranchers had been a part of it. I remembered something that Cressie Green had said: If you come to know and work a patch of land, you'll find you don't own it, it owns you.

The Zumwalt Prairie, a place I had come to know and learn from and deeply love, indeed had become a part of me. Saving it for future generations will be difficult. But there *is* hope. It lies in working together.